Bette Davis

Bette Davis

*The Performances That
Made Her Great*

PETER MCNALLY

McFarland & Company, Inc., Publishers
Jefferson, North Carolina, and London

Frontispiece: Bette Davis during her halcyon days. (Peter McNally collection)

LIBRARY OF CONGRESS CATALOGUING-IN-PUBLICATION DATA

McNally, Peter, 1934–
　　Bette Davis : the performances that made her great / Peter McNally.
　　　　p.　　cm.
　　Includes bibliographical references and index.

　　ISBN 978-0-7864-3499-2
　　softcover : 50# alkaline paper ∞

　　1. Davis, Bette, 1908–1989 — Criticism and interpretation.　I. Title.
PN2287.D32M36　2008
791.4302'8092 — dc22　　　　　　　　　2008000645

British Library cataloguing data are available

©2008 Peter Van Vleet McNally. All rights reserved

No part of this book may be reproduced or transmitted in any form or by any means, electronic or mechanical, including photocopying or recording, or by any information storage and retrieval system, without permission in writing from the publisher.

Cover photograph: Bette Davis as Marie Roark in *Bordertown* (Photofest)

Manufactured in the United States of America

McFarland & Company, Inc., Publishers
　Box 611, Jefferson, North Carolina 28640
　www.mcfarlandpub.com

In memory of my parents,
Edward J. McNally and
Marie P. Bentley

Table of Contents

Preface — 1
Introduction — 3

The First Tier

1. *The Letter* (1940), A TALE OF A LIAR — 9
2. *All About Eve* (1950), BEST PERFORMANCE — 22
3. *Dark Victory* (1939), ACTING VICTORY — 38
4. *The Little Foxes* (1941), STAR VERSUS DIRECTOR — 51
5. *Now, Voyager* (1942), A WOMAN OF INDEPENDENCE — 63
6. *What Ever Happened to Baby Jane?* (1962), HOLLYWOOD HORROR IN KABUKI — 78
7. *A Piano for Mrs. Cimino* (1982), A CONCERTO FOR DAVIS — 91
8. *The Old Maid* (1939), THE 19TH CENTURY AND ILLEGITIMACY — 102
9. *The Virgin Queen* (1955), AGAIN, A QUEEN — 114

10. *The Private Lives of Elizabeth and Essex* (1939), First and Forever a Queen — 123

11. *The Whales of August* (1987), The Greatest Star and the Greatest Star — 131

12. *Jezebel* (1938), The Legend Begun — 140

The Second Tier

13. Not to Be Overlooked, Twelve Other Significant Performances in Not Always Significant Films — 153

14. In the Final Analysis — 221

Afterword — 231
Appendix I: Personal Data — 233
Appendix II: Nominations and Awards — 235
Appendix III: The "Woman's Picture" Factor — 237
Appendix IV: Missed Opportunities — 239
Appendix V: Film Chronology — 241
Chapter Notes — 243
Bibliography — 247
Index — 249

Preface

DAVIS: THE ARTISTRY OF BETTE DAVIS

> *"I don't think any actress has given as many multifaceted performances"*[1]
> — George C. Scott
>
> *"Still may be the greatest actress of our time."*[2]
> — James Mason

Over twenty-five books have been written about Bette Davis: biographies, film compilations, appreciations, two autobiographies, and memoirs. Why another? The subtitle of this book, *The Performances That Made Her Great*, should explain the need.

Among all the volumes of print about Ms. Davis and her acting in films, theater, radio, TV and on recordings, this is the first to analyze specifically her performances in her top work. As with all artists, whether painters, writers or actors, the key to analysis is to view the best of the person's creative output and subject it to critical appraisal, not to view the lesser works (or in some cases outright failures) of a person's career.

An analysis of Picasso is the analysis of his greatest art. This does not preclude acknowledging his lesser work, but the emphasis should be placed upon what makes him great — his masterpieces. The same rule applies to acting. An actor's greatness is measured by his or her greatest achievements. In judging actors, it is difficult to measure them against actors in history because we only have word-of-mouth and written reactions of historical contemporaries. Even in twenty-first century terms, it is not simple to judge actors, especially those whose careers were spent on stage in live theater. Again, we have to rely on verbal witnesses who were critics of the time.

In the case of Ms. Davis, the major portion of her career was as a film actor. The record is available to view at any time. She, and her performances, can be analyzed according to prevailing and existing standards of her time, as well as to determine what stands the test of time. One can view properties chosen, and view critical assessment.

Ms. Davis' acting career deserves such critical study in order to measure her greatness on her own individual basis.

Introduction

> *"The real actor—like any real artist—has a direct line to the collective heart."*[1]
> — Bette Davis

    A niece of mine, who was an officer in the U.S. Army (and a paratrooper) once said to me, knowing I was admirer of Bette Davis, "I watch her movie *Now, Voyager* over and over again, and cry every time."

    When she said this, I was astonished. My niece was in her thirties, a thoroughly modern woman in the 1980s. I never thought younger people would even know who Bette Davis was, let alone admire her movies, but that's the beauty of videotapes and now DVDs. One can watch old movies as if they were freshly made just for you. One can see performances that your parents or grandparents thought were great, and either agree or wonder how anyone could praise acting that you find inadvertently funny or worse, god-awful.

    When my son was growing up, we played tapes of classic movies for him (as well as ourselves) to view. He told his fourth grade teacher that Gene Kelly was his favorite movie star, having seen *Singin' in the Rain* over and over again. And this in spite of his having seen Harrison Ford in *Indiana Jones*, and *Star Wars*, two of his favorite movies.

    When I grew up in the thirties, forties and fifties, we only saw movies once, at the movie palace. For me that was the State Theater in Easton, Pennsylvania. The city had three other theaters, with one devoted to B-westerns

(Roy Rogers, et al.) but I never went there. The A-pictures were the ones I wanted, and was allowed, to see.

I first remember seeing Disney's *Ferdinand* and *Snow White and the Seven Dwarfs* (whose witch scared me to death). Then I begged my father to take me to see a reissue of *Frankenstein*; I hid under the seat when the little girl drowned, but asked my father to tell me when it was over so I could come back up.

My mother was an actress in community/college theater and occasionally took me to movie matinees. I was eight when she and my father took me along to see *Now, Voyager* in 1942. At the theater I spied a lobby card with a picture of Davis. I inquired, "Is she in this movie?" If she was, I didn't want to see it. Well, my mother lied and in we went. People didn't arrive on time for movies as they do today. If you came late, you just stayed for the next showing until you saw the part you missed. That meant getting through a newsreel, previews, a travel talk by Mr. Fitzpatrick, a Pete Smith specialty and a cartoon. We were seated just as Charlotte Vale (Davis), the old maid, descended her family staircase. We first saw her Oxford shoes, her thick legs, her tiny-printed spinster dress, her lace cuffs and finally her frameless eyeglasses on her bushy-eyebrowed-face. As her face came into view, I turned to my mother and loudly stated, "You lied." My mother merely responded with, "Shh." I was furious, but I waited and watched and listened. As an eight-year-old, I was fascinated. So began my life-long admiration for the actor Bette Davis.

My view of Davis then was a view of Charlotte Vale, and I must surely have sympathized with her lover's little girl, especially when she was cared for by Davis. I particularly recalled the scene when Davis lets a party roast wieners on a stick in the family fireplace. I wanted to try it at home, in our small colonial two-bedroom house.

Davis, at this time, was in her halcyon days. Both critics and the populace took her seriously. I recall that friends of my parents, all professional people, and their friends from the field of the theater in New York, all went to see the latest Davis picture and afterwards discussed the film and her performance. Davis was the "First Lady of the Screen."

When I came to adulthood in the mid–50s, with the exception of *All About Eve*, Davis' career was in decline, as was her popularity.

Davis told Joseph L. Mankiewicz, her *Eve* director:

> I am neither Lady Macbeth nor Portia; I'll play either at the drop of a hat anywhere.... Me, I'm an actress. And I do appear upon the screen, that big. What I say or do, and how I look, is what millions of people see and listen to. The fact that my performance is the end result of many other contributions as well, matters to them not at all. If I make a horse's ass of myself on that screen, it is I —

Bette Davis — who is the forty-feet by thirty-feet horse's ass as far as they're concerned. Not the writer, not the director, the producer or the studio gateman — nobody but me. I am the representative horse's ass for all concerned.[2]

Discerning moviegoers still went to see her in *The Catered Affair* and *Storm Center*. She drew crowds on Broadway to Tennessee Williams' New York Drama Critics Circle Award-winning play *The Night of the Iguana*. When she left the play, audiences dwindled. Prior to that, in 1959–60, she and her husband, Gary Merrill, toured the U.S. in *The Word of Carl Sandburg*, drawing capacity audiences across the country.

Her movie career rebounded with the horror film *What Ever Happened to Baby Jane?* in 1962.

Her total career from 1928 to 1989 included plays, radio, TV, and records, but the majority was spent in motion pictures.

This book will offer in-depth analysis of her top twelve films, with comments sprinkled throughout concerning many of her other movies that comprise her 100-plus motion picture career. A chapter apiece will be devoted to her twelve greatest films, which cover a time period from 1938 to 1987, when she made her last completed movie. Each chapter will look at the picture's script, direction, camera work, and performances, particularly as they relate to the finished film and, in particular, Ms. Davis' performance.

A separate chapter will deal with twelve other Davis films which are regarded as excellent more for Davis' performance than the overall quality of the movie.

A final chapter will summarize Davis' career in light of the time, her peers, actors of other times and places, and, most importantly, her persona.

Finally, this introduction would be remiss if it didn't state, up front, that the author regards Ms. Davis as America's finest female actor and intends to reinforce this notion via the analysis of her best work.

The First Tier

"...[I] Davis films were ever shown chronologically, they would reveal the face of the anima in its transcendent beauty and totemic awesomeness."[1]
— Bernard Dick

1

The Letter (1940)

A Tale of a Liar

> *"Davis gives what is very likely the best study of female sexual hypocrisy in film history."*[1]
> — Pauline Kael

Six years after her breakthrough role in *Of Human Bondage*, Bette Davis had matured, and brought her refined acting skills to bear on what many consider her finest performance: Leslie Crosbie in *The Letter*. It would be another ten years before Davis again had such a literate script, a director she trusted implicitly, and the opportunity to give a performance of which she was justifiably proud.

An almost film noirish scene: Malaysia, a rubber plantation, nighttime. Behind the credits, the camera pans to a thatched-roof shed containing many native people playing a game at a table, conversing, sleeping in hammocks. A rubber tree drips liquid into an attached pot.

In the background is a house with a large veranda. Moonlight illuminates the southeastern Asian tropics. A pistol shot rings out. Birds flutter, the natives sit up and look about. A man stumbles from the main door toward the steps. A woman, dressed in a long evening gown, follows and fires a second shot. The man hurls down the steps. The woman reaches the front rail and fires four more bullets into the man lying on the ground below. She has advanced to the lowest step. The gun clicks. She drops the pistol, a grim look on her face as she eyes her target.

The moon appears from behind a cloud. She turns her head to look up, eyes wide open, a moment of fear. She retreats to the top of the stairs.

The natives rush forward and the head boy, actually an older man, bends toward the dead man and says, "Mr. Hammond."

The woman, Leslie Crosbie (Davis), the mistress of the plantation, tells the head boy to come inside where she instructs him to send someone to the district attorney's office and to Mr. Crosbie on Plantation Number Four. "Tell him there's been an accident. Mr. Hammond is shot."

Leslie then turns toward the other people at the door, telling them to leave. She retreats to her bedroom. The head boy looks around the living room and picks up a small circle of crocheting, drops it and leaves.

Leslie is heard sobbing in her bedroom.

Played by Davis, Leslie is a deceitful woman, a passionate woman. Apparently defined by her British colonial circumstances, she is the wife of a successful rubber plantation manager, Robert (Herbert Marshall) who, as we learn, loves her greatly.

Davis has immediately shown us, taught us, all we need to know of this murderess. Her gait is determined as she pursues her victim. Her eyes only show fear once, as moonlight illuminates her face. Inside the house, she remains very still, with her back to the head boy, as she orders him to inform her attorney and her husband of the accident. Only then does she turn and forcefully tell the others to leave, giving orders to her servants.

Her emotion only breaks when she is behind closed doors. We hear her sobbing in the privacy of her bedchamber.

This is a portrait of an extremely controlled woman, only revealing her fears to the moon and crying behind closed doors. Davis has set her character, that of an aristocratic English plantation wife in a British colony near Singapore.

The inside of the house reveals her reserve and orderliness. The crochet circle is symbolic of the web she will weave.

She appears to be an attractive woman in her thirties, wearing a modest gown, but her coiffure speaks volumes. The hair covers her head slickly, rolled up at the edges, making the hair look like a protective helmet, with no looseness in the style.

The tense, tightly-woven story shows how Leslie has been living a lie. She's been having an affair with the plantation overseer, Geoff Hammond (David Newell). He is married to a Eurasian, and has apparently tried to break off his relationship with Leslie. In a jealous passion, she kills him and then tries to deceive her husband, and everyone else, by saying she shot him in self-defense to prevent a rape.

When her husband, Robert, and her lawyer, Howard Joyce (James Stephenson), arrive, Leslie unlocks her bedroom door and comes into the living room. An assistant district attorney (Bruce Lester) and a police officer have been waiting for some time.

1. The Letter *(1940)*

Leslie has changed her clothes. She now wears a long-sleeved, full, white shirtwaist above a long, dark skirt which reaches to the floor and has prominent pinstripes running down its length.

"I'm so frightened," she says swiftly, going to throw herself in Robert's arms. Then, almost immediately, she turns to Joyce, thanks him for being there, and asks after his wife, Dorothy.

After she greets everyone, ever so politely, ever so British, her lawyer says she must tell what happened to the assistant district attorney and the police because someone has been killed.

Without much reluctance, Leslie reclines on a pillowed sofa to recite her specific, precise recollection of the events leading to Geoff Hammond's death. Her calmness only breaks once — when she comes to Hammond's attempted rape. "I can't go on." It's a cry against the outcome of her action, not from fear of the circumstances in which she finds herself.

In telling her story, Davis is very precise in how she defines her character, again very quietly, only twisting her handkerchief at the beginning to betray her nervousness and determination to control the situation and her emotions.

Basically, she looks to the side while speaking, only occasionally looking directly at Robert or Howard for confirmation of a point she is making about the overseer.

In fear-ridden sorrow she finally cries, "I'd give anything to bring him back to life!"

After her recollection is over, Leslie cooks a late supper or early breakfast for them all. As they sit at the table, Joyce explains that Leslie has to be arraigned and go to prison because a man has been killed, and there's only one charge possible — murder.

Leslie takes this revelation much more calmly than Robert, who is in despair that his wife will have to face prison.

Leslie rises, goes to a venetian-blinded window and stares up at the moon. Striped shadows fall across her body.

As she is calmly packing to leave, Robert tells her she is the best wife a man could ever have.

As they drive away, the head boy, who had run away, and Hammond's widow are in the tropical foliage watching the car disappear before they go to look at the dead body.

A week later the distraught Robert visits Joyce in his law office. Joyce's administrative assistant, Chi Jon (Victor Sen Young), is introduced as a "clerk [who is] perfect help." Robert and Joyce discuss Hammond's strange hidden life, the owner of a gambling house as well as husband to a Eurasian.

After Robert leaves, the clerk reveals to Joyce that he has a copy of a letter sent to Hammond by Leslie on the day of the murder, contradicting her denial of any communication with him for three weeks.

Joyce takes the letter to confront Leslie in jail. Leslie greets him with effusion, saying her stay in jail has been very pleasant, allowing her to work on her crocheting. Davis shows herself to be lively, almost happy and very pleasant to everyone around her. The jail matron obviously respects her. When she leaves them alone, Joyce confronts Leslie on the issue of the communication. All the while Leslie continues working on the significantly larger bed coverlet.

Hammond notes how strange it is that Leslie has told her story exactly the same every time which is unusual. Then he asks her if there was any communication between Hammond and her.

"Haven't written to him?"

"No."

He pushes her, "Note? To come see you?"

"Impossible!"

He shows her the letter.

"A forgery," she responds.

He persists.

Confident at first, Davis continues crocheting, talking pleasantly and smiling. At the first mention of communication, she removes her spectacles and stops crocheting.

With his persistence, her voice rises and she looks directly at Joyce, denying the possibility. When he produces the letter, at first Davis is calmly passive because it isn't Leslie's handwriting. And she says it is a forgery.

Davis stands to read the contents. Joyce warns her of the consequences if the defense sees this. She responds irrationally that there's no damning evidence.

Joyce replies about the specific contents, telling Hammond to park away from the house and the demand to see him. There's a short intake of breath and Davis faints, falling to the floor.

When Leslie, on an examination table in the nurse's office, revives, Davis again plays her very calmly, her left arm (not the right arm of truth) raised against the wall.

"I'm afraid I've made a mess of things." She suggests he could get the letter for her. Joyce, the moral center of the movie, declares his honesty and his duty to his profession. "No, I can't."

Leslie has started to tell the truth. She rises from the table, pleading for his help. She turns to search his face and desperately plays her last card. For the sake of Robert, she pleads for Joyce to find a way to secure the letter.

Davis' face is all anxiety, her voice tender with care for Robert. Joyce reacts with a positive reply to save her. She falls into his arms to thank him. It feels as if she has been very close to him in the past, not just as client and lawyer. Davis shows us this relationship.

At this point, she is tightly reining in her emotions, seemingly in control, manipulating not only her feelings but her lawyer's as well. This is a woman who will do whatever it takes to preserve herself and the perception of her reputation and outward appearance.

Davis only allows desperation in her voice as she begs Joyce to save Robert from embarrassment.

Joyce ends by saying, "I'm just going to try to save your life," but the real thought is expressed, "Strange, a man can live with a woman for ten years and not know the first thing about her."

Joyce has to speak to Robert to get the money, $10,000, required for the letter. His clerk adds two conditions: 1) The letter is to be delivered to Leslie directly by Mrs. Hammond at the latter's house and 2) Leslie must deliver the money personally. The clerk allows that he will receive $2,000.

When Joyce reveals the situation, but not the cost, to Robert at the club, particularly that Leslie has forgotten about the note, Robert states, "...it's not like her; she never makes a mistake." He asks Joyce if it's the right thing to do. Joyce answers it's "not right, but expedient."

Prior to the trial, the court allows Leslie to spend the intervening days at the Joyce's residence. On the night of the letter transaction, Leslie is still making considerable progress on her lace bed coverlet, much like a spider spinning a web. Joyce asks her why she crochets. "It soothes me," Leslie replies behind her spectacles. He remarks on the concentration required, saying he's trying to understand her. Leslie pauses and turns toward him, "...why, because I'm so ... evil?" He doesn't comment.

But it's much more symbolic than that. The web she is "spinning" is her protection from outside threats. Just as a black widow spider spins her web to attract and kill her food sources, the spider also attacks her mate. Leslie has attracted two mates, her husband of over ten years and Geoff Hammond, the overseer. Perhaps Robert and Leslie who are childless haven't really mated. Yet she and her lover have mated for the past several years, and when he tried to leave her, she murdered him. Although she hasn't killed her husband, she has ruined him through the scandal, and she is spending his money to get the letter.

Leslie constructs a web of lies to protect herself, just as she crochets a bed coverlet. She even takes the coverlet to jail. No male is safe in her presence, not even Joyce, her lawyer, who confronted her about the evidence of the letter.

Leslie wears a lace mantilla which basically hides her face when they go to Mrs. Hammond's. While waiting in the antique shop at Mrs. Hammond's,

Davis, as Leslie Crosbie, peers at a pair of daggers as her lawyer (James Stephenson) looks on in *The Letter* (Photofest).

Leslie fondles a pair of daggers. Joyce and she are then escorted by his law clerk into Mrs. Hammond's house. They enter a room where opium is being smoked. When Mrs. Hammond (Gale Sondergaard) enters, Leslie is requested to remove the mantilla from her head. Then she is requested to approach Mrs. Hammond to give her the money. Only when Leslie is confronted by another equally strong woman is she unable to protect herself. Mrs. Hammond sees the true Leslie. She further demeans Leslie by dropping the letter to the floor, requiring Leslie to kneel down to retrieve it. Leslie finds a worthy adversary in another woman, not a man. One should note that the mantilla Leslie wears to hide her face is not the bed coverlet she has been crocheting. They are two separate items, both used as protection.

Upon rising, Leslie, in a soft but steely voice, says, "Thank you," not "I'm sorry." And leaves.

Throughout these scenes there is very little dialogue, none of it from Leslie. Davis uses her body and her non-expressive face to show Leslie's coldness and determination. Her face is emotionless, yet we know she is holding back a furnace. This is the kind of acting at which Davis was a master.

1. The Letter *(1940)*

At the trial, Joyce falters in his summation, ending with "...justice will be done." Leslie is the picture of composure throughout, wearing a large, wide-brimmed hat which protects her from full view. Joyce's law clerk is inscrutable while awaiting the verdict; Leslie is again crocheting. Shadow stripes fall across the wall, and Robert as well.

Leslie is stoic as she stands to hear the jury's verdict, not guilty. The law clerk, all smiles, congratulates Joyce. Leslie smiles until she sees Mrs. Hammond with the head boy.

The climactic scene of the film involves Robert and Leslie at the celebratory party at the Joyces, where they've been guests. Robert has learned of Leslie's love for Hammond, and the cost of retrieving the incriminatory letter, which he reads in Joyce's presence. He returns later in the party to their bedroom. He is not sober. He finds Leslie crocheting, but she has been unable to continue, so is just sitting in a chair. She actually challenges Robert by saying, "There's no way you could forgive me." Teary-eyed, she looks at Robert. He replies, "If you love a person, you can forgive them anything. What about you? Do you love me?"

Leslie goes to his arms, on her knees in front of him. "Yes, I do. No," she counters, then cries out, "I can't, I can't!" She looks straight into his face and reveals, "I still love the man I killed," her eyes frightened and teary.

Davis knew this would be the killer blow for Robert. She fought William Wyler's direction, saying a woman couldn't possibly look directly into a man's eyes and make that statement, but she acquiesced to his direction for this powerful moment. When revealing the truth, Leslie could be cruel and, as she said earlier, evil. Her whole body crumples as Robert leaves the room.

The play rightfully ended here, with two people caught in a web of lies, doomed to be together. But Hollywood in 1940 had a code. Leslie had to be punished (as if their situation weren't punishment enough!). Before the evening is over, Leslie will again submit to the other woman. She walks out onto the treacherous moonlit terrace where Mrs. Hammond and a man are waiting to take revenge. She is indeed murdered — by her female equal.

As she wanders out toward the terrace gate, she encounters the couple. The man grabs her from behind and she cries out, but the party music muffles the sound. The moon disappears and she is stabbed with a dagger. Mrs. Hammond and her accomplice leave. They encounter policemen who stop them.

The movie ends as we see Leslie's body on the ground by the gate, the coverlet on the rail near the house, now a shroud.

Except for the unneeded ending, the screenplay by Howard Koch, based on W. Somerset Maugham's story and play, is compelling and literate. The camera work by Tony Gaudio is superb, catching all the tropical and colonial moods.

Davis was never more character-centered or subtler, underplaying what could have been manneristic and hysterical. It is a tightly-controlled performance.

The opening scenes reveal Leslie's primary character trait as one of compulsive control. Even after telling her lawyer, the assistant D.A. and her husband of her ordeal, she is able to cook them a supper and serve it as a proper Englishwoman who is innocent and following the social dictates of a colonist in her position.

Leslie's fate is shown through lighting, costuming and set design. Shadow stripes from venetian blinds fall across her body as she looks out a window. The long skirt she wears is striped. Even the furniture has horizontal stripes. All is reminiscent of prison stripes in this black and white movie.

Throughout the film, Leslie crochets the bed coverlet. A mantilla/shawl envelops her, protects her, when she goes to Mrs. Hammond.

Davis used not only her face and eyes but her whole body to express Leslie's torment and determination. At only one time does she drop her façade and give vent to the truth. When Robert forgives her, her body and face crumble, as she passionately tells him she still loves the man she killed. Of course, she immediately realizes she has thus condemned herself to a life of emptiness. She and her husband would be exiled from their country, their culture and each other, becoming outcasts living, to them, a completely foreign existence, protected only by their lies, a prison worse than death.

There is nothing but defeat on Robert's face.

Davis kept the whole movie brilliantly tense, even erotic with its sexual tension. Her adultery seems understandable given the stick her husband seems to be. It is only with his forgiveness and her confession that we see what a really good person he is and what a manipulative, evil woman she is, the personification of the colonial imperialist who rapes the Asians for their resources.

This is the movie to view if one wishes to see the degree to which Davis could use her acting skills to submerge a character within her being, to capture a character in all her facets. As with all great star acting, Davis is Davis, but you'll never see another Davis movie with this person inside.

In *Mother Goddam,* Whitney Stine writes, "[D]irector William Wyler ... is the liability if an actor's performance is at fault; he is the one to censure — or to thank — for the finished effect."[2]

Charles Affron, in *Star Acting,* declares:

> ...an actress who learned that every gesture counted, and whose sense of measure is transmitted to us as knowledge, Leslie Crosbie in The Letter, is a character partially defined by self-possession, and is emblematic of Bette Davis, crisply disarranging the tranquility of the night with her pistol, and then recounting her

1. The Letter *(1940)*

Leslie (Davis) and her husband Robert (Herbert Marshall) discuss Leslie's acquittal of murder with their lawyer, Joyce (James Stephenson) (Photofest).

lie so well that she makes lucidity itself a truth.... William Wyler's limpid images are animated by Davis, who helps us find out where everything is.[3]

In *Acting Hollywood Style,* Foster Hirsch maintains that "Bette Davis in *The Letter* (1940) ... plays a character in hiding.... [W]e are placed in the position of becoming an investigator, sifting clues and hints and peeling away layers of subterfuge in order to determine the truth."[4]

Katherine Cornell and Gladys Cooper on stage, and Jeanne Eagels on screen, performed in *The Letter.* It was also remade for TV with Lee Remick, and as a theater revival with Carrie Nye. In all, Davis overshadows your thoughts of Leslie because she nailed the part in an excellent production with other consummate actors. No one else measures up. Who could you see playing it today? Perhaps Meryl Streep, maybe Nicole Kidman, but is either willing to be a total liar and/or bitch?

Emmanuel Levy, in *Oscar Fever,* allows that "Bette Davis once said that her two Oscars for *Dangerous* and *Jezebel* didn't mean much because they were for the 'wrong' films; she would have been more grateful to win for *The Letter* and *All About Eve.*[5]

Davis said she felt World War II destroyed James Stephenson's career. He died six months later. He certainly was the moral center of this movie, not Herbert Marshall. He even makes you wonder if there was more going on beyond the lawyer-client relationship with Leslie.

It is noteworthy that the Asian roles, with the exception of Sondergaard, were played by Asians and not stereotypically, but as fully developed characters. Sondergaard was excellent as well, even though I'm sure an Asian (Anna May Wong) could have played her role.

This was Davis' second feature under William Wyler's direction. During the first, *Jezebel* (1938), they had an affair, but Wyler subsequently married. Davis was between marriages. She had been divorced from her first husband in 1939 and would not marry her second husband until December 31, 1940. Still friends, Wyler and Davis had great professional respect for each other. *The Letter* shows the gratifying results.

There were rumors that Davis had an abortion during the early filming and that it was Wyler's, but it was another man's. Davis was not averse to love affairs. In fact, she apparently had a short affair with Anatole Litvak, the director of *All This and Heaven Too*, her preceding film, as well as with Howard Hughes and, on this film, Bruce Lester.

The theme of the movie is mendacity: lies multiply.

Leslie spins her web of deceit as she crochets a web of imprisonment, entangling everyone. She's completely egocentric, even when not appearing to be so. Her hair is a helmet. It protects her from people knowing her thoughts and emotions. Her nervousness is only given away by her face which she hides behind spectacles, a mantilla or a hat and her hands when telling the story of the murder.

Self-knowledge is apparent when she finally reveals herself to Howard, not Robert.

Alexander Walker, in *Bette Davis*, says:

> ...[M]any consider [*The Letter*] the finest she ever made: The role of a woman who, conversely, spends the whole picture concealing her thoughts, lying to cover them up. Deceit becomes Davis marvelously; it sharpens her femininity. She never seems more desirable than when she is lying her way out of a crisis with a ready tongue and, if that fails, falling back on wiles and pleas that are pitched at the males she basically mistreats and despises.[6]

Wyler was borrowed from Sam Goldwyn; his contract allowed him to quit if Davis was a no-show. He wanted Gregg Toland (*Citizen Kane*, 1941) for cameraman, but Warner Brothers overruled him. Wyler also wanted a three-week rehearsal period but was given three days. It was a Hal Wallis production with Robert Lord as associate producer. Lord was the previous screenwriter on Wallis' productions of *Jezebel* and *Dark Victory*, and most of Davis' Warner Brothers productions until Wallis left the studio in 1942.

With the exception of *The Whales of August*, almost all of Davis' movies were plot driven, gothic tales, romances, comedies or gangster films.

Davis would say of Leslie Crosbie in *The Letter*:

> It's a great part, a very wonderful part, but I saw Katherine Cornell do it on stage. She did it in New York in 1927. I was so fascinated by her acting genius that I saw the play twice, and I can recall every vivid detail of her performance. But, you see, I'm not at all like Kit Cornell. I had to make this part mine, all mine, my very own. It was the hardest thing I ever tried, because I kept remembering Cornell in the part.

Others considered for the part were Merle Oberon, Barbara Stanwyck, Claudette Colbert, Joan Crawford, Vivien Leigh, Marlene Dietrich, Katharine Hepburn, Frances Farmer and Greer Garson.

Herbert Marshall, who played Robert, had been in the earlier Paramount movie as the murdered lover.

The picture went three days over schedule but came in under budget, which was unusual for a Wyler film. He was notorious for multiple takes, upwards of forty in some cases. Then Hal Wallis would often print his first take.

The approach Davis used for the film was what she always did. She memorized the entire script — every scene, everyone's part. She always knew what came before a scene being filmed and what came after.

In *The Letter* her performance is a study in deep control. Except for her outburst to Robert when she reveals she still loves the man she killed, her voice never rises. In fact, much of the drama and tension comes from her silence and noticeable suppression of emotion. Only through her facial expressions, particularly the font of human emotion, the eyes, and very few nervous gestures do we learn about Leslie and what she's thinking.

Leslie uses deceit to frame her truth in the constant reiteration of her story of the event of the murder and what led up to it. Her fear is visible when she first looks up at the moon, and later when she faints under her lawyer's inquisition about the letter. However, she obfuscates her real fear by shifting her apparent concern over to her husband, as false as it is.

Davis' physical demeanor throughout the film is one of an upper-class British subject. Her voice and tone is always lady-like and precise with a discernable English accent. Emotions are kept under wraps, so Davis has only her eyes to help us decipher Leslie's anxiety and fears. She keeps her hands busy crocheting the web-like coverlet. She covers her eyes with glasses so that we must look through the glass darkly.

Much of the film takes place at night in moonlight, or indoors in darkness, such as the scenes at the Eurasian's dark house. Even the welcoming home party at Joyce's home is at night, and there is not a lot of artificial light either. Shadows are often cast across both Leslie and Robert. They are a doomed couple.

Max Steiner's score is suitably Asian and it underscores scenes rather than intrudes. In fact, Wyler often uses silence or natural sounds of the jungle for effect. It's particularly noticeable when Leslie visits Mrs. Hammond to deliver the money for the damaging letter. All we hear is the muted tinkle of hanging wind chimes.

In this scene and in her scene with her lawyer, Joyce, in jail, Davis shows the power of her skill, as she is very still at times and very quiet.

Although her performance gives hints along the way as to Leslie's true nature, her apparent reasonableness with everyone leads them, and us, to believe she is an honest, loving wife to her husband. Even after her confession to Joyce as to the truth of the letter, it is remarkable to see how sympathetic she still remains. Even her final disclosure to Robert is couched in terms of her not wanting to hurt him with the truth of her feelings.

Then Davis reveals Leslie's true colors, not through her confession that she still loves the man she killed, but by the calm disclosure to Joyce when he tells her that Robert will forgive her. She calmly says, "I know."

Here is a character totally loved and admired by her fellow colonists. They respect her and her husband as paragons of how British colonists should behave. Yet she breaks every social code of behavior that they regard as a superior way of life — the English life. They could even forgive murder, but not betrayal of class. One does not commit adultery with a lower-class, married man, and if one does, then one does not call attention to it by an uncontrolled, passionate killing. That was Leslie's sin. Her behavior was unacceptable and she knew it. Davis knew it and allowed us to see she knew it, as well as showing us a woman whose fear inevitably led to her undoing.

Even without the final revengeful murder of Leslie, Davis shows us how Leslie had ruined every life she touched, not just her husband's, but her lawyer's and those of his family and her entire colony. Even Mrs. Hammond, the only adversary as strong a she, will inevitably pay the price for her murder of Leslie.

Leslie ultimately could not finish the bed coverlet with all her crocheting, her weaving of her web. The bed where the most intimate actions of a couple take place was finally left exposed for all to see — empty. Davis finally let us see Leslie fully exposed as she exposes her inner being, a woman subject to her suppressed emotions, her true self.

William Wyler, her favorite director, kept a tight control on Davis, the actress, which only made her performances more intense and lasting. It allowed the truth of her performance to speak loudly. He knew the character and the actor thoroughly, allowing Davis to perform at her best.

At this point in her life, Davis' personal life gave her the maturity to essay this role in a much fuller way than she would have been able to do earlier in her career. Her acting skills were fully honed. Just a year earlier, she had gone through a messy divorce, brought by her first husband. She had had a "secret" affair with Wyler while they were filming *Jezebel* in 1938, and later had an affair with Anatole Litvak, her director on *All This, and Heaven, Too*. None of these affairs could be out in the open because of the mores of the time. Yet it would appear Davis, as she said, had a great need for love. When she had an abortion while making *The Letter*, she honestly didn't know who the father was. Davis was suffering some torments herself. This was a person who said she was raised in a strict Yankee way from New England, but her actions belie her words. She was a woman who was openly passionate, a woman in love with love who couldn't openly show it. And yet, she basically wanted to be loved as she felt her father never had. It informed much of her life, especially her relationships with men.

Cast: Leslie Crosbie — Bette Davis; Robert Crosbie — Herbert Marshall; Howard Joyce — James Stephenson; Dorothy Joyce — Frieda Inescort; Mrs. Hammond — Gale Sondergaard; John Withers — Bruce Lester; Prescott — Cecil Kellaway; Adele Ainsworth — Elizabeth Earl; Mrs. Cooper — Doris Lloyd; On Chi Jen — Victor Sen Yung; Chun Hi — Willie Fung; Head Boy — Tetsu Komai; Fred — Leonard Mudie; Driver — John Ridgely; Robert's Friends — Charles Irwin, Holmes Herbert; Geoff Hammond — David Newell; Well-wisher — Douglas Walton.

Production: Hal B. Wallis — Producer; Robert Lord — Associate Producer; William Wyler — Director; Howard Koch — Screenwriter; W. Somerset Maugham — based on his play; Tony Gaudio — Cinematographer; Max Steiner — Musical Score; Leo F. Forbstein — Musical Director; Orry-Kelly — Gowns; Carl Jules Weyl — Art Director; George Amy — Editor; 1940; Running time — 95 minutes.

2

All About Eve (1950)

Best Performance*

> *"Barring grand opera, I can think of
> nothing beyond her range."*[1]
> —*Joseph L. Mankiewicz*

For *The Letter*, Davis received many critical reviews stating that it was the best role of her career. But in 1950 Davis created the role of Margo Channing in a script written and directed by Joseph L. Mankiewicz. It was a mutual admiration society for both parties, with the critics throwing their hats in the air.

A bookend movie, *All About Eve*'s opening is mirrored at the finale. We first see a celebration, a theatrical awards ceremony, taking place in what appears to be the Players Club in New York City. A narrator, the drama critic/columnist Addison DeWitt (George Sanders), is explaining the scene and introducing the major players of the film as well. The camera moves from dining table to table as we meet the characters. Margo Channing (Bette Davis) is an attendee, not an award winner, but DeWitt, and Davis' acting, make it clear she is a star. DeWitt states, "She entered the stage at age five, in *A Midsummer Night's Dream*, stark naked. She has been a star ever since."

The female winner of the top acting award is one Eve Harrington (Anne Baxter), who has won the Sarah Siddons statuette† for a role originally intended for Channing. This high comedy tells the story of how Harrington used, and

---

*Original title by Mankiewicz.
†An award later made real in Chicago and given to Davis, presented by Baxter.

was used by, theater people to achieve success. Within a year, she rose from being a nobody to a top star of the stage.

The playwright's wife, Karen Richards (Celeste Holm), begins a narration which leads to an introduction of Eve, the star-struck, youngish woman waiting in the rain outside the theater stage door from which Margo exits nightly. Karen takes Eve backstage to meet her idol, Margo Channing.

Bill Sampson (Gary Merrill) gives Eve the lowdown on what theater is after she implies that going to Hollywood is a sell-out to true theater. He, acting like the then-current hot director Elia Kazan, tells her theater is every kind of entertainment — the circus, grand opera, ballet, the movies, vaudeville, etc. "You may not like them all, but they're all theater for someone."

It should be stated, unequivocally, that although this film is set in the theater world, it could really be about movies, and is a close first-cousin to Billy Wilder's masterpiece, *Sunset Boulevard*. Whereas Wilder's heroine is a has-been, a silent screen star living in a fantasy world, Margo Channing is a realist, a working actress, which is a vast difference. Gloria Swanson appears in ninety percent of *Sunset Blvd.*, whereas Davis is not even in fifty percent of *Eve*, but she dominates the film totally. As one critic said in the nineties, she is bodacious!

After Eve is introduced to Margo, they develop what seems to be a friendship. At the airport, Margo and Bill discuss Eve when she leaves them alone before Bill's depar-

An iconic publicity shot of Davis from *All About Eve* (Peter McNally collection).

ture. They have both been taken in and feel protective toward her. Margo takes Eve under her wing as a secretary-companion, much to the chagrin of Margo's maid-dresser, Birdie (Thelma Ritter), who doesn't trust Eve at all.

At the theater, after a performance, Margo indulges Eve when she catches her holding up her costume and bowing to a backstage mirror. "Perhaps, we'd better let Mrs. Brown get the costume, Eve."

When Margo is awakened at 3 A.M. by a phone call from Bill in L.A., every crease and line of her face reveals her sleepiness, but also her 40-ish age. With no makeup masking the heavy circles and bags under her eyes, Davis lets us see her age and surprise at his unexpected all. Eve had placed the call earlier because it is Bill's birthday. Margo ends the call with a sarcastic remark, "I'll check with Eve," and lights a cigarette while worried concern shows on her face.

When finally confronted by Margo, Birdie says, "It's like she's studying you, night and day, like you were a blueprint." The seeds of doubt have been planted, and Margo finally realizes that Eve is literally trying to take over her career as well as her lover, Bill Sampson.

Sampson went Hollywood to direct a movie. Upon his return, unbeknownst to Margo, Eve has arranged a coming home/birthday party. At the cocktail party, a first for a Hollywood movie, Margo and Bill start to quarrel because he hadn't come upstairs to see Margo when he first arrived, but talked to Eve. Davis shows her comedic skill with her inclination to have a chocolate from a covered candy dish. She looks at the candy, looks away, then turns to them again and pops one in her mouth, chewing and continuing her verbal quarrel with Bill. This cocktail party is the central moment of the film.

When discussing his new play, *Footsteps on the Ceiling*, with Lloyd (Hugh Marlowe), a somewhat drunken Margo bares her soul to him and asks him about the play. She is concerned about the twenty-something age of the lead. She then admits she's turned 40, and that Bill's 32. "Suddenly I feel like I've taken all my clothes off." However, she assures him she will honor her commitment.

She has a tiff with Bill, over her perceived view of Eve, whom Bill keeps referring to as just a kid. Margo exits to her bedroom after having told Eve to stop treating her like the Queen Mother. Sampson follows and DeWitt quips, "Too bad. The third act will be played off-stage."

Channing has requested her producer, Max Fabian (Gregory Ratoff), hire Eve as a secretary, which he promises to do. Margo has promised to read at an audition with a starlet, Miss Caswell (Marilyn Monroe). Being Margo, she is very late, an hour and a half, for the audition and runs into Miss Caswell's mentor, DeWitt, in the theater lobby. DeWitt informs her that her understudy, Harrington, read with Caswell. He also informs her that Eve was brilliant, all "fire and music."

Channing is livid because she had no idea Eve was her understudy. She proceeds to the theater auditorium and skillfully sets everyone up for her fury, which ends with her and Sampson finishing the argument alone on a stage-set bed. She reveals her deep uncertainty about their relationship because he is six years younger than she. When Sampson finally says he's leaving, she asks, "Where are you going? To find Eve?" With that he replies, "That finally makes it all believable," and leaves. It is a complete rift.

At the Richardses' (Hugh Marlowe and Celeste Holm) invitation, Channing goes for a weekend at their Westchester country home. On the way to the train station to return to the city, Richards' car runs out of gas (arranged by Karen to let Eve go on as understudy) and it's winter. When Lloyd goes to get gas, Channing unloads to her best friend, Karen. She apologizes for her recent behavior and explains her fervent wish to be a wife to Bill.

When Eve makes a pass at Bill in her dressing room after her unscheduled understudy performance, he rejects her firmly. "Haven't you heard? I'm in love with Margo." "You hear all kinds of things," she replies. He finally answers, "Just consider it an incomplete forward pass," and leaves her as she, frustrated, tries to rip apart her wig.

Addison, who's been listening, appears at the door and invites himself in. She asks him to take charge. "I believe I will," he answers.

The next day, Karen walks into "21" to meet Margo for lunch. Margo, habitually late, is not there yet, but Karen runs into DeWitt, who tells her to read his newspaper column while waiting. She is shocked by what she reads and leaves.

At Margo's apartment, Margo is reading aloud Addison's review of Eve's performance to Karen, commenting trenchantly on the unlikely possibility of getting all the critics to see that particular performance. She is plainly devastated. Sampson appears, rushes to her and takes her in his arms. "It's all right, baby. Bill's here."

The two couples subsequently meet at the Stork Club where Channing and Sampson tell the Richards that they are to marry. A toast is made to the bride and groom to be, Margo and Bill. Karen asks what she'll wear. Margo says, "Oh, something simple, a fur coat over a nightgown."

They notice Eve with Addison at another table. When Addison raises his glass toward them as a toast, Margo reacts by raising a scallion in their direction and taking a big bite out of it.

Eve sends a note to Karen, requesting that she meet her in the ladies' room, which she does. Eve blackmails Karen to secure a part in Lloyd's new play.

When Karen reappears at their table, they all notice that Eve and Addison are leaving. Margo looks at them and says, "There goes Eve, little Miss Evil. She left good behind. The four of us together. Lloyd, don't be mad, I don't want to play Cora." Karen laughs uncontrollably.

The remainder of the film shows Eve and her aggressive behavior to become a star. Things fall into place, because Margo does turn down the Richards' new play. Eve makes a pass at and apparently succeeds in entrapping Lloyd Richards. However, DeWitt knows this because he listens well and has dug up Eve's past from Karen and elsewhere. While in New Haven for the tryout he establishes the fact that Eve belongs to him and him alone. He establishes his control over her in her hotel suite. He knows everything about her, including the lies about her origins and how she has treated everyone who had actually tried to help her. She becomes hysterical and declares she can't go on that night. He tells her she'll give the performance of her life; and she does.

The film flashes back to the awards ceremony, ending with Eve's award. People rise to leave and congratulate her. She has told the assembly that she is leaving for Hollywood, but she won't be gone long for her heart is in the theater. Margo congratulates Eve and says, "Don't worry, Eve. You can put that award where your heart ought to be." She turns and leaves with Bill. Eve is stony-faced, silent.

Davis always said the key to her performance was a remark from director Joe Mankiewicz who told her, "Margo was a dame who treated her fur coat like a poncho." And that's the way she played her, right from the first scene in the theater dressing room when she asks Birdie where the fur coat is. Birdie replies, "Right where you left it," on the floor by the chaise lounge.

Eve begs off attending the after-ceremony party and DeWitt drops her at her hotel. A young girl, a fan, has gotten into her suite and surprises her. At first Eve is going to evict her, but relents and lets Phoebe (Barbara Bates) make her a drink. The doorbell rings. DeWitt has returned Eve's award, which she left in the cab. Phoebe tells Eve it was a cabdriver. Eve tells her to take the award to her bedroom to pack. Phoebe goes into the bedroom, dons Eve's evening coat, holds the Sarah Siddons award in her hands and bows to the triple looking-glass. The image multiplies. The film ends.

All About Eve came ten years after Davis had made *The Letter*. She had been the reigning queen of Hollywood, referred to as the fourth Warner Brother. During this time, 1938–1948, she had had her pick of scripts at Warner Brothers. She had made many successful films, critically acclaimed and popular, such as *The Great Lie, The Little Foxes, Now, Voyager, Mr. Skeffington*, and *Watch on the Rhine*. But she had hit a brick wall with a series of flops, weak films starting with *Winter Meeting* in 1948 and ending disastrously with *Beyond the Forest* in 1949. Her 18-year residency with Warners ended.

Worst of all, it was a vast surprise to her that there were really no offers of work. She had not aged well, had a reputation of being extremely temperamental and was not considered box office. Hollywood was also going through a tremendous change. The studios had been divested of their ownership of theaters, and television was replacing movies with home entertainment. She was offered *The Story of a Divorce* at RKO, later known as *Payment on Demand*. She made it in 1949, but it wasn't released until January 1951, after *All About Eve*. During the final filming days of *Payment*, Darryl Zanuck sent her the script for *Eve*. It was a "Mae West"! The cast had already been assembled; Claudette Colbert was Margo, but she had had a skiing accident, injuring her back. Gertrude Lawrence and Marlene Dietrich were among those considered as replacements.

Davis jumped at the role. She read the script and immediately realized it was the best script she had seen in years. Truthfully, it was the best since *The Little Foxes*, even though she was never pleased with *Foxes*. She had to join the cast in San Francisco within a week of her finishing *Payment* because of the rental dates of a theater there, only available for a certain time period. Davis showed up with a bad case of "laryngitis." When Joe Mankiewicz heard her, it was a surprise. But he told her to keep that voice throughout the picture, which was perfect for the role. Truth be told, she injured her vocal chords screaming at her third husband, William Grant Sherry, with whom she was splitting. Such are the accidents of the theater! None of the other stars were of Davis' caliber. Only Monroe went on to become a major star. Davis got Edith Head to design her wardrobe, beautifully contemporary. It was done in haste, however, and Davis' famous party dress did not fit properly. It was not supposed to be off-the-shoulder, but it worked for the character, so they left it alone, and it worked well for the low-busted Davis. Davis and Merrill's affair was initially unknown to Mankiewicz. Their antics offended as least one cast member—Celeste Holm. When Davis and Merrill married they adopted a daughter and named her Margot, after the role. Merrill also adopted Davis' daughter, Barbara Davis Sherry, who at 15 reverted to her initial surname, Sherry.

What did Davis bring to this role, other than an injured voice? Plenty: ten years as a real star, with roles of every description; the knowledge of twenty years as an actor, and the ambition to be a great actor; the knowledge of success and failure, and of hardships; fighting with Warners to get and maintain a career; a toll on her personal life, including three marriages, none of which lasted; financially supporting her mother and sister; and no children until May 1947. At this point, she only wanted to be remembered for her work.

As she said to Mankiewicz, "You resurrected me from the dead." Contrary to rumors given to Mankiewicz, she showed up on the set letter-perfect and reveled in her role. The entire cast knew they were in a masterful comedy. She brought her star acting to Margo Channing. There was much talk about a real-life basis for Margo. Mankiewicz declared the inspiration Peg Wolfington (a famous 19th century English actor); others said Davis' characterization was close to Tallulah Bankhead. The movie was actually based on Mary Orr's short story, which had been influenced by Elizabeth Bergner, a Broadway actress, and her husband.

It really makes no difference, for it is Davis who stamps the role emphatically as hers and hers alone. Other actors may essay this role, and have, but the measurement comes back to Davis. She was quoted as saying she was not the role. She later felt that Gary Merrill married Margo, not her, Bette Davis. She also said, in agreement with others, that this probably was her best performance. Mankiewicz declared, "Working with Bette was ... from the first day to regrettably our last, an experience as happy and rewarding as any I have ever known ... she's intelligent, instinctive, vital, sensitive — and above all, a superbly equipped professional actress who does her job responsibly and honestly."

When Davis was awarded the American Film Institute's Lifetime Achievement Award, Mankiewicz was one of those paying her tribute. He went on, at length, with various stories about Hollywood. One thing he made clear was that he thought Davis was deserving of the award. He said, "Barring grand opera, there is nothing that Bette could not do." She was the first woman to receive this prestigious award, her predecessors being James Cagney, a Warner Brothers alumnus; John Ford, the director best known for his westerns with John Wayne; Orson Welles, the boy genius of *Citizen Kane*; and William Wyler, her favorite director, who also directed *The Best Years of Our Lives*. The last also spoke at her AFI ceremony, stating, "Yes, she was difficult, difficult like me. She wanted everything to be the best."

Her performance as Eve is excellent, but whether it's her best is arguable. What it is is the accumulation of her twenty years. One sees it all in this film, her wonderful intelligence, acting technique and her value as a person with humor. As Michael Merrill, her son, says, this is his favorite film of hers because it offers portrayals that are the closest to her and his father, Gary Merrill. So, as much as she denied the role's similarity to her own persona, her son and the moviegoers identify Margo with Davis, and rightly so. She admitted she had to constantly remind herself it was Margo she was playing, not herself. Davis was a true superstar, with all that that entails. She was a major actor, had a temperament, and was at the stage in her career where Channing was, over 40 (actually 42) and ageing, something unaccepted in Hollywood, where youth was all. She was going through a messy divorce, and she fell in

The major cast of *All About Eve* on 20th Century–Fox's backlot. From left: George Sanders, Gary Merrill, Davis, Anne Baxter, Celeste Holm and Hugh Marlowe (Photofest).

love with Merrill, six years her junior. She knew what it meant to fight for a legitimate career. She knew what it meant to do crap and be able to pull off a performance by surmounting a poor script and inept direction. She knew the treachery of a theatrical, albeit movie, career. But most of all, she knew the joy of success, of being number one. She brought all this to the role of Margo, in spades. Just look at the enormous smile on her face as she and the rest of the cast cross the back lot arm-in-arm.

In the opening scene of *Eve*, Davis establishes her character immediately, without speaking a word. Dressed in a fur-trimmed gown, sporting long youthful hair and glittering jewels, she's smoking a cigarette as only Davis can. DeWitt's arm appears as he reaches over to add soda to her drink. She sweeps her arm right across the bottle, cigarette in hand, eyes hooded, deftly rejecting any dilution, a bemused look upon her face. Margo's been here before; it's old hat to her, and what we realize is that, at last, she's happy. She has what she wants, career recognition and now her love, her husband, Bill Sampson. This is star acting; this is Davis.

Davis always used her face fully to express her emotions. Her evident disdain for Eve's acceptance speech is apparent. Everything is in character. She is Margo, a superstar, reveling in her husband receiving a director's award for *Footsteps on the Ceiling*, but aware of the troubles he and the playwright had in producing Eve's award-winning performance, in a play originally written for Margo.

Charles Affron, in *Star Acting: Gish, Garbo, Davis,* states, "The accumulation of years as an actress, rather than a star, accounts for Margo Channing's center of gravity.... The prodigiousness of the actress [Davis] and her assumption of characterization and existence are the core of *All About Eve*.... In *All About Eve* she enacts her reasons for acting."[2]

In her scene in the theater dressing room Davis is loud, raucously laughing with her maid and her playwright. She changes to grand dame when introduced to her fawning fan, Eve. She can't maintain this posture long, however, and even brings sympathy to Eve's life story. Finally she returns to her down-to-earth nature when her lover/director shows up. She's someone with a sense of humor, a human being, not just an actress. Mankiewicz asserted, "...Margo, *the Actress* ... was — and is — a woman whose need to act equates with her need to breathe. Who, when she isn't 'on'— just isn't, at all."

Davis let herself be photographed as never before with harsh lighting, in cold cream and a wrapper. She changes into a fur coat and "star" look as they leave the dressing room. She looks fifty years old, even though she is probably more beautiful in a contemporary way than we've ever seen her before or after.

Davis maintains her down-to-earth character as we subsequently see her chewing on a chicken drumstick while narrating the positive changes brought to her life by Eve. She is content, at ease and happy.

When awakened by a late-night phone call from Sampson, who is in Hollywood, Davis wears no makeup, revealing baggy eyes, unkempt hair, and the pain in her eyes when she realizes she's forgotten his birthday. After she's hung up, she realizes she has a problem with "Little Miss Evil." Eve had prearranged the phone call to Bill for his birthday and also planned a coming home/birthday party for him, all unbeknownst to Margo.

Birdie Coonan (wonderfully played by Thelma Ritter) is an ex-vaudevillian. Margo and Birdie get together in the dressing room and in her bedroom as Margo dresses for Bill's cocktail party. Here is Margo's true confidante, the one who tells her the truth, the one who is unimpressed with all the theatrical phoniness and is truly concerned with Margo's well-being. They enjoy each other, trust each other, both as characters, and, most importantly, as actors. (One thing never acknowledged was Davis' indebtedness to Ritter when she played Aggie Hurly in *The Catered Affair*; the Bronx accent was Ritter all the way.)

Davis deftly handles the scene with Baxter the morning after the late-night phone call. Talk about cat and mouse! Margo never loses her temper nor lets Eve know she suspects something. She just keeps giving Eve more rope with which to hang herself. Davis does it all from a sitting position in bed, drinking coffee and smoking a cigarette. It isn't until Eve leaves that we see her mounting anger at Eve's motives as she eyes Birdie.

The welcome home cocktail party is where Davis claims, rightfully, the picture as hers. Her "dressing cocktail" with Birdie assisting her is priceless. As Birdie helps her dress, Margo asks Birdie about her past love with a French man. Birdie replies that there wasn't a thing that man didn't know about love. Margo laughs. Birdie asks, speaking about men, if Margo knows that Bill had arrived. Margo gulps down her martini and rushes to the stairs, descending them at a clip, but deliberately slowing down for her entrance. Her disbelief at Sampson's not coming to her, her hurt, shows, but she can't show it to Bill, until finally she can't stand hearing anymore about "the kid" (Eve). The click in her brain has occurred. She sashays up the steps from the sunken living room, stops, looks back at Karen and Bill and says, "Fasten your seat belts. It's going to be a bumpy night!" Exit. Then she, Channing — pure Davis, caustically greets DeWitt and Caswell.

Affron states, "She [Davis] amazes us with her dexterous passage between a role about performance and the performance of a role, and with her ability and courage to both use and demonstrate the tricks of her art and her life."[3]

This is just the beginning. The results are seen much later, when Margo, seated on the piano bench, holding a martini in two hands, asks the pianist to play "Liebestraum" for the fifth time. She is maudlin and full of self-pity. Her bent head, face and body show it.

At a request from her producer, Max Fabian (Gregory Ratoff), Margo leads him to the pantry for a Bromo Seltzer. Richards (High Marlowe) comes upon her. She levels with him about her age and desire not to attempt the role of Cora, a twenty-five-year-old.

Finally, we see Margo, drunk, angrily tell off Eve. She unloads her wrath upon Eve and proceeds upstairs to bed, all the while using the force of her voice for the right effect, and deliberate looks and body movement — no mannerisms — to display the actual feelings of a hurt, deceived woman, albeit a drunk one.

Foster Hirsch, in *Acting Hollywood Style*, explains, "Only once in the film do the verbal gloves come off, in the scene in the back [sic, actually front] of the stalled car in which Margo talks about being fulfilled as a woman. Physically confined — Davis can't do physical shtick in the back [sic] of the car — she speaks her character's (dated) sentiments with a no-frills simplicity."[4]

It is worth noting that Davis had never had such unflattering lighting before. Every line and crease and sagging jowl shows in this film. Milton Krasner had never photographed her before and Davis let him see the whole aging process that had occurred within her. As we know, in retrospect, her hard life had caught up with her; smoking and drinking have a hardening effect on a person's aging. Fortunately, for Davis, she fell in love soon after filming started. The hard-living Gary Merrill was also a heavy drinker and smoker. Their chemistry clicked, and a headlong affair began, which resulted in Davis' fourth marriage and the one that lasted the longest — ten years. But true to the script of *Eve*, the six-year difference in their ages (for one thing) eventually worked against the marriage.

What makes her performance in this film is that it was so close to her personality and she had perfected her acting skills to allow the character to reveal herself through the superb dialogue and the astute direction of Mankiewicz. There was no need for mannerisms or theatrics in order to cover a weak script. Davis always believed acting was larger than life and here was a prime example of this attitude in Margo. Of course, there were differences from Davis' real persona and Margo Channing, but you can believe it wasn't a stretch for Davis to enact Margo in all her emotions. She had them all herself. The movie happened at precisely the right time in her life and career.

There was talk that this revived her career, while others said it was the climax. In truth, it was both. She did get more worthy roles, but not much until 1962 and *What Ever Happened to Baby Jane?* She returned to Broadway with mixed results and was off the screen from 1952 to 1955. She subsequently won only a few major roles worthy of her talents. She even mistakenly turned down Hal Wallis' offer of the lead in *Come Back, Little Sheba*, an Oscar winner for Shirley Booth. Davis received an Oscar nomination in 1952 for her work in the highly underrated *The Star,* the year Booth won.

Davis went to Broadway in 1952. She was offered the mother's role in Broadway's *Look Homeward, Angel* but had to drop out when she fell down a flight of stairs and injured her back in 1954, the beginning of back problems which would affect her later in life, particularly when she was forced to leave *Miss Moffat* in 1974.

All About Eve is the only Davis film that is consistently regarded as a great film. Even other pictures in which she has given great performances lack the distinction awarded this film by critics. It is peculiar because as great a witty comedy as it is, it is a typical Mankiewicz script, very heavy on talk and not very fluid as a movie. Its greatness lies in its performances and wit and depiction of the theater in general.

In *Cult Movies*, Danny Peary writes, "Margo is quite extraordinary: she is vain, but self-effacing, strong enough to hold her own during the course of an argument but vulnerable to its after effects; self-reliant one minute and dependent the next, wanting to be stroked like an alley cat that finds it too difficult to fend for itself all the time."⁵ The critic Peter Travers says, "*All About Eve* ... takes unapologetic glee in the shimmer and sophistication of its language."⁶

One thinks of Eleanora Duse's career which was quite similar. She, like Davis, was a star attraction who performed in many noteworthy plays, but not the classics, and through the force of her ability and talent gave exemplary performances.

Eve provided Mankiewicz with writer and director Oscars for the second year in a row. Previously it was for *A Letter to Three Wives*, which had one *Eve* cast member, the unseen other woman, Celeste Holm. George Sanders won a best supporting actor award for his turn as DeWitt in *All About Eve*.

Thelma Ritter and Celeste Holm were nominated for their supporting roles, and both Baxter and Davis were nominated for Best Actress. None of them won, most likely in Davis' and Baxter's case because Baxter was the studio star and Davis wasn't. That most likely took votes away from Davis, who probably was in competition with Gloria Swanson for *Sunset Boulevard*. So, up popped Judy Holliday, for *Born Yesterday*, who won. Davis did, however, win the New York Film Critics' Award, for the first time, after several ballots. She had been a runner-up for *Dark Victory* in 1939. Another Best Performance award Davis received for *Eve* was at the Cannes Film Festival in May 1951.

Eve, the Oscar winner, was not a blockbuster hit even though it was a critical success. At first, 20th Century–Fox tried reserved seat showings in New York. This was not the way moviegoers went to the movies. In those days, people arrived when they arrived and if they'd missed the beginning of a movie, they stayed for the next showing until it reached where they came in. When they gave up the reserved policy, the studio then released it to art houses in other cities; it did not have first-run house distribution and theaters only took what they wanted; block booking was over. *Eve* didn't even play some towns because it was thought to be too sophisticated for rural areas.

> [It's a] funny business, a woman's career. The things you drop on your way up the ladder, so you can move faster. You forget you'll need them again when you get back to being a woman. That's one career all females have in common—whether we like it or not—being a woman. Sooner or later we've got to work at it, no matter how many other careers we've had or wanted.... And, in the last analysis, nothing is any good unless you can look up just before dinner or turn around in bed—and there he is, without that, you're not a woman. You're something with a French provincial office or a book full of clippings. But you're not a woman ... slow curtain. The end.

In *All About Eve*, Margo says these words to her dearest friend, Karen, while they are stuck in a car which has run out of gas on a country road in Westchester en route to the train station to get Margo back to the city for an evening performance in Lloyd Richards' play, *Aged in Wood*.

Margo sums up her character's thoughts and feelings about life, revealing her great need for Bill Sampson as her husband, not just to be a successful actor.

In real life Davis had similar feelings. She had achieved enormous success as an actor, but had hit an extremely low point in her departure from Warners. *All About Eve* was a miraculous lifeline thrown to her by Mankiewicz. She knew it was one of the best scripts she had ever read.

Within weeks of shooting, Davis also received her second personal lifeline. Her co-star, Gary Merrill, fell completely in love with her, to the extent that he said in his autobiography that he walked around with an erection for two weeks after their meeting.

For Davis, this was her idyllic work situation, a great script and someone to love at the same time. She told Barbara Walters, later in life, that to have a love affair while working added to her performance and well-being. Walter queried why the latter wouldn't be a distraction. Davis just smiled and said to the contrary.

In her later years, Davis continually repeated that her work was her life and that she wished to be remembered as a good worker. It was seldom that she admitted she wished she had also had a lasting love relationship. But with Walters, she did. She said it was the great disappointment of her life that she hadn't had "someone to watch over me."

Nowhere is this better expressed than in Margo's speech to Karen. And nowhere does one see Davis so literally alive and sincere as she is in this scene. By this time in the filming she had fallen in love with Merrill, or, as she ruefully said later, she fell in love with Bill Sampson and Merrill fell in love with Margo Channing. She allowed that she was far less glamorous than Margo Channing and far more domestic than Merrill suspected. In the end, this marriage lasted longer than any of her other three marriages, and Merrill never married again either. She kept his photograph prominently displayed at her future homes.

At the Sarah Siddon Awards in New York, where Eve is to receive her Best Actress award, Margo is basically silent, as we hear an elder statesman actor (Walter Hampden) introduce Eve, and while Addison DeWitt is heard in voice-over. When he focuses on Margo, the camera does likewise. One sees a beautiful, mature woman at the table, giving little attention to the speaker. She's been there before; she's won her awards. She is a star, smoking a cigarette as only Bette Davis could.

What we learn throughout the film's unraveling is that Margo is now a completely satisfied woman, at least with herself and her new husband, who's been awarded a Best Director award for *Footsteps on the Ceiling*. She couldn't be happier. She has the one thing she was lacking before this night, the man in her life. All is right with her world and with Davis' too.

Karen's narration focuses on how Eve became a part of their lives, her first introduction to Margo — in Margo's dressing room. The camera lets one see from where the raucous talk and laughter emanate. Margo narrates a story of her experience with a southern interviewer.

Margo is dressed in a theatrical wrapper, with her hair still bound by strips of cloth to hold it in place under her wig. Her face is still covered in stage make-up and she's puffing away on a cigarette. She's regaling Lloyd and Birdie with her remembrance of the interview. Her sleeves are rolled up and she's all business, just as an actor backstage after giving a performance would be.

When Karen begs Margo to see Eve, Margo immediately puts on a phony grand dame accent and manner as she extends her hand to greet Eve. She couldn't be more phony and grand. Even Birdie comments, "I'll leave the room 'til you're back to normal!"

As Eve tells her trumped-up, sad life story, Margo realizes the sadness and "truth" of Eve's life and changes her attitude and voice entirely to show her true compassion for Eve. Davis makes this change with absolute ease. She drops her theatrical manners and peers at Eve with intense interest and even sympathetic tears. Davis shows one what an understanding and down-to-earth person Margo really is underneath the theatrical persona she hides herself behind. There is no over-emoting, just simple acceptance and concern. One sees it in her eyes and her body language, and it's perfectly believable.

When Margo realizes what a threat to her Eve really is, she resorts to false superiority and actual child-like behavior because of her doubts. At the central scene of the cocktail party, she proceeds to insult everyone there, including her real friends, and really taunts and tests her love, Bill. She becomes blatantly drunk, which is her excuse for her rude behavior. Fortunately, her best friend, Karen, calls her up short when Margo treats Eve abominably.

Although not admitting the wrongness of her behavior, she excuses herself to go to bed. Bill asks her if she needs some help as she starts up the stairs. Margo turns toward Eve below and says, "No, but Eve would help me, wouldn't you, Eve?" Eve replies, "If you'd like." The last word comes from Margo: "I wouldn't like." And she turns to resume her flight. Fortunately, Bill realizes her vulnerability and fear and follows her upstairs.

Davis has a field day in this scene, drunkenly telling off everyone in sight, playing the role of theater goddess to whom everyone must bow. But underneath it, one can see her fear and feeling of inferiority, especially when she admits, in a rude way, that she doesn't have the unyielding grace of Karen, who went to Vassar, because her father needed her behind the notions counter at Woolworth's.

Her fallen face, hooded eyes and deliberate walk shows the inner feelings of Margo and, yes, Davis. Both were fearful of losing their happiness with a younger man.

Davis again shows Margo's deep-seated fear and vulnerability after she reads Addison's ecstatic review of Eve's performance in Margo's role when the latter fills in as an understudy. Margo is standing in her living room, dressed fashionably because she was supposed to meet Karen for lunch. She angrily reads the review aloud to Karen and commenting on it, hits the newspaper with her hand to emphasize her points. She's hurt as well as angry. She, her talent, has been attacked; her being has been attacked.

Bill arrives, whom she hasn't seen for a short while because of a mutual misunderstanding regarding Eve. He has read "that tripe" and now realizes what an underhanded bitch Eve is. He races across the room and surrounds Margo with his arms, his love, his protection. They hold each other and kiss. Karen says she feels *de trop* and leaves as they hug each other again.

Davis again shows how she can so completely make us understand and feel for this wronged woman. Standing alone, she merely reads the review aloud with amazement and hurt over the attack on her. She looks to Karen, but just to ensure her friend is listening. She is confused and wonders aloud what Actor's Equity or her lawyer can do, but she realizes these are only words of desperation. Nothing can be done. The damage has already been inflicted. She doesn't cry out to Karen to help her. Karen just being there is enough,

It's only when Bill arrives that she allows herself to show her hurt as she sobs aloud. Her protector has arrived; that's all she needs or wants.

Of course, it was acting, too. Because when they had their final embrace, it was prolonged to the point where Mankiewicz called out, "Cut! Cut! This isn't swing and sway with Sammy Kaye!"

Margo's concern is every woman's concern, especially in American society, as it was in the 1950s and even today, the fear of getting older in a culture which worships youth. Yet Davis showed us forcefully how much more interesting, how complex a mature woman is, and essentially how attractive she is. Physical beauty is only skin deep, whereas true inner beauty is far more intriguing. Adults should not be afraid of being adults, being who they are, not what they were — something our society finds difficult to accept, especially when applied to a woman.

Alexander Walker, the British writer, in *Bette Davis: A Celebration*, sums up his take on *All About Eve*:

In particular she [Margo] learns what it is to come to terms with the one enemy she can't out-act — age. The whole screenplay is conceived with this universal truth in mind: it is about the sole truth Broadway [Hollywood] recognizes, and the film underlines it again and again.... Margo in this sense is a sort of Everywoman: in all other senses, she remains Bette Davis.[7]

Cast: Margo Channing — Bette Davis; Eve Harrington — Anne Baxter; Addison DeWitt — George Sanders; Karen Richards — Celeste Holm; Bill Sampson — Gary Merrill; Lloyd Richards — Hugh Marlowe; Birdie Coonan — Thelma Ritter; Miss Caswell — Marilyn Monroe; Max Fabian — Gregory Ratoff; Phoebe — Barbara Bates; Speaker at dinner — Walter Hampden; Girl — Randy Stuart; Leading man — Craig Hill; Doorman — Leland Harris; Autograph seeker — Barbara White; Pianist — Claude Stroud; Clerk — William Pullen; Frenchman — Eugene Borden; Reporter — Helen Mowery; Captain of waiters — Steve Geray; Well-wisher — Bess Flowers; Stage Manager — Eddie Fisher (never seen).

Production: Darryl F. Zanuck — Producer; Joseph L. Mankiewicz — Writer and Director; Milton Krasner — Cinematographer; Alfred Newman — Musical Score and Director; Lyle Wheeler and George W. Davis — Art Direction; Thomas Little, Walter M. Scott — Set Directions; Edith Head — Costumes for Miss Davis; Charles LeMaire — Costumes; Edward Powell — Orchestration; Barbara McLean — Editor; Ben Nye — Makeup Artist; Fred Sersen — Special Photographic Effects; W.D. Flick, Roger Herman — Sound; 1950; Running time: 138 minutes.

3

Dark Victory (1939)

Acting Victory

"Who's going to want to see a picture about a girl who dies?"
— Jack L. Warner[1]

Jezebel won Davis an Oscar in 1938, but in 1939 she had four superior roles in four disparate movies. It took much power of persuasion on her part and Casey Robinson's to convince J. L. Warner to produce this classic movie, *Dark Victory*.

Edmund Goulding, her director before and after this movie, guided her throughout her tragic performance, at the zenith of her career. Nowhere is it more apparent that a film adaptation of an inferior stage play can become a classic than in this film *Dark Victory*. Often described as a woman's picture or a weepie (see Appendix III), *Dark Victory* is much maligned because, in fact, the film is a dramatic tragedy in the Grecian classical sense. If it had been a male character in the lead role there would have been no question about the tragic quality of this highly undervalued movie. According to Bernard Dick in his introduction to the book *Dark Victory*:

> *Dark Victory* is a woman's film primarily because a woman is at its center; it is a classic because we are all at the center, sharing a woman's confrontation with her mortality as if it were our own.
>
> If there is an art to living, there is also one of dying.
>
> Except for *Dark Victory*, no woman's film has ever shown how that art can be mastered because no woman's film — and few films of any type — have ever had a protagonist like Judith Traherne who was willing to master that art.[2]

3. Dark Victory (1939)

The screenplay was crafted by Casey Robinson from a play by George Emerson Brewer, Jr. and Bertram Block, which flopped on Broadway (with Tallulah Bankhead in the lead). One significant thing Robinson added at Goulding's request was a best friend for the heroine, Judith Traherne, Ann King, played by Geraldine Fitzgerald. King acts as a Greek chorus, voicing the sorrow and pity about the heroine's tragic condition thereby allowing the heroine, Judith, to be freed of self-pity and able to act heroically. Davis acknowledged, "Mr. Goulding, this true genius of film-making ... worked on the script."[3]

Traherne is one of the roles for which Davis had to fight. Her studio boss, head of Warner Brothers, Jack Warner, couldn't believe anyone would want to see a movie where the heroine goes blind and, even worse, dies at the end. Davis and Hal B. Wallis, the producer, were able to convince Warner to give it the green light.

Not only was 1939 a bonanza year for Hollywood, but it is considered by movie critics to be the best year of movies ever. Everything from *Gone with the Wind* to *The Wizard of Oz* appeared that year. It was, in all likelihood, the premiere year for Davis as well. She starred in four of her best films, *Dark Victory*, *Juarez*, *The Old Maid*, and *The Private Lives of Elizabeth and Essex*. She could have been nominated for an Oscar for any of those performances. But only for *Dark Victory* did she receive a nomination, in addition to its Best Picture nomination.

In later years, she regularly maintained that *Dark Victory* was her favorite film. It was a large financial, as well as critical, success.

After filming started, the production was almost shut down because of Davis. She had just gone through a particularly messy divorce from her first husband, Harmon Nelson, and was full of guilt and anguish. She felt that her nerves were on the edge of a breakdown, and that she couldn't devise the performance which she thought the role demanded. After viewing the early rushes, however, Wallis told her to stay nervous; her performance was just right for the part. Goulding was able to help her accomplish one of the best, most subtle performances of her career. In *Bette Davis: A Celebration*, Alexander Walker stated that Davis had "a quality she had never displayed on the screen — one that attracted the epithet of 'stoic,' even 'beautiful.' That quality was *resignation* ... she surrenders to the only thing a Bette Davis character would have admitted was invincible — which is death itself."[4]

Judith Traherne (Davis), a Long Island socialite, is an independent, strong-willed young woman who excels at horseback riding and other high society pursuits, bridge, theatergoing, nightclubbing, smoking, and drinking. But there is a problem in Traherne's charmed, carefree life. Something is affecting her vision, causing headaches and blurred vision. Traherne tries to ignore it until she is thrown by a horse when she misleads him into a jump. Later that same day, she falls down a flight of stairs.

After Judith falls, Dr. Parsons (Henry Travers) takes her, along with Judith's secretary and friend, Ann (Geraldine Fitzgerald), to see Dr. Frederick Steele (George Brent), a Park Avenue neurosurgeon. The doctor is on the verge of retiring from practice in order to move to Vermont so he can participate in brain cell research. He is reluctant to see Judith, as his nurse, Wainwright (Dorothy Peterson), reminds him he must leave to make his train.

A tortured Davis as the tragic heroine of *Dark Victory* (Photofest).

Dr. Parsons pleads with Steele to see Judith, the girl he brought into the world. His request is rejected and Dr. Steele walks him to the waiting room. Judith hears his dismissal and rises to leave.

Dressed in a fur-trimmed coat-dress with a matching hat, she moves toward the door.

"Wait, Judith," Dr. Parsons tells her, and then introduces her to Dr. Steele. He takes her hand and looks at it while she flippantly describes his patients as his guinea pigs.

"How did you get those burns?"

Judith looks at her fingers, "I never noticed them until now."

He looks into her eyes, then tells her he'll look at her briefly and takes her into his office, closing the sliding doors against Dr. Parsons and Ann.

"I haven't much time," he says.

"I haven't much time either," Judith replies, letting him know her time is just as valuable as his.

He has her sit in a chair facing some windows. He raises a shade and watches Judith. She squints, but says nothing.

"Does the light bother you?"

"No," she answers.

Judith takes a cigarette from her case, but when she starts to light it, she cannot focus correctly. Steele reaches for her hand and helps her.

When she tries to light his cigarette, the same action occurs. Steele has to hold her hand. "That light is in your eyes. You're squinting."

He lowers the shade. "How long have you had these headaches?"

Judith finally admits her problem. She's nervous and frightened. She twists her hands and her voice is shrill. It's lost its authority. She's vulnerable.

"How long have you had them?"

"For a long time, three or four weeks."

She is in such denial that she finally rises and defiantly tells him, "I'm young and strong and nothing can touch me!"

As she starts for the door, he tells her she is frightened.

"That isn't true!" she replies. She returns to him, realizing she needs his help and is hearing the brutal truth.

He kindly tells her he'll conduct a few tests and has her sit on a table while he tests her reflexes. She laughs when he taps her knee. "I always do that. I just find it funny." He smiles at her and continues. He checks her eyes and is concerned with what he sees.

She says, "I've been told they're a nice color." No answer. "Do you agree?" He allows an affirmative reply and tells her there'll be one more test. He asks her to close her eyes and hold out her hands while he puts objects in them for her to identify. She says, "I don't know," when she puts an object in her right hand, but she can identify what is placed in her left hand: a pencil, a cube, and finally a piece of silk cloth. He says, "Now, I'm going to try to fool you." He places a rough burlap-like cloth in her right hand. "You can't fool me ... still silk."

When she opens her eyes, she can see his concern. Wainwright enters to urge him to leave to catch his train.

Judith looks at him with pleading eyes. He returns her look and tells Wainwright, "Cancel the tickets, there'll be another train."

Judith softly responds, "Thank you."

She also apologizes for her original behavior toward him. He tells her she's been a good sport.

When she asks what she can do, Steele tells her to continue her normal daily routine, with only one difference: "You'll be seeing a lot of me."

"I'll bet you'll be a frost at a party," she laughingly replies.

Through this crucial scene, Davis changes from an arrogant socialite to a frightened woman in denial, to a brave woman, grateful for the doctor's ministrations. There is no abrupt change; rather, it is gradual—a learning experience for Judith. Davis displays her initial imperviousness, then spars flippantly with Steele about her Long Island life, shows concern (in her close-ups) over her inability to light the cigarette, demonstrates denial as she tries to believe she is well, and finally reveals her acceptance and gratitude at the doctor's care.

Steele has diagnosed a brain tumor, and an operation ensues, with apparent success. In addition, Traherne and Steele fall in love. Unbeknownst to Traherne, however, the prognosis is bleak. Her cancer will recur and death will occur within a year. The doctor confides this to Ann, Traherne's secretary, but not to Judith.

Judith accidentally discovers the tragic news while in the doctor's office where his things are being packed for their move to Vermont. The office is in similar disarray as on her first visit. She enters, beautifully outfitted in a silver fox fur jacket and matching hat on top of her piled-up hair. She's bright and cheery with Wainwright and asks if she can help.

Wainwright tells her the doctor will meet her at the restaurant for lunch. Wainwright goes to help the movers, and Judith looks around the outer office, then proceeds to Steele's inner office, all smiles. She sits at his desk and reads one of his framed degrees aloud. Her voice is proud and happy. She starts to straighten the letters on his desk, talking aloud to herself about how they will be useful people in the world. As she stands to set the pile of letters aside, she notices a manila folder with her name on it. "Judith Traherne," she says and sits down again to read the letter in the folder. Her face crumbles as she sees "Prognosis: Negative." She flips through a few more letters from other doctors, each saying, "Prognosis: Negative."

"Wainwright?" she calls.

"Yes."

"What does prognosis mean?" she asks as she comes to the doorway.

"The future of a case."

"What does negative mean?"

"It means the outcome is ... hopeless."

Judith darts through the outer office door. Wainwright turns in her desk chair and suddenly realizes what she has said. She stands and gasps, clapping her hand to her forehead in dismay.

Again Davis deliberately shows how a person's emotions can change radically without histrionics. Just a simple slouch and crumbling of her face indicates the shock she has received. Her quiet questioning of Wainwright and simple darting out the door displays all the emotion necessary to see her desperation.

In that short scene Judith goes from being a happy, relaxed woman to a woman of steel as she swiftly marches from the office — from her happy life to one of tragedy. She shows it all in her face and body.

The scene that follows the revelation takes place in a restaurant. Traherne is at a table, drinking one martini after another. First, her fiancé, Dr. Steele, shows up. They spar verbally as he tries to discover what is bothering her. When her friend, Ann, arrives for lunch and asks if they shouldn't order, Traherne replies that she will have a helping of prognosis negative! She downs her drink and leaves King and Steele sitting in stunned silence.

Dressed to the nines in her fashionable silver fox jacket and hat, Davis' Traherne is the epitome of 1939 glamour. Without a false movement, she uses her body, and especially her distraught, disbelieving face, as she grabs her fox muff and imperiously leaves the table and restaurant, to reveal a proud, regal, stalwart as well as hurt and angry woman who's been deceived by the two people she loves the most.

Finding peace and forgiveness is not easy for Judith. She must go through a period of anger and denial as she carouses with her friends, especially Alec (Ronald Reagan), and drives herself to perform well in horse riding at tournaments. She's rude to everyone, alienating many of her friends. Her behavior leads men to believe she is a very loose woman.

At one tournament, after the race is over and Judith has won a cup, she changes from her riding habit to an evening gown and continues to drink at the bar even though she receives pleas for her to accept her award.

On her way out, she runs into Steele, who says he's been looking all over for her. Judith lashes into him for his betrayal, very angrily assaulting him. He replies, "I know how you feel — anything to strike back at me. But don't do it this way.... Judith, I want you to find peace. Death when it comes ... decently ... beautifully ... finely."

When she leaves to accept the award, Alec sees Steele and invites him to go for a drink. A group of men pass them and one makes a disparaging remark about Judith. Alec calls him on it and the man swings at him. Steele punches him and he lands on the floor.

Upon arriving home, Judith goes to the stable to see about a sick horse, "Jessica's Girl." Her groom, Michael (Humphrey Bogart), and she return to the warm tack room where she forces him to talk to her. Finally she says, "You're making love to me, aren't you, Michael?"

Michael acknowledges it and moves in and kisses her, but Judy pushes him away and reveals that she is going to die.

The iconic shot of Davis as Judith Traherne when she faces death beautifully and finely (Photofest).

She remembers what Steele said. "When it comes, it's got to be met finely, beautifully..." She has forgiven him and realizes her love for him.

Davis exposes the character's coming to terms with death: disbelief, denial, isolation, anger, bargaining, depression, and finally, acceptance.

Steele and Traherne marry and live in Vermont, where he continues his medical research, with her loving support. A fall weekend comes when Steele is to travel to New York to deliver his medical research. At the same time, Judith's eyesight begins to fail. She knows it is the sign that the end is hours away, but she doesn't let her husband know. She sends him on his way. Ann, nearby, realizes what is occurring. Judith even sends her away. As she climbs the stairs to her bedroom, she hugs her two English setters, sends them away and crawls onto her bed after saying a prayer. The housekeeper appears and covers her with a comforter, then draws the shades. Charles Affron, in *Star Acting*, expresses it well, "The best is saved for the famous final shot and the culmination of the heroine's looking ahead, her strength to grasp the future.... It is her [Davis'] bravery and strength, not Judith Traherne's, that constitute the film's real victory."[5]

3. Dark Victory (1939)

A major opportunity was missed with these final scenes. Someone allowed Max Steiner, the composer, to ascend those stairs with Davis with "heavenly" music and a "heavenly" choir. How much better if it had been done in complete silence, with only natural sounds.

Davis was completely believable as the beautiful socialite without a care in the world who is transformed into a selfless, responsible person, concerned about other humans, not just herself.

In real life it may have helped that she and Brent had an affair during filming. She always maintained that love gave an edge to her performances. Originally Spencer Tracy had been considered for the doctor's role but, for once, Brent seems ideally cast (and, of course, the love affair probably helped his performance too). A very handsome Irish man, Brent supposedly fought with the IRA and was a long-time contractee with Warners. He played opposite Davis in many films including, *Jezebel, The Old Maid* and *The Great Lie*.

Edmund Goulding had helped make Davis a star. In *That Certain Woman* in 1937 he made sure she received star treatment, and he later directed her again in *The Great Lie*. He really gave Davis the sympathetic treatment she needed, as a person, while acting in *Dark Victory*. But he couldn't prevent Ronald Reagan from refusing to play the gay character he was supposed to be. As Judith's friend, Alec, he obviously is not romancing her, but then neither does he appear gay; he's just a cipher who drinks companionably with Judith.

After the completion of the film, Davis admitted she asked for a private screening and said she couldn't suppress a grin on her face when she emerged from the screening room. She knew her work was superior. Affron confirms her feelings by saying, "The face ... is possessed by a will and an intelligence that concentrate physique, pattern and moment.... Davis' Judith Traherne becomes ours. No other interpretation is imaginable, so unswerving and sure is the version she created." The New York Film Critics acknowledged she would have won the best actress award that year if it hadn't been for Vivien Leigh in *Gone with the Wind*. Even Davis, the runner-up, said she was "gone with the wind." As was well-known at the time, she had almost been given the role of Scarlett. In fact, the American public had voted her the number one choice for the role. She regretted the loss for the rest of her life.

Foster Hirsch writes in *Acting Hollywood Style*, "Bette Davis ... provides [a] prime example of how charged, wordless off-screen looks function in talking pictures ... the look is the visual center of the performance and also carries the story forward. In these moments of heightened intimacy between player and camera, actors in effect become co-authors."[6]

The public very nearly did not get to see Davis in *Dark Victory*, even after all the pre-production acrimony among Davis, J.L. Warner and Casey

Robinson as to whether or not the movie would be produced. Davis had been constantly pursuing the role, but when the production started, she was one nervous woman. She had just gone through a divorce initiated by her first husband, Harmon O. Nelson. During the ending of their union, she had had an affair with her director of *Jezebel*, William Wyler, and later a short affair with Howard Hughes.

Arriving on the set, she was full of guilt and remorse over the way she had treated Nelson. As the shooting progressed, she felt she was on the edge of a nervous breakdown. Admittedly, a highly energetic, not to say volatile, young woman, she told Edmund Goulding of her concern. He and Hal Wallis watched the early rushes and concluded that her nervousness was exactly what she needed for her character. She came across perfectly. It was this nervousness that Davis could integrate correctly into Traherne's character, especially when the character feels betrayed by her doctor and her best friend, Ann.

Because movies are rarely shot sequentially, but filmed using a set that may be seen in several disparate scenes, the *Dark Victory* sequences which took place in Dr. Steele's office were filmed one right after another. They involved Judith's first visit to Steele, and the scene when she discovers her true condition of "prognosis negative." If these were two of the scenes initially filmed, Traherne would have been nervous, upset and even near hysteria. It would be understandably taxing for Davis to control her own personal emotions under these circumstances so soon after the emotional turmoil of her divorce.

Fortunately, Edmund Goulding had worked with her before. He was aware of her personality and what a highly emotional woman she was. He was a very insightful director who came to Warners from M-G-M, where he had worked with their top female stars, notably Greta Garbo in *Grand Hotel*.

During her first visit to Dr. Steele, Judith, although trying to hide her fear, exhibits her nervousness and fear all through the preliminary examination. She twists her hands, won't engage the doctor with eye contact, and reveals a high-pitched anxiety in her voice.

The second scene begins with Judith excitedly looking forward to her marriage with Steele and their move to Vermont. When she comes across the file showing her negative prognosis, however, it changes her whole demeanor. Fear and anger strike her all at once, because she can't believe she hasn't been told the truth by her doctor/fiancé or her friend, Ann.

All of her personal feelings could be called upon by Davis at this time but, as she said, it was probably very upsetting to her because she felt out of control.

During filming, she and her co-star, George Brent, began an affair. Davis even admitted that when they were doing the scene where she is admitted to the hospital for her operation, she and Brent could not look at each other without breaking up. She, like her character, had fallen in love. Actually, this wasn't an entirely new feeling. Ever since she had come to Warners in 1932 and acted in some of her earliest films, she had felt a great attraction to Brent. But he married Ruth Chatterton, an older Warners star from the twenties and thirties.

Hollywood actors falling for their co-stars or directors, given such an intense bonding experience over a four-to-six-week shoot, was considered a common occurrence. And just as usual was the affair lasting no longer than the production itself. Little was said publicly during Hollywood's Golden Age because the studio publicity agents worked overtime protecting their stars from scandal and the American public's wrath.

If one views *Dark Victory* carefully, one can almost tell how these two personal events affected Davis' performance. Here was a complex, varied character, Judith Traherne, who suffers a tragedy but also displays her serene happiness once she has married Steele.

Stills taken by George Hurrell show a tortured face, a tragic mask created by Davis. Her eyes have a haunted, fearful look. Yet other photos show her as what Hurrell called a most beautiful woman. In fact, the latter stills show a Davis as never seen before or since. She had a serene loveliness.

At the beginning of the film, Judith is a head-strong, confident woman. Look at the way she treats her secretary/companion, Ann, as less than an equal. She is full of energy and dismisses her headache as a hangover. She takes a call from her stable boy, Michael, and berates him for not following her orders. She argues with him about the value of a horse's worth. She defiantly rides the horse, but misleads it in a jump. She only later admits that to Ann and only because of her blurred vision.

Traherne tries to dismiss her family doctor's concern and bounds out of her bedroom to fall the length of the stairs. All this time, Davis portrays Traherne as an energetic woman who thinks she's completely in control of her life. Even at the surgeon's, her immediate reaction is to leave the office. A person like her cannot be ill.

Her nervousness rises when the doctor takes her into his inner office for the exam. She covers her fear with sarcasm and bravura remarks.

When Steele finally asserts she is certainly ill, seriously ill, Traherne tries to escape but is stopped by Steele's obvious sincerity and seriousness.

Davis shows a full range of emotions throughout the examination scene, finally culminating in her acceptance that she must face her problem if she is to solve it. Davis' energy is palpable throughout the scene as Brent gives her a calm, solid character to act against. The script, and Goulding, gave them the leeway to expose their interior emotions.

The hospital scene, prior to Traherne's operation, again pits Davis against

Brent as he handles his patient firmly but with care. A triangle is formed when Ann is allowed to become the best friend of Judith, and Steele's support, as Judith is acclimated to the hospital and her forthcoming brain operation. Goulding photographs the three of them together in the second shots.

Davis again is quite energetic, full of questions about why she has to follow hospital rules; but the new connection with Brent lets her flourish with the love she expresses through her smiles, laughs and looks as she banters with him. Davis shows us that Traherne now has a person in addition to her friend, Ann, whom she trusts implicitly. Actually, they are a threesome, each supporting the others.

After the apparently successful operation, Traherne throws a party for her friends and invites Steele. Everything goes quite well and she lovingly gives Steele a pair of cuff links.

However, afterward Ann makes an appointment to see Steele. He tells her of Judith's true diagnosis. Judith wonders where Ann has gone, and the maid inadvertently tells Judith that Ann has gone to see Steele. Judith is suspicious and jealous. She has revealed her feelings toward Steele to Ann in a telling scene. She's the old Judith who can't stay still. She walks in and out of the room, all the while talking about and seeking Ann's approval.

When Ann arrives home, Judith accuses her of lying when she said she was going shopping. Fortunately, Steele arrives soon after and Ann goes upstairs. He has brought Judith a gift. She falls into his arms, losing her insecurity, knowing he loves her.

It was not unusual for Davis to credit films as parallel to her personal life, perhaps because it helped her to explain her own reactions to her life experiences. In the Actor's Studio misguided use of Stanislavsky's theory on acting, such a comparison rings true. But Davis eschewed "method acting." She preferred being theatrical. She did not search her inner self for a character's motivation. The playwright's or screenwriter's words were her inspiration. She took this character and subsumed it into her own persona, then acted it all for us to see.

At her age of 32, she did not have a Long Island socialite's background, nor had she suffered a brain tumor. But she could empathize with that role and bring her emotional feelings to express Judith's character and audiences believed in her realistic, though theatrical and bigger than life, portrayal.

Davis and Brent continued their rather long affair beyond this picture, but she maintained that secretaries got in the way. When she finished the series of four pictures in a row, she went to her beloved New England for a rest after June 1939, when she'd completed *The Private Life of Elizabeth and Essex*. Her affair with Brent was over, and she met her second husband, Arthur Farnsworth, in New Hampshire. Brent and Davis acted together again in the 1940s movies *The Great Lie* (1941) and *In This Our Life* (1942).

3. *Dark Victory (1939)*

In *Dark Victory* all the factors — a great Casey Robinson script, Edmund Goulding's direction, Davis' divorce and subsequent love affair with Brent, the great photography of Ernest Haller — came together to enhance one of Davis' greatest performances.

Frank S. Nugent, of the *New York Times*, wrote:

> Miss Davis is superb. More than that, she is enchanted and enchanting ... a great role — rangy, full-bodied, designed for a virtuoso, almost sure to invite the faint damning of "tour de force." But that must not detract from the eloquence, the tenderness, the heart-breaking sincerity with which she has played it. We do not belittle an actress to remark upon her great opportunity, what matters is that she made the utmost of it.[7]

(Nugent felt Davis should have received an Oscar for this role rather than the previous year's *Jezebel*.)

James Skelly Hamilton, in *The National Board of Review Magazine*, said:

> ... Bette Davis is the answer. It's her show, her special kind of show all the way through.... She has never before seemed to be so entirely inside a part, with every mannerism and physical aspect of her suited to its expression. If she has deserved medals before, in parts of more dramatic validity, she deserves the prayerful gratitude of *Dark Victory*'s authors.[8]

The picture was nominated for an Oscar, along with Davis' performance and Geraldine Fitzgerald's in the supporting category. Also nominated was Max Steiner for his original score. None of them won. In those days ten pictures were nominated for Best Oscar, rather than today's five. Davis was beaten by Vivien Leigh, and Fitzgerald by Hattie McDaniel, both for *Gone with the Wind*. Fitzgerald, a superior talent, would never win an Oscar.

Davis, alone, was starred* above the title in the film's credits. Even Brent, who'd been at Warners and was a star before Davis came to the studio, was featured in smaller print below the title.

Warners' top designer, Orry-Kelly, created Davis' elegantly modern costumes, including fox furs, a fur-trimmed coat-dress, and smart casual wear when the couple settles in New Hampshire. Davis was gowned very glamorously, and George Hurrell took some publicity stills of her at this time that are extraordinary. In *Mother Goddam*, Whitney Stine says, "When she came to the portrait gallery, George Hurrell saw something different in her face. 'You're beautiful, Bette,' he told her and proceeded to take a series of pictures that would be the most outstanding of her entire career. He captured a delicate, appealing quality."[9] Davis was in her halcyon days.

It was soon thereafter, when Frank Capra was working at Warners (probably on *Arsenic and Old Lace*), that Davis spotted him in the studio dining

---

*Featured actors were listed below the title. Those above were starred.

room. She called out to him, "What have you got for me, Frank?" He replied, "You've got it all, Bette!"

John Springer, in *They Had Faces Then*, opines "...the star of the thirties — and into the forties, too — Davis, it was."[10]

Cast: Judith Traherne — Bette Davis; Frederick Steele — George Brent; Ann King — Geraldine Fitzgerald; Michael O'Leary — Humphrey Bogart; Alex Hamin — Ronald Reagan; Dr. Parsons — Henry Travers; Carrie Spottswood — Cora Witherspoon; Miss Wainwright — Dorothy Peterson; Martha — Virginia Brissac; Colonel Mantle — Charles Richman; Dr. Carter — Herbert Rawlinson; Dr. Driscoll — Leonard Mudie; Miss Dodd — Fay Helm; Lucy — Lottie Williams.

Production: Hal B. Wallis — Producer; David Lewis — Associate Producer; Edmund Goulding — Director; Casey Robinson — Writer; Robert Haas — Art Direction; William Holmes — Editor; Ernest Haller — Cinematographer; Max Steiner — Musical Score; Leo F. Forbstein — Musical Director; Orry-Kelly — Costumes; 1939; 105 minutes.

4

The Little Foxes (1941)

STAR VERSUS DIRECTOR

> *"I never meant Regina to be a violent woman or a fiery woman..."*[1]
> — Lillian Hellman

"I hope you die. I hope you die soon. I'll be waiting for you to die." Regina Giddens (Bette Davis) angrily speaks to her heart-weakened husband, who has just returned from a sanitarium. They are in his old bedroom where Regina has had his things moved, anticipating his return.

She stands her ground, never flinching, as she attacks Horace (Herbert Marshall) with her hatred for him, especially now, because he has rejected investing in a scheme with his two brothers-in-law to build a cotton mill in partnership with a northern industrialist. This period drama takes place in 1900 in the deep south.

Regina and her brothers, Ben (Charles Dingle) and Oscar Hubbard (Carl Benton Reid), have been waiting for Horace's return to get $75,000 from him, their banker, to seal the deal. Discussion of the deal with Horace in his bedroom, at Regina's insistence, has exhausted him. The brothers realize that this is an inopportune moment, and they leave.

In 1940, Davis worked for William Wyler for a second time, playing Leslie Crosbie in *The Letter*. In 1941, she anticipated another association with Wyler in the adaptation of the successful play, *The Little Foxes*. For only the second, and last, time, Warners loaned out Bette Davis, this time to Samuel Goldwyn for this production. The first time had been to RKO for *Of*

Human Bondage in 1934. Now seven years later, Davis was the top star of Warners, and Jack L. Warner made a deal to borrow Gary Cooper for *Sergeant York* in return for Davis' services. Regina was a strong role, executed onstage by Tallulah Bankhead. Written by Lillian Hellman, *The Little Foxes* was a drama of greed, avarice and post–Civil War southern mendacity, to be directed by Davis' favorite director.

One must address this movie with the question, "What went wrong and what went right?" for it is the key to an unexpected masterpiece of ensemble acting.

For good or for bad, Davis saw the Bankhead performance on Broadway and subsequently felt it was the definitive characterization, the only way the role of Regina Giddens could be portrayed. (Zoe Caldwell remarked in *I Will Be Cleopatra*: "When I have seen an actress totally define a role, I am satisfied I don't want to play it.")[2] William Wyler had other ideas. He felt Regina needed to show some warmth and charm in order for her to be convincing in how she manipulates her family to get what she wants. In addition, he was displeased with the makeup Davis and Perc Westmore had developed for Regina, a calamine white lotion, even though it was correct for the period. It did not photograph easily. The battle began.

The opening of the movie clearly establishes that we are in the Deep South in a well-to-do southern mansion, the mansion of the Giddens (Horace and Regina, and their daughter Zan). Regina's brothers live nearby, one of them, Oscar, has a wife, Birdie (Patricia Collinge). We zero in on a family, composed of the Hubbards and Giddens, complete with a black servant. We hear Regina's voice of authority calling from a balcony above to her daughter, Alexandra (Teresa Wright), who is about to be sent north to retrieve her father from a sanitarium. That evening, Regina and her brothers entertain a visiting northern industrialist, William Marshall (Russell Hicks). Regina turns on what charm she can muster to help her brothers convince the industrialist to invest in a local cotton mill, the key factor being low wages which the local black people will willingly take.

Birdie, married to the avaricious brother, Oscar, has watched her life drift away from her antebellum Southern plantation upbringing to become an alcoholic. She has even come to hate her only son, Leo (Dan Duryea). She escapes by drinking wine and living in the fantasy of the past.

Ben, the eldest Hubbard, has led a life completely devoted to avarice and greed. His only family is his brother and sister, and he is not close to or intimate with either. He feels superior to both and is particularly misogynistic toward Regina. There is no love lost among the three of them.

One never learns what kind of parents the three of them had. One can only conjecture from their behavior, and Birdie's few comments, that there was little love for any of them. None of them knows how to love another human being, only how to manipulate others in the name of greed. They use people, even each other, to achieve their goals. Only Horace has been able to impress his better nature, and his internal strength, upon his daughter Zan, much to Regina's surprise.

In a scene following the dinner given for the northern industrialist Marshall, Regina turns on the charm. For the most part, Davis is seated on a Victorian settee. Through simple looks, sly smiles, or a foot kicking her brother, she shows how charming she can be with the industrialist. She takes in every detail and controls what is happening, editing her brothers' remarks, indulging in her sister-in-law Birdie's and her daughter Alexandra's musical recital, controlling the conversation and the length of the after-dinner social gathering. There is never a misplaced action, look or tone of voice. Davis uses all her skills as an actress to reveal her character and let the viewer understand her words and actions, particularly through body movements and facial expressions. One can always "read" Davis' eyes and face, especially her oft-used technique of an outward-looking stare. Regina's thoughts can be "read" this way.

She knows she has charmed Mr. Marshall. She knows she has ultimate control over her brothers. She also believes she has control over her husband, Horace, and her daughter.

Even after Marshall leaves, when she and her brothers quarrel over Horace's yet-to-be investment in the project, one can sense the brothers' unwillingness to cross her.

After Horace's return from the sanitarium where he's been recovering from a heart attack, he rejects their plan. He tells Regina he has no desire to become a wealthier man, that he and Regina have all the means necessary for them. He also says he has no intention of cooperating with her brothers' scheme which will be completed with "slave labor."

Before Horace's return from the sanitarium, however, Leo, Regina's nephew, has stolen railroad bonds from Horace's safety deposit box at the bank where he works as a clerk for his uncle. He did this with the approval of his father (Oscar) and his other uncle (Ben) in order to meet a deadline for investment prior to Horace's return. (The brothers' scheme was advanced without Regina's knowledge, and Horace accidentally discovers the theft after he goes to get his will from his safety deposit box.) The two brothers thus believe they have the upper hand, but they are still reluctant to cross Regina.

Horace tells Regina, "We'll just sit by and watch the boys get rich." Regina, furious, says, "We'll have to talk about it, just you and me."

They continue to fight as Zan comes inside from the terrace. She is frightened for her father. But the fighting stops and Regina comes downstairs to ask Ben for more time.

Horace appears at the top of the landing, listens and returns to his bedroom.

Regina appears and Horace says, "It's a great day when you and Ben cross swords. I've been waiting for it for years."

Regina, completely defeated, turns on him and unleashes her wrath.

That next day, Horace visits his bank. After leaving the bank with his safety deposit box, Horace tells Cal (John Marriott), his servant, to return to the bank and deliver a message to the manager that he is to go to Mobile and bring back his attorney.

At home, Horace has placed the box on a table in front of the living room settee. Regina returns from her dressmaker to find him sitting there. She berates him for being in her part of the house, but he ignores her remarks, saying he has something he wants her to see, that someone has taken $75,000 worth of Union Pacific bonds from his bank box. Regina looks at him incredulously and asks, "What kind of joke are you playing now? Is this for my benefit?"

She sits on the settee and opens the box to discover he has told the truth, that Leo has stolen the bonds so Ben and Oscar can use them to invest with Mr. Marshall.

Regina leans back and laughs, "Well, this will make a fine little scandal. A scandal to hold over their heads. How could they be such fools?" She laughs again.

But Horace ruins her thoughts, telling her there will be no scandal because it will be a loan from her ... not an investment. "For once in your life, I am tying your hands."

Regina responds, "You must hate me very much."

"Why did you marry me?" he asks.

"I only have contempt for you. I was lonely ... yes, lonely ... not in the way people usually mean. I was lonely for all the things I wasn't going to get! I thought you'd get the world for me."

Regina rises from the settee and crosses over to the window, looking out. "You are a soft, weak fool," she says. "I'm lucky, Horace. I've always been lucky. I'll be lucky again."

Horace's face registers a twinge of pain, then a more severe reaction. He reaches for his medicine bottle on the table by his wheelchair. He opens the bottle, but, in his haste, he drops it and the bottle spills its liquid contents. He gasps to Regina, "Get me the other bottle upstairs."

Regina sits on the settee, staring past him with a rigid look on her face. She moves not a muscle.

4. The Little Foxes *(1941)*

Regina Giddens (Davis) waiting for her husband, Horace, to die (Photofest).

Horace's call for Addie (Jessie Grayson) is barely a whisper. Agonizingly, he rises from the wheelchair and crosses slowly behind Regina toward the stairway.

Regina continues to face straight ahead, acknowledging Horace's departure only by moving her eyes left to where he has been. She hears a dish fall from the hall table, sits up a little and continues to look to her left.

Horace tries to climb the stairs, but only makes it a few steps before he collapses.

Regina waits a full three seconds, an eternity, then rises and rushes toward the stairs, calling for Addie and Cal.

In *Stars*, Richard Dyer feels there are two moments where Davis shows the interior thoughts of Regina when she refuses to fetch Horace's medicine:

> ...she remains motionless and her expression does not alter ... only two performance signs of Davis to discuss, facial expressions and posture ... in many respects indecipherable, mouth closed, eyes "straight ahead" ...the posture rigid. There is ... a formal pace. The total stillness is striking ... repression, the deliberate suppression of all expression of emotion ... thereby to emotion itself.... the next shot ... close-up of her face ... movement of eyes to their left, an intense emotion — contrary and intense. We learn the character of Regina is not pure evil. Regina has to operate within the *house*.[3]

This is serious drama, a study of greed and its consequences on the human soul, a powerful play from a distinguished playwright, Lillian Hellman, who also wrote the basic screenplay.

What went wrong? 1. This was about a financially declining southern family. The set and clothes show a family who must be wealthy, with no financial problems. It belies the basis for the greed and materialism exhibited by the characters. 2. The excellent cast, with the exception of Davis and Herbert Marshall, were the New York cast intact. They'd played their parts to perfection. Davis was a movie star, albeit a great actress, but she had not the months of performances under her belt. 3. Davis, the star, disagreed with the director, William Wyler, as to her characterization; and she had the power, as a star, to play it her way. She actually shut down production for over three weeks when the division became unbearable. Davis maintained she returned because of her professional duty to do so.

What went right? Or, better yet, what went right because of what went wrong? 1. Sam Goldwyn prevailed in the choice of the opulent set and beautiful costumes, yet the viewing public wasn't distracted from the story or the characters. The set was really a non-issue. What worked was that the set and costumes were the correct period, and the actors used the set and costumes to enhance their roles. In particular, Davis had never looked this way before. Her hair, an upswept pompadour of the Victorian era, and her eyes, narrowed by heavy eyeliner, gave her the right look for a strong, determined woman.

2. Because Davis was a consummate actress, she played well with the other Broadway actors. Tellingly, her character dominates the others, including her brothers. Davis had a star quality that none of her co-stars had; they were not Hollywood stars at all. So she not only became part of the ensem-

ble, she added dramatic weight to the scenes in which she played. There are few, if any, real close-ups of Davis in this movie. With the ensemble approach, Davis not only blended in, but she did so without mannerism or upstaging. Her very stillness, at times, drew the audience to her character. She was the complex one, not the others. Gregg Toland's deep-focus photography allowed one to see an entire scene in all its detail.

3. Although Davis says she played Regina the only way it could be played, as Bankhead had, Wyler, through the use of ensemble acting, either forced her or allowed her to see the necessity of variation of character in her performance beyond displaying mere avarice, greed and yes, lust for power and wealth. Finally, we see her fear and loneliness. It is a multi-faceted performance, all true to the character. In *Acting Hollywood Style*, Foster Hirsh comments, "...Wyler understood the star's power is in fact intensified by being leashed, with few close-ups and forced to share the spotlight, Davis internalizes the character's rage and her own ... she gives a tight, brittle, murderously subdued performance."[4]

Later in life, Davis still did not recognize Regina as one of her best performances, but audiences and critics did.

Charles Affron, in *Star Acting*, succinctly describes Wyler's exact direction, using the house set, furniture and windows to underscore the film's main thrust about the Hubbard family's quest for power and greed. We witness the sister, Regina Giddons, her two brothers, and her husband, their placement in rooms and upon the main staircase signifying the pinnacles of power as they play out their destinies in their dark, cruel world.

Affron states, "She [Bette Davis] sees all, just like Wyler's ideal audience. The freedom of directorial perspective and the accuracy of the actress's glance meet at the centers of images that are turned to the movement of the camera and the throbbing stillness of Davis's being."[5]

With Horace now dying, Regina comes downstairs to confront her brothers and Leo. She realizes she now has complete control over her brothers. Horace was unable to carry out his threat to adjust the will so his Union Pacific bonds would go to her only as a repayable loan from her brothers. Her ace is that she knows exactly what happened, and confronts them, demanding 75 percent of the profits from their joint investment.

She laughs when they leave. Just minutes later, when Horace dies, Regina again comes downstairs to confront Ben, Oscar and Leo. "If I don't get what I want I'll put you all in jail.... You boys are sort of working for me now."

Zan realizes what an evil woman her mother is, and ultimately, stands up to her. She has joined the group, upset over her beloved father's death. Regina tells her to go to bed, but Zan says she wants to ask some questions, and she stays, hearing the whole discussion.

Ben finally says, "The world is open for people like you and me."

Zan tells Regina she is not going to Chicago with her.

"If I say not?" Regina replies.

"Say it, Momma. Say it and see what happens."

Regina slowly walks halfway up the stairs, turns and says, "Alexandra, would you like to sleep in my room tonight."

"What's the matter, Mama? Are you afraid, Mama?"

This is a telling remark from Alexandra to her mother. Regina is left alone, unloved and unwanted. What Regina doesn't realize, even at the end, when she faces loneliness and fear, is that she has severed what every human being needs, love from another human being. She has become inhuman even to her daughter. She will be tolerated by her brothers because she has the power, but she will have no love from anyone. We see her fear in the last close-up of her face behind a lace curtain, as she watches her grown, maturing daughter leave with her fiancé, David Hewitt (Richard Carlson). There is nothing but fear in her eyes as she stares out the window, no self-knowledge, just fear. She is left with her material possessions only—a life that will most likely lead to psychosis, similar but different from her sister-in-law Birdie.

This is Davis at her peak—no mannerisms, part of the ensemble cast, letting the character be revealed through her. It is great acting under a great director.

Alexander Walker, in *Bette Davis: A Celebration*, feels, "By suppressing Davis's emotions, Wyler exposed her genius."[6]

Under perfectionist director, William Wyler, the equally perfectionist actor, Davis, developed the multi-faceted character of Regina, even though the director and she were at loggerheads throughout the production. They never worked together again, even though Davis always maintained Wyler was the best director she had ever had and that she would have jumped into the Hudson River if he so directed.

What is strongly evident in *The Little Foxes* are two resources the actor effectively used to great advantage. She used these resources in other films, but here one sees the major effect they have on her performance.

Davis clearly understands the importance of the set, or house, in this film. The house is her domain. It is where she exerts her power. Regina controls all the situations, the scenes, in her house.

In the opening dinner sequence, without Horace, she is in charge of the dinner party in the dining room. She decides on the topics of conversation. She decides who will speak and basically what they have to say in response to the guest, the northern industrialist. She decides when dinner and dinner conversation is over, and when the party will move to the parlor for coffee and musical entertainment, provided by Birdie and Zan.

Davis is alert to everyone's needs, carefully watching and listening to everyone's talk at the table. She admonishes her brothers, always ingratiating herself and her family with Mr. Marshall. Small, smiling glances are bequeathed to Mr. Marshall throughout the meal.

In the parlor, while Birdie and Zan play the piano, Regina is prominently featured on the room's only settee. One arm is gracefully across the rounded back, and Regina sits with her legs crossed, the better to kick Oscar and laugh softly when Oscar dozes off. As she kicks Oscar's foot, she looks charmingly at Marshall.

When the brothers again start to discuss the cotton mill, Regina circumvents the potential overkill by telling them it's time to say goodnight to Mr. Marshall.

Davis is all grace and smiles for Marshall, but she keeps her eyes on all of them, her brothers, Birdie and Zan. She doesn't miss a trick.

Everyone watches Regina to see if they're doing well. She is the leader of the pack. She's the one who provides the southern hospitality and the assurance that her husband will be involved.

Davis uses stillness through the scene as others move around or cause a commotion. She is the "eye of the storm."

Davis allows the furnishings and the house to become powerful props for her character. Her Victorian settee is like a throne for displaying the queen of the household. She is comfortable in it and she rules from it. It is part of her materialist greed.

Before Horace comes home, she has the servant, Hal, remove Horace's bedroom furnishings to his old room, not the marriage room. She isolates Horace from her domain and later attacks him for being in her part of the house.

Regina issues commands from her bedroom balcony to Zan down below on a terrace; she issues commands to her brothers from the main staircase and, most fatally, she controls all the actions in the parlor, her part of the house when she allows Horace to die, remaining seated on her settee as Horace desperately tries to get medicine and help from the servant, Addie, when he suffers the final major heart attack.

Davis dominates the scene when Regina argues with her brothers over the stolen bonds. She resorts to rising above them on the stairs and issuing her proclamations.

When Zan challenges her mother, she must come up to meet her part way on the stairs. It's the one time Regina is defeated, as her maturing daughter refuses to do her mother's bidding.

The house itself is like Regina's castle; here she is all-powerful. But outside in the real world she has trouble controlling others, including her sister-

Davis and Teresa Wright on the set of *The Little Foxes*, with Carl Benton Reid behind them (Photofest).

in-law, Birdie and her daughter's boyfriend. They are able to defy her when she is out of her domain.

Davis not only was expert at using the setting to enhance her characterization, but, in this film, more than any others, she uses stillness to display her control and power.

4. The Little Foxes (1941)

When confronted, she uses stillness to the point of rigidity to offset any attack. Only Horace seems able, at times, to cause her to lose control. He thwarts her initial attempt to let her brothers have the $75,000 for investment. However, she still believes she will be able to persuade him to invest. What she really does is punish him and limit his access to certain areas of the house.

Even with the revelation of Leo's theft, though, she realizes she cannot persuade Horace to use the money as investment. It is only then that she angrily attacks Horace, saying she never loved him. This causes the heart attack and puts Regina/Davis in her position of stillness and control. Sitting rigid on the settee, she only moves her eyes as she grasps the arm of the settee and waits for him to collapse.

From then on, Regina bides her time with stillness and control until finally she has complete domination over her brothers. Even when she loses her daughter, she stares out an upper story window at Zan and David's departure. Her face, behind a lace curtain, is stiff with loss and fear.

This is an actor who knows the great power of expressing inner emotion through absolutely stillness, through the window of her eyes.

Erich von Stroheim would have loved working with her because it was just as important to her character development to be costumed and made-up correctly as it was to express the emotions of a character. People asked Stroheim why he provided historically correct silk underwear for his Prussian soldiers in one movie when no one would see it. His answer is perfect. The actors will see it, feel it, know what a Prussian soldier of that era felt. It helps with the performance.

Davis depended on appropriate costuming for her myriad characters. In fact, she felt the overly rich costumes diminished the effectiveness of the movie presentation of *The Little Foxes*. There should have been a desperateness to these characters who no longer had the wealthy aristocratic life to which they aspired. That is the reason Oscar married Birdie, because of her aristocratic background. Regina married Horace for his banker's money. Their dress in the film should have reflected their lack of wealth.

Their scheme with the northern industrialist is to return them to the wealth they felt entitled to, a southern aristocracy of money. All three Hubbards, including Regina, are desperate not to be thought of as merchants, but to be raised to the level of Birdie's old plantation aristocracy, and they believe they can achieve this through money.

Davis understood these feeling to some extent herself. She always referred to herself as a New England Yankee, but she knew she wasn't a Cabot or a Lodge. However, she aspired to their old New England beliefs, instilled in her by her mother's family and her father's success as a Harvard lawyer. Her success as an actor allowed her the financial wherewithal to basically maintain her Yankee beliefs and live the "New England" life, even in California. Her homes were always filled with New England antiques and various British objects, especially at Laguna Beach and the eastern retreat, a converted barn, she had in New Hampshire, "Butternut."

Britain's Dilys Powell thought *The Little Foxes* was "enormously helped by its chief player. Bette Davis has never given a finer performance than as the cold murderess."[7]

Jan Herman, in his biography of William Wyler, *A Talent for Trouble*, feels, "...seen today ... it has more impact than either of 1941's *How Green Was My Valley*, or *Sergeant York*. Neither of those can hold a candle to it on any artistic level...."[8]

Bosley Crowther, in the *New York Times*, called it "...the most bitingly sinister picture of the year.... Miss Davis' performance in the role which Tallulah Bankhead played so brassily on the stage is abundant with color and mood."[9]

Cast: Regina Giddens — Bette Davis; Horace Giddens — Herbert Marshall; Alexandra Giddens — Teresa Wright; David Hewitt — Richard Carlson; Birdie Hubbard — Patricia Collinge; Leo Hubbard — Dan Duryea; Ben Hubbard — Charles Dingle; Oscar Hubbard — Carl Benton Reid; Addie — Jessie Grayson; Cal — John Marriott; William Marshall — Russell Hicks; Sam Manders — Lucien Littlefield; Lucy Hewitt — Virginia Brissac.

Production: Samuel Goldwyn — Producer; William Wyler — Director; Lillian Hellman — Screenwriter; Arthur Kober, Dorothy Parker, Alan Campbell — Additional scenes and dialogue; Gregg Toland — Cinematographer; Meredith Willson — Musical Score and Direction; Orry-Kelly — Costumes; Stephen Goosson — Art Direction; Daniel Mandell — Editor; 1941; Running time — 115 minutes.

5

Now, Voyager (1942)

A Woman of Independence

*"Untold want, by life and land ne'er granted, now, voyager, sail
thou forth, to see and find."*[1]
—Walt Whitman

"I'm just a fool," Charlotte cries, "just an old fool. These are an old maid's tears of gratitude for the crumbs [of love] offered. No one has ever called me darling before." She, Charlotte Vale (Davis), has exposed her complete vulnerability, her human need for affection, to Jerry Durrance (Paul Henreid), the man with whom she has fallen in love while on a cruise ship to Rio de Janeiro.

Davis shows her complete ability to expose herself as a woman and actor in this truthful and touching scene from the 1942 movie *Now, Voyager*, probably Davis' most popular film. The major wartime audiences were composed mostly of women, and they loved this film which, in those bygone days, was called a woman's picture, even a tear-jerker. Today, we'd say it was a film about a woman, or a romance.

What audiences and critics overlooked at the time (and some still do!) is that the major thrust of this drama is to show the growth of a woman, how she attains purpose and independence, against prevailing cultural and familial dictates. The heroine is a daughter of Boston aristocracy who eventually rejects her clan's rule to marry a suitable aristocrat. She is willing to give up her mother's wealth to be true to herself. She undergoes psychotherapy to better understand herself and her importance, her ability to be useful. She sacrifices a love affair to be helpful, instead, to a disturbed child's growth.

Emotions are paramount in this film, based on Olive Higgins Prouty's popular novel. Davis had to fight, once again, to get this role, a role where she is anything but a bitch. Hal Wallis, in his autobiography, *Starmaker*, asserts, "Bette Davis wanted to play the part, and we finally went with her. She was our last choice, and a lucky one."[2] Irene Dunne, Norma Shearer and Ginger Rogers had been approached. One can readily see why Davis was so attracted to the role of a woman of Boston, an unattractive woman who turns into a beauty, a woman who finally has to act independently — all things pertinent to Davis' life. It is probable that Davis wished her life had been like Charlotte's in some respects. She had a love-hate relationship with her own mother. Although she was married at the time to Arthur Farnsworth, he would die mysteriously a few months later. She was still the breadwinner of her extended family, which included her mother and her sister.

The film, directed by Irving Rapper, an Englishman, opens with a shot of the solid stone mansion of the aristocratic New Englanders, the Vales of Back Bay Boston. It is raining. Charlotte's mother (Gladys Cooper) and her daughter-in-law, Lisa (Ilka Chase), are discussing Charlotte's apparent nervous condition. Charlotte is a neurotic spinster under the domineering control of her mother. Lisa has invited a psychiatrist, Dr. Jaquith (Claude Rains), to visit and meet the family, specifically Charlotte. Charlotte's mother has neither sympathy nor understanding for her troubled daughter, a daughter born late in her life and who's much younger than her two brothers.

As the film begins, we do not see Charlotte until her mother sends a servant to Charlotte's bedroom to tell her to come downstairs for tea. Charlotte is alone in her third-floor room, carving an ivory box. Upon hearing the servant knock and call, she carefully puts out a cigarette in a saucer, then wipes the saucer clean with a tissue and drops the tissue into a wastebasket. All we see is her hands; not a word is spoken.

Charlotte descends the impressive marble staircase, and one sees only her slow-moving oxford-clad feet, stockings and the lower part of her print dress. Her feet hesitate on a lower step as she discerns her mother's irritated voice, coming from the drawing room.

The camera pulls back to reveal Charlotte in full, standing above the two steps leading down to the drawing room. She is rather heavy in appearance. She clutches her hands, twisting a handkerchief, and her face — tight lips, heavy brows, unattractive rimless eyeglasses, her hair severely pulled into a bun — reveals that she's frightened. Still not a word.

As she enters the room, she is berated by her mother for being late. When she is introduced to Jaquith, she says not a word. Her mother apologizes for her rudeness and says, "Has the cat got your tongue?" No answer.

Charlotte moves beyond her mother, as she continues looking at the doctor.

When Charlotte hears that he is a psychiatrist, and hears him say he helps persons choose the right forks on the road of life, the conversation becomes too much for her. She looks at her mother with trepidation and leaves the room.

Jaquith quickly follows her, saying he'd like to see the house, and follows her up the stairs, all the while describing the house in terms of personification. When they reach the second floor, she turns to him and utters her first words, "Introverted, doctor?"

All the fear and insecurity need no words. Davis has shown by the movement of her whole body, and particularly her facial expressions, every frightened emotion Charlotte has been feeling.

All the while Rains has been talking, Davis eyes him suspiciously and listens intently. When he requests to see her room, she tells him it is on the floor above and leads him up the stairs. Arriving at her door, she reaches in a pocket in her dress, saying, "Note, doctor, she locks her door." He, in turn, suggests it's her right to do so, for her room is her castle. Opening her door, Charlotte sardonically says, "My castle, doctor."

Commenting on the solidity of her furnishings, built to last a lifetime, he espies her ivory boxes and comments admiringly on their craftsmanship. Charlotte's face changes as she responds to his compliments. She allows that he may have one, except for the one she feels has a flaw in its lid, caused when her mother had sent for her at an earlier time and she slipped with her carving tool.

Jaquith responds with how admirable her work is and how he would be too clumsy to carve. She moves slightly toward him, her face aglow, and softly says, "I think you are the least clumsy person I've ever met."

When he spots cigarette butts in a wastebasket, he requests a cigarette from her. Still on the defensive, she accuses him of spying, as he sees what she hides from her mother and the world.

She hysterically forces him to look at a photograph album she was about to hide, showing her long-ago cruise which she took with her mother when she was twenty. Her mother thwarted a shipboard romance with a ship's officer.

At the end of the tale, Charlotte cries out, "My mother, my mother, my mother!" Through her tears she asks Dr. Jaquith if he can help her. He declares she doesn't need his help, to calm herself and return to the drawing room for tea. He thanks her for the gift of the ivory box she has given him and leaves.

In the interim, Charlotte's niece, June (Bonita Granville), has arrived

Claude Rains, as Dr. Jaquith, admires Charlotte Vale's (Davis) ivory handiwork in *Now, Voyager* (Photofest).

and meets Charlotte as she's reentering the drawing room. June sarcastically taunts Charlotte. When Charlotte tries to pour the tea, her hands shake, as do the cup and saucer. June says, "What's this? Aunt Charlotte has the shakes. She must have a hangover!"

Davis sets the teapot and cup and saucer noisily on the table, looks up and cries out, "You like making fun of me. You always make fun of me." With a desperate look, she rises to a crouch and half-runs from the room, crying.

Mrs. Vale emphatically states, "No Vale has ever had a nervous breakdown." Jaquith replies, looking her straight in the eye, "Well, there's one having one now." He suggests a restful stay at Cascade, his sanitarium, to help Charlotte choose the right forks in the road of life.

In this early part of the film, the background is clearly delineated. Davis expresses Charlotte's hesitancy, feeling of unworthiness, insecurity and desperate need for love, especially apparent in this non-demonstrative and verbally abusive family, personified by her mother and niece. Only her sister-in-law, Lisa, understands the desperation of the situation and is proactive on Charlotte's behalf.

Claude Rains, Davis' favorite leading man, is smooth, calm and well-spoken as the psychiatrist. He remains even-tempered with Charlotte's mother, the figure of authority who is used to being deferred to. This fine English actor never gave a bad performance and was particularly good as Job Skeffington opposite Davis in *Mr. Skeffington*.

Stairway entrances play a significant part for Davis in this film (and many others). Her careful descent tells so much about Charlotte when one first sees her feet. Later, one sees the transformed Charlotte as she comes down the gangplank of a cruise ship, again viewing just her (now fashionably well-clad) feet. This approach is used again when her uncle and brothers and their wives see Charlotte walk down the family staircase for a formal dinner to which they've been invited. There they see, for the first time, Charlotte transformed into a beautiful and confident woman.

Davis handles each descent in a physically different way. She was a great believer in the use of the entire body for acting. She claimed she learned body movement from Martha Graham, the famous dancer, who taught at the John Murray Anderson School Davis attended in New York.

The cruise ship, headed to Rio de Janeiro, is where Charlotte encounters the outside world for the first time after her sanitarium stay. This is significant because her last cruise, with her mother, was an unmitigated disaster. This one is the antithesis of the former. On her own, alone, she meets Jerry Durrance (Paul Henreid). It is unclear why he is on this particular ship, but it seems to have been an expedient way to travel to South America for his business during wartime. While sightseeing together in Rio, his destination, their taxi driver has an accident in the mountains. They are stranded one night in a hillside cabin while the driver goes for help. One assumes their affair is consummated from the symbolic fire which they have built to keep warm. They decide to "bundle," an old New England term for sleeping together with a board between them. Obviously, they didn't have a board, and the camera focuses on the blazing fire, a cinematic symbol for sexual heat. The morning shot shows spent, smoldering ashes.

Paul Henreid became a life-long friend of Davis. It was she who was responsible for his getting a second screen test after the first one showed him as "an oily European."

Jerry is married to a hypochondriac, and his youngest daughter is obviously an unwanted child whom he doesn't know how to help.

Even after their mutual demonstrations of love, Charlotte resumes her trip to Buenos Aires and subsequently returns to Boston, realizing their affair must be terminated because Jerry cannot divorce his wife because of his love and concern for his daughter.

Upon her return, Charlotte's mother is appalled at Charlotte's physical change and demeanor. She threatens disinheritance, but Charlotte only listens and handles her calmly. In *Acting Hollywood Style*, Foster Hirsch states, "When Charlotte is transformed into a fashionably-dressed woman of the world, she doesn't sound like 'Bette Davis' in full cry but speaks instead in quiet, cultivated tones, a voice with just the right inflection to deliver Davis' most romantic line, 'Jerry, let's not wish for the moon. We already have the stars.'"[3]

Lisa introduces her to a "suitable" widower, Elliott Livingston (John Loder), a proper Bostonian. The relationship appears destined for marriage. However, Durrance, now an architect, appears in the city, and even attends a dinner party and a symphonic concert with them. Later that evening, calling from the Back Bay train station, Durrance declares his love for her, but thinks it best for him to leave so she can find happiness with Livingston.

Charlotte subsequently breaks her engagement to Livingston. Her mother is incensed by Charlotte's news. She is so disturbed, especially in light of Charlotte's determination, that she has a heart attack and dies.

Charlotte's guilt sends her back to Dr. Jaquith's sanitarium where she encounters Jerry's depressed daughter, Tina (Janis Wilson). Reacting deeply to Tina's problems, Charlotte gains the psychiatrist's permission to help her.

With time, Tina and Charlotte bond completely, and Charlotte brings her to Boston to live with her for an indefinite stay, with the doctor's and parents' permission. Even though they realize they cannot have each other, Charlotte and Jerry accept that the love they have for the child will be a bond for them.

The ending is hard to swallow, seeing that Charlotte has no other relationship in her life. Many viewers probably projected that Jerry would eventually divorce his wife and marry Charlotte. Davis suggested Charlotte would end up with Dr. Jaquith.

The plot and relationships seem very sentimental, almost soap operaish. It is the consummate acting of Davis, Rains and the supporting cast that move this movie to a believable level. Bernard Dick, in his biography of Hal Wallis, notes:

> Although Davis was not on Wallis' short list, it is to his credit that he offered her a role, that, perhaps, for the first time in her career, revealed her myriad talents as she changed from a dowdy maiden aunt, bullied by her mother and mocked by her niece, to a glamorous sophisticate who is alternately flirtatious, witty, headstrong, sensual and, in the final scenes with her lover's daughter, poignantly maternal ... it was a matter of shading. *Now, Voyager* required a more diverse palette; in Davis' care, that palette existed, although its colors were not always evident...[4]

The film's main interest comes from following Davis' characterization of Charlotte, who changes from an insecure, dominated woman into a caring, useful, responsible adult, something rarely seen in movies at the time when a woman was always subservient to a man and his needs. Love and marriage to a man solved all women's problems.

In *Star Acting*, Charles Affron declares:

> She triumphs over the collection of absurdities that pass for the peripetics of this "modern psychological drama." It is a triumph that insures *Now Voyager*'s place among the most satisfying of her films.
>
> Whoever is responsible, *Now, Voyager* has the consistency of style and even more surprisingly the taste that continues to give pleasure to its viewers.
>
> ...Davis on the brink of a nervous breakdown is a sight to behold, and she brings to her rendition of the frustrated, mother-hating virgin a tautness and lack of compromise that ... constitute some of her best footage.
>
> ...Both she and her director capitalize upon her potential energy, which is an inexhaustible store that must be dosed out to avoid stridency.[5]

Two vital scenes between two talented actresses, Davis and Cooper, allow their relationship as mother and daughter, and as two strong women, to become thoroughly understandable.

The first is Charlotte's reentrance to the Vale family home after her return from the sanitarium and her South American cruise. While she was away, her elderly mother has had some heart problems, and a live-in nurse, Dora (Mary Wickes), warns Charlotte that her mother is waiting like a bear for Charlotte's return.

When Charlotte enters her mother's presence, she is hesitant, and rightfully so. Her mother attacks immediately. She looks at Charlotte appraisingly, saying, "It's much worse than I thought." She forces Charlotte to turn around in order to scrutinize her new appearance — she is beautifully dressed and coiffed, slender, and using facial makeup. Finally, her mother pronounces that Charlotte's changes are due to her illness.

Mrs. Vale has retained a seamstress to alter Charlotte's old wardrobe, in particular a dress for Charlotte to wear at that evening's dinner with her uncle, two brothers and their wives.

Through it all, Davis remains calm but steady in her eye contact with Cooper, telling her that she is a changed woman. Finally, rather than argue, she leaves her mother's bed chamber.

When Mrs. Vale comes to find Charlotte before dinner, she discovers Charlotte has not moved into her father's old bedroom where her furnishings have been moved, but is in her old third-floor room. Mrs. Vale is aghast at Charlotte's newly-purchased evening dress, upon which Charlotte has attached a three-camellia corsage sent that day by Jerry. The arrival of the camellias gives her the self-confidence to listen to her own desires and conscience, to defy her mother and even to move back to her old third-floor room. She disregards her mother's verbal abuse because she has finally received the love and respect she deserves.

Mrs. Vale is furious because of Charlotte's move, new dress, and the mysterious appearance of the corsage (there was no card). She accuses Charlotte of being an uncaring daughter. When Charlotte responds that they can go down to dinner together, her mother declares that she doesn't want to go with her, but wants to go down alone. Charlotte's mother descends the stairs part way, twists her ankle and falls to the second floor.

Hurriedly, Charlotte follows and calls for help, for Dora. A doctor is sent for.

Charlotte is then in her mother's bedroom with the doctor who is attending to Mrs. Vale's torn ligament. Mrs. Vale complains that she can't hear the whispering.

Davis shows Charlotte to be a still-caring daughter, loving and concerned. Sitting at the foot of the bed, her voice registers care as she quizzes the doctor about her mother's condition.

Finally, her mother barks at her, "Have you no manners, Charlotte? There are guests downstairs, waiting. Tell them they may come to see me, one or two at a time."

Charlotte walks down to the first floor. Her relatives are astonished when they see her transformation. Charlotte smilingly and effusively greets them and controls the situation entirely. Lisa has invited a widower, Elliot Livingston. Charlotte even suggests a fire be lit in the drawing room. Aghast, one brother, Lloyd, states that he can never remember it being lit. "High time it was," Charlotte replies.

When the evening is over, everyone is complimentary to Charlotte. They have been astonished by her. Elliot remains to ask if he may call.

Mrs. Vale is awaiting Charlotte in her bedroom, but Dora has given her a hot toddy with a sleeping potion. Mrs. Vale tries to threaten Charlotte's financial security if she won't conform to her wishes. But she soon falls asleep, with Dora rubbing her head.

The second telling scene comes after Charlotte has rejected Elliot's offer of marriage. Mrs. Vale has found his proposal very proper for the uniting of two aristocratic Boston families. When Charlotte arrives at her mother's bedroom, Mrs. Vale is sitting in a chair near a window. Charlotte approaches her and sits in a rocking chair. She shares her decision to break the engagement. Mrs. Vale immediately attacks her, suggesting that not loving a person is no reason not to unite the two families. She calls Charlotte a selfish old maid. Finally, Charlotte responds that she was never wanted as a child, never loved.

In this scene, Davis starts off in an agreeable, confiding mood, explaining her broken engagement. But when Cooper demands that she stop rocking (the boat!) and berates her, Davis' face and eyes change. She has the spine and self-worth to prevent her mother from getting away with her demeaning remarks and attitude. Davis' face and stride are strong as she crosses the room to leave, as are her words. She declares, "Dr. Jaquith says that sometimes tyranny is the expression of maternal instinct.... It's been a calamity on both sides." She turns and tries to apologize, to ask for her mother's companionship, for her to act like a mother instead of a dictator.

Throughout the film one can see that Charlotte's character is very much like her mother, intelligent, determined and independent, but Charlotte will never let her persona become dictatorial or unkind. She works for the goodness and kindness her power can bring to others, to help them, not hurt them. She has a will just as strong as her mother's.

When Davis and Cooper are acting together, one sees true professionals. Their facial expressions tell it all, and their voices articulate the characters beautifully. Both give quiet, subtle performances. Voices may be raised, but there is always class, no yelling or histrionics. Davis said Cooper was basically a stand-offish person but an excellent actress with whom to work.

At the end of the movie, a "wienie" roast is held in the Vale drawing room fireplace. Modern popular music is playing, and there is a lot of talking and laughter. Tina, Jerry's daughter, who has been staying with Charlotte, is having her first party. Both Jerry and Dr. Jaquith are there. Dr. Jaquith tells Charlotte that the new wing at his sanitarium will be named for her because she has given them the money. She will be on the board of directors. It's obvious the two get along very well. One can see they are comfortable with one another.

The final scene is between Jerry and Charlotte in the library, away from the others. Jerry is going to remove Tina from Charlotte's care. His argument is that a woman may only be fulfilled through the love of a man. However, Charlotte makes him realize that Tina is his gift to her, so she can care for her as if Tina were their child. She has to reject his love because of her promise to Dr. Jaquith not to be involved with Tina's father. They may not have each other but they have a love for Tina.

Charlotte knows fulfillment comes from being true to oneself— a strong independent woman and a useful person. She rejects sentimentality completely. Charlotte's rejection of Jerry asserts her independence.

Her final line, "Jerry, let's not wish for the moon. We already have the stars," is not as cryptic a statement as some would have it. Symbolically, the moon has stood for love. She's rejecting his "moon-love." Everyone has a multitude of stars. Even we, the viewers, have the star(s), namely, Davis herself.

Davis played both mothers and daughters, before and after, but this film is unique in that she, as Charlotte Vale, had to delineate one of cinema's most complex daughters against the most domineering of mothers, played by Cooper. As actresses, both were considered top talents. Miss Cooper had been a renowned British actress and was perfectly cast as the Boston matriarch of the Vale family. Davis, from Massachusetts, knew about Boston aristocracy first-hand. Her father was a Harvard law graduate. Plus, she had a very complicated relationship with her own mother.

During this period, in 1942, Davis' film career was at its zenith at Warners, even though she initially wasn't offered the role of Charlotte. As she acknowledged, who better could capture this role than herself?

During filming, Davis had to play Charlotte at two ages, as a young twenty-year-old and, for the most part, as a 29-year-old. Her actual age was 34, and she needed a superb cinematographer, which she had in Sol Polito. She never looked as sophisticated as when she blossomed from her ugly duckling phase into a swan. As an eighteen-year-old, her face belied her older age, but careful photography and her acting overcame the obstacle.

One first sees Charlotte when she is at her worst, heavy, nervous, afraid, and physically plain as a maiden aunt. She is continually berated by her rigid mother, a true Bostonian matriarch.

Charlotte appears in her mother's drawing room for afternoon tea, where she is requested to pour tea. Davis, in this early part of the film, displays her ability to show inner desperation through her silence to her mother's questions. Everything is controlled emotion.

When Rains follows her to her third floor bedroom, she reveals her fear via self-deprecating remarks and her constant references to her mother. Davis raises the emotional quotient when she comes to feel that Rains is "spying" on her.

In the flashback, Davis acts young and can hardly control her romantic love for a shipboard officer. She even defies her mother's admonition not to mix with the ship's tourists. Her romance is short-lived because her mother and the ship's captain discover the couple in a tryst in a freighted car.

Davis reveals her devastation and desperation as she tells her mother that she loves the officer. Treated like a naughty child, she is sent to her cabin, while the officer is severely reprimanded. Davis is energetic and lively as a late teen, searching for a love she has not received from her mother.

Back in the present, the 29-year-older spinster asks Dr. Jaquith for help.

When Charlotte subsequently breaks down, no one follows after her. Mrs. Vale is mortified at her daughter's behavior and angrily tells Jaquith that no Vale has ever had a nervous breakdown.

Throughout this tea scene and the flashback, one completely understands the mother-daughter relationship. Mrs. Vale is completely domineering and maintains absolute control over Charlotte and the household. She thinks she has controlled Charlotte's reading habits, her mode of dress, her entire life.

Charlotte regards her mother as a tyrant and is cowed by her. Her only defiance against her is revealed by her smoking privately in her bedroom and her reading of unapproved books, hidden in her bedroom.

No sign of maternal affection passes Mrs. Vale's lips, only ridicule and sarcasm.

Cooper pulls this role off beautifully because one can see she believes she is doing everything for her daughter's benefit and can't understand Charlotte's behavior or ingratitude. She treats everyone as an inferior — she is a Vale.

Davis shows Charlotte as she must feel. She recognizes Charlotte's complete dependency on her mother for everything in her life. She knows she's a Vale, but also recognizes her mother's treachery. Even though she follows all her mother's restrictions on the surface, she suffers inner turmoil, finally succumbing to a breakdown.

After recovery, Charlotte, with the help of her sister-in-law, goes on an ocean cruise to South America. Still unsure of herself, she meets Jerry Durrance on a day excursion in Rio de Janeiro. She is asked by the cruise director to let Durrance accompany her. In her mind, she remembers her mother's admonition to regard tourists as unworthy of a Vale's presence. The screen shows Cooper's face superimposed over Davis' face. It is a revelation when Davis smilingly tells Henreid, "I'd be delighted to see whatever you wish." It's a first baby-step to independence from her mother's tyranny.

One realizes right there that Charlotte can be as strong as her mother. In fact, they are similar; forthright, intelligent women.

No longer a teenager, Davis conducts herself as a sophisticated lady, true to her class and upbringing, throughout the cruise. Even in her brief affair she shows restraint. The biggest emotion shown is a tearful gratefulness when Henreid gives her a small gift and calls her "darling." Davis is contained and quiet, whether she's happily in Henreid's presence or tearfully bidding him adieu.

What changes is the confidence she has in herself, which is expressed when her sister-in-law and niece meet her at the pier upon her return to New York. She is smiling, happy, and making her good-byes to people, including several attractive men she's met onboard. Most importantly, she's able to tease and joke with her niece who heretofore treated Charlotte with derision. Davis shows her growth in her posture, her relaxed mood, her confident smile and verbal ripostes.

Larger and more significant is the test of the mother-daughter relationship between Mrs. Vale and Charlotte. Confident, Charlotte remembered what she has been taught by her psychiatrist about her own worth and rights as a human being.

When Mrs. Vale informs Charlotte of how she expects her daughter to behave in her household, and again dictates what she'll wear and in what room she'll sleep, Charlotte does not argue with her nor confront her. She only tries to explain that their relationship has changed, which, of course, is what Mrs. Vale fears most. Rather than argue, Charlotte simply leaves the room.

Throughout the scene Davis displays her confidence through her calmness and her steady, reasoning voice. Cooper shows her disconcertedness by her anger and demands. Both actresses have an opposite to play against. Davis always gave her fellow actors that needed encounter.

In the follow-up scene, Charlotte, against her mother's wishes, has repaired to her old third-floor bedroom, signifying she will not take her late father's room and will not take her late father's position of husband to her

Charlotte (Davis) placating her mother (Gladys Cooper) (Photofest).

mother. She chooses to wear a very sophisticated gown for dinner, attaching a camellia corsage sent to her by Jerry.

When Mrs. Vale comes up to her daughter's room, angry at Charlotte's defiance and refusal to use her father's bedroom, Charlotte again refuses to rise to her mother's level of anger. Mrs. Vale is so upset that she refuses Charlotte's offer to descend the stairs together. But she realizes she can't seem to provoke Charlotte to either anger or acquiescence.

Charlotte shows her still-present love for her mother when she rushes to her side when her mother falls on the stairs. Davis' voice rises in frightened concern for her. In her mother's bedroom, Charlotte is the concerned adult asking the doctor about her mother's condition, a pulled ligament. She eagerly takes on the maternal role. Of course, Mrs. Vale is not about to relinquish her matriarchal role and berates Charlotte for keeping the family dinner guests waiting.

After the dinner is over, Charlotte's reappearance in her mother's room gives Cooper and Davis a chance to play a significant scene which allows for apparent changes in their relationship. Mrs. Vale tries to coerce Charlotte into being the "slave-daughter" she wants by telling her she'll be the most powerful and wealthy Vale when she dies.

Davis, standing at the foot of the bed, next to Cooper, but above her, smiles rather than disputing her, and allows the nurse to rub her mother's head and neck while a sleeping pill takes effect. Cooper confusedly keeps talking, but the nurse tells her she is not understood and shoos Charlotte from the room.

Davis and Cooper complement one another, and now partake in some role reversal. Davis has become the caretaker, a role she relishes, and Cooper likes being taken care of, though she'd never verbalize it.

The most powerful scene for the two actresses comes later when Charlotte discloses her decision to reject a proper Bostonian marriage proposal, although a small scene prior to it cannot be overlooked.

Charlotte has begun seeing a Bostonian widower, of whom her mother approves. Charlotte, dressed in an evening gown, glamorously coiffed and made up, is arranging some roses in a vase for her mother, who is sitting in a chair next to the table. Mrs. Vale is again being feisty with Charlotte about her camellia corsage and about her fiancé. Charlotte continues arranging the roses, never uttering a word of disagreement, but smilingly listening to her mother ramble. Finally, as Charlotte's ready to leave, she approaches her mother with a goodbye and says pleasantly, "There's no one like you, Mother, and there never will be."

Mrs. Vale is quiet and obviously nonplused. But she accepts it; that's what she enjoys — no one is like her. In this small scene, Davis and Cooper are able to show that there is caring, if not outright love, between them. Cooper shows that Mrs. Vale is pleased her daughter is about to marry a suitable suitor, even though she is confounded by it. She obviously is respectful of her daughter and, underneath, pleased with the swan far more than the ugly duckling. Davis, through her quiet dignity and loving manner toward Cooper, shows how well she can express familial love for her mother. She recognizes how similar they are. Her confidence allows her to reach the stature of her mother.

The climactic scene, of course, is the revelation of Charlotte's decision to break the engagement. Mrs. Vale is incensed, not for Charlotte, but for herself. She lets the invective flow all over her daughter, who has calmly told her about the breakup, once again trying to be kind to her mother, regardless of her own hurt, but to no avail.

Cooper has raised the volume quite a few decibels, and Davis is given a chance to naturally react, to show her hurt and reveal some unpleasant truths about their mother-daughter relationship. But she even modifies that when she reaches the door and turns to say how well they've been getting on, only to find her mother has had a fatal heart attack. Davis shows, in her face, all the guilt she feels as she calls to the nurse for help. Dora tries to reassure her.

Davis and Cooper more than respected each other as actors. They showed how they loved working with one another. They were two professionals.

Thereafter in the film, Charlotte comes to realize her own natural instinct as she cares for and comes to love Jerry's daughter. One also sees her natural abilities come to the fore, not only in her becoming a successful Vale by working with Dr. Jaquith and his psychiatric institution, but via her absolutely mature handling of Jerry when he appears to take his daughter out of her care. She is way beyond Jerry; she is an aristocrat, albeit a justice-seeking woman.

Davis never had a more fulfilling role, or one that called for such a rounded performance. She made many other mother-daughter films (*The Old Maid* and *Strangers: The Story of a Mother and Daughter*, to name two), but none offered as complete a study of a woman as *Now, Voyager*. As Charles Affron concluded:

> ...Davis teaches us strength through her ability to stamp its quality on the attractive claptrap of *Now, Voyager*. Indeed, Davis calls for our strength along with our handkerchiefs, and we can see clearly even when our eyes are awash with tears.[6]

Cast: Charlotte Vale — Bette Davis; Jerry Durrance — Paul Henreid; Dr. Jaquith — Claude Rains; Mrs. Vale — Gladys Cooper; June Vale — Bonita Granville; Lisa Vale — Ilka Chase; Elliot Livingston — John Loder; "Deb"

McIntyre — Lee Patrick ; Mr. Thompson — Franklin Panghorn; Miss Trask — Katherine Alexander; Frank McIntyre — James Rennie; Dora Pickford — Mary Wickes; Tina Durrance — Janis Wilson; Manoel — Frank Puglia; Dr. Dan Regan — Michael Ames; Leslie Trotter — Charles Drake; William — David Clyde.

Production: Hal Wallis — Producer; Irving Rapper — Director; Casey Robinson — Screenwriter; Olive Higgins Prouty — Based on her novel; Sol Polito — Cinematographer; Warren Low — Editor; Max Steiner — Musical Score; Leo F. Forbstein — Musical Direction; Orry-Kelly — Gowns; Perc Westmore — Makeup Artist; Robert Haas — Art Director; Fred M. MacLean — Set Decoration; Robert B. Lee — Sound; 1942; Running time: 112 minutes.

6

What Ever Happened to Baby Jane? (1962)

HOLLYWOOD HORROR IN KABUKI

> *"The two stars didn't fight at all on Baby Jane....*
> *Miss Davis was wonderful in it, too."*[1]
> — Robert Aldrich

Nothing Davis did in films could be a further stretch from the subdued, subtle performance of Charlotte Vale in *Now, Voyager* to the bravura acting in this gothic horror, *What Ever Happened to Baby Jane?* Whatever one says about this film, and no matter how campy it became, one has to realize it was a tremendous success at the box office and garnered Davis her tenth Oscar nomination. With time it has been reevaluated, and rightly so.

Davis, playing former child star Baby Jane Hudson, threw discretion to the winds and went over the top in a riveting performance, as she shows us a self-deluding, alcoholic, mentally unstable has-been who lives under the largess of her crippled sister, Blanche, a former 1930s movie star, played by Joan Crawford.

Though both Davis and Crawford are excellent in their roles, Davis is loud, bitchy and bawdy, while Crawford is suffering, weak and frightened. Davis clearly dominates the film with her showier role. It is with deliberateness that they are seen as children first, when Baby Jane is involved in vaudeville with their father.

Preceding the title credits, Baby Jane performs a number, "I've Written a Letter to Daddy," accompanied by her father, Ray (Dave Willock), on the piano. She sings and dances. While receiving the audience's applause, her sister, Blanche (Gina Gillespie), is seen with their mother, Cora (Anne Barton), in the wings. The look of hatred is evident on Blanche's face. Her mother tries to mollify her, telling her to remember that Jane really loves her. Blanche replies, "I won't ever forget, you bet I won't forget."

Blanche, the older sister, is understandably resentful of her younger sister's large success as Baby Jane Hudson (Julie Allred), a singing, dancing child performer, blond and precocious, much like Shirley Temple. Jane is completely spoiled by her father, while her mother tries to be protective of Blanche.

The film moves forward to 1930s Hollywood. Blanche (Joan Crawford) has become a successful movie star while Jane (Davis) is relegated to trashy B-pictures and appearing in those only because of Blanche's power as a successful studio star. A producer and public relations man reveal that Blanche's pictures are not revered, nor is she, by the industry. The two film clips shown, provided by early Davis and Crawford movies, do nothing to convince us that either was a talented actress.

When the accident is shown which causes Blanche's disability (she is unable to walk), it is not possible to see how she was hurt. One is led to believe that Jane drove their car, while drunk, into Blanche as she tried to open their driveway gate. The credits play over the accident as we move to the present.

So far one hasn't seen either Davis or Crawford acting in the "present" movie.

At the neighboring house to the Hudsons', a Mrs. Bates (!) (Anna Lee) and her daughter, Liza (Barbara Merrill), are watching an old Hudson (Crawford) movie, *Sadie McKee* (c. 1934) on TV. They are enthralled. Mrs. Bates takes a bouquet of gladioli over to the Hudsons, for Blanche. Blanche is watching the same movie. Jane answers the kitchen door and is surly and unwelcoming in accepting the flowers. When she goes upstairs to answer Blanche's buzzer, she finds Blanche enthralled, and delighted that the neighbors like her movie. Jane mocks her and reminds Blanche that she (Jane) also made a movie at the same time, a love story, never released in the U.S.

Our introduction to Jane is unpleasant. Physically, her face looks like a Kabuki actor's, heavily made up with a grotesque amount of lipstick and mascara. Her hair is apparently blond, parted in the middle and sporting lots of childish ringlets.

Over the years, Jane has developed a not-so-surprising hatred for her sister, whom she believes she, herself, had crippled in the car accident when she was drunkenly driving in the mid-thirties. They have since lived in Blanche's mansion. It's now 1962, and Jane discovers that Blanche has been receiving

Joan Crawford and Davis in a publicity shot for *What Ever Happened to Baby Jane?* (Photofest).

fan mail because of her old films' exposure on TV. Blanche is planning to sell their house and have Jane hospitalized because of her alcoholism and increasingly unstable actions.

Foster Hirsch, in *Acting Hollywood Style*, asserts, "When Bette Davis adopted the mask of a sadistic hag to conduct a reign of Grand Guignol terror against her crippled sister in *What Ever Happened to Baby Jane?*, she tilted melodrama into the realm of horror film, eliding two genres which at their outer limits, often overlap."[2]

The relationship between Blanche and Jane is set immediately. Although Blanche apparently holds the purse strings, she is more than physically crippled, she is bedridden or in a wheelchair, and dependent on Jane for her food and care. All these years she has been living a lie — the lie that Jane was responsible for the car accident that crippled her. So, in a way she is a victim not only of Jane, but of her past actions toward Jane.

Jane's unpleasantness with the neighbors sets her character, further revealed by her slovenly, scuffed-slipper walk and her long frilly kimono-robe. It appears she hasn't washed her face in the past month. She starts her attack by serving Blanche her dead pet canary for lunch.

As well, Jane decides to make a comeback as a cabaret act and advertises for a piano accompanist. When she dresses up to drive to the newspaper to place the ad, she dons some weird apparel — a beret (with her hair pulled back with a barrette), a beauty mark on her cheek, a flimsy dress and high ankle-strap shoes. She even acts coyly and flirts with the young ad clerk.

Critically, one must judge this movie for what it is, primarily a horror movie in the same vein as *Psycho*, designed to frighten as well as cause laughter with its macabre humor. The mood is set by the production's tone, which is similar to film noir. Within the Hudsons' dark mansion the sisters are basically recluses who live outside reality.

Early in the film, Jane shows her dependency on alcohol. In the kitchen, Jane has just finished working on her horoscope. A large map of the zodiac is on the wall. She reaches for a drink and then yawns. Later in the morning, she checks a cupboard for liquor and finds nothing but empty bottles. She calls the liquor store, only to learn that Blanche has given them instructions not to fill any orders from Jane.

Jane tells the clerk to wait while she gets Blanche on the phone. Davis sits up straight in the hall chair, takes a deep breath, changes her sullen face into a smile, and imitates Crawford's smooth, syrupy voice on the phone, saying there must be a mistake. Although Davis must have lip-synched Crawford's voice, the facial contortions, and the false cheer and simpering smile, are dead-on. It's an inkling of the black, cruel humor to come. Subsequently, Jane rips Blanche's phone from the wall in her bedroom. When Jane receives the liquor, she eagerly pours herself a large shot glass of scotch and belts it down.

The key to Jane's behavior is her absolute childishness. In the music room, she sits at the piano, looking through old scrapbooks of herself as a child. Drinking as usual, she launches into "I've Written a Letter to Daddy," gets up and approaches the full-length mirror. As she sees herself as she really is — an old, ugly hag — she breaks down in tears, crying out, "They never loved you enough." She is brought back to the present by Blanche's buzzer.

In Davis' face there is the loneliness of a child — the voice of a child's cry, and the fear of the way she appears behind her facial mask. These emotions change to hatred as she responds to her sister's call.

Being a paraplegic needing a wheelchair, Blanche is unable to leave her bedroom to go downstairs. Jane sets upon her tortuous path to destruction, both of Blanche and herself. Jane dismisses Elvira, the cleaning woman, for the day. When Jane brings her dinner, Blanche can't bring herself to lift the silver cover. Jane then refuses to bring Blanche's breakfast the next day because she hasn't eaten her dinner. Jane lifts the dinner lid and proceeds to mock Blanche for not eating by taking a pork chop and devouring it herself. Then she removes the tray, telling Blanche she'll have to wait for lunch because she didn't eat her "din-din."

After bringing Blanche her lunch, Jane removes the phone from its cradle downstairs and leaves the house. While Jane is gone, Blanche types a note requesting help, adding a warning it should not be shown to her sister. She manages to toss it out her iron-grilled window onto the drive separating them from their neighbor, Mrs. Bates. She does this just before Jane returns home.

Coming from the garage, Jane encounters Mrs. Bates. While talking with her, Jane picks up Blanche's note.

Blanche tries to talk with Jane about their future and selling the house. Wise to her plans, Jane says, "Blanche, you aren't ever going to sell this house. And you aren't ever going to leave it either."

Jane returns to serve her sister dinner. It appears okay, for the dinner plate is covered by a silver lid. Blanche tries to talk with Jane about their relationship, but Jane already knows of her plans to sell the house and also the plan to hospitalize her. She then encourages Blanche to eat her dinner, leaves the bedroom and waits outside the closed door. Blanche, desperate with hunger, hesitantly lifts the silver cover, only to discover a dead rat. She turns, hysterically whirling around and around in her wheelchair, screaming. Jane is in the hall laughing hysterically over her sadistic act.

When Edwin Flagg (Victor Buono), a piano accompanist, comes for an interview with Jane, Blanche buzzes from her room to find out who is below. Angry, Jane rips the buzzer cord from her wall. Returning to Edwin, Jane tells him her daddy said, "You could never lose your talent. You can lose everything else, but you can't lose your talent!" She takes Edwin to the music room and sings "I've Written a Letter to Daddy" for him as he plays the piano.

The next day she goes to the bank to get money to pay Edwin. She returns to find Blanche has succeeded in tortuously descending the stairs to call her doctor for help. Jane arrives just in time to hear her on the phone. She immediately attacks Blanche, furiously beating her, kicking her in the stomach and even her head.

The next morning Elvira (Maidie Norman) appears, and Jane dismisses her, saying they won't need her any more. Elvira asks to see Blanche but is told she is sleeping. She leaves, and we watch her wait for her bus, as does Jane. After the bus picks up Elvira, Jane drives away to retrieve her costumes from the dry cleaner.

When she returns, she finds Elvira, who had retained her key, at Blanche's locked bedroom door trying to remove the hinge pins with a hammer and screwdriver in order to get in. Jane tries to stop her, but is unsuccessful. Elvira demands, "You've got to act like a grown woman, just like everybody else." In a baby voice, and with child-like petulance, Jane refuses. Elvira threatens to call the police. Jane relents, and in a frightened baby voice says, "I didn't mean any harm." She has reverted to her child-like behavior, abandoning adult reasoning and responsibility, becoming just a pitiful child who then responds to Elvira's adult behavior with irrational violence. When Elvira enters the bedroom, she sees Blanche with her arms tied to an overhead pulley and her mouth taped with duct tape. Blanche is whimpering and struggling, trying to communicate to Elvira the danger posed by Jane, who hits Elvira over the head with a claw hammer, killing her.

When Edwin returns that next evening, Jane does not allow him in. He gets drunk and returns later, loudly demanding to see her. The police arrive. Jane allows Edwin in and tells the police it's okay. But when he hears Blanche knock over a bedside table upstairs, he demands to see what's going on. Jane tries to stop him, but can't. When he sees Blanche tied and gagged, he runs from the house.

As demented as Jane is, she realizes the police will return. She manages to get Blanche out of the house in her wheelchair and drive to the beach.

As the sun rises, Blanche is able to tell Jane, before she dies, that it wasn't Jane who caused the long-ago accident but she, herself, who tried to run Jane down and slammed the car into the wrought iron gates, thus crippling herself.

Robert Aldrich, the director, then allows Davis, for the only time in the film, to appear pretty. The lights are focused to dispel her age and hatred as she gets ice cream cones for her sister and herself, then dances gracefully on the beach as a crowd and the police gather around her. She has succeeded in returning to her childlike state, slipping into complete insanity.

When Jane ventured out of the house into the real world, she had no logical way to deal with it because she has led a show business fantasy life, even after Blanche's accident. Their money kept both of them secure as long as they stayed within the home. But over those years, both have lost touch with the real world, especially Jane, an alcoholic slipping more and more into dementia.

The only "normal" person they have any regular contact with is their house cleaner, Elvira Stitt. Even the doctor Blanche finally contacts appears to have no handle on their troubled relationship, nor the danger that Blanche is in.

Jane doesn't deal with any relationship in a realistic way. She lives in an angry, alcoholic haze even when she tries to carry out a fantastic plan of creating a Las Vegas act based on her childhood vaudeville act. She also sees the piano player, Edwin Flagg, she hires as a potential lover. Her behavior becomes childlike after she murders the cleaning woman, and she expresses herself in childish emotions, seeking help from Blanche, whom she has been torturing. Her life and reason have completely slipped away from her.

Davis neatly shows all of Jane's emotions — her hatred for her sister, her childlike wish for love, her delusion about returning to the stage, her fear of adult authority, her sadistic behavior when she can't have her own way. She is a childish creature, striving for the love she never received from her parents, particularly her father, who only saw her as a stage success, not a real daughter. She never matured into an adult woman.

All her actions are childish. Aside from the horrific happenings, she is a tragic/clown figure. Dressed and acting like a demented clown, Davis creates a figure who is, in the end, Kabuki-like. From the beginning, one realizes Jane is a doomed person.

Some have said *What Ever Happened to Baby Jane?* is a descendent of *Sunset Blvd.* because Norma Desmond was also a recluse who fantasizes about a comeback in movies, and who eventually kills her gigolo and falls into dementia. There are similarities, but the latter is not of the horror genre; rather, it is a biting satire of Hollywood, and carries a very cynical attitude.

The better comparison is Alfred Hitchcock's *Psycho*, made a few years before *Jane*. The thrust of both movies is to entertain and frighten audiences with shocking events, and to make them laugh at macabre happenings, i.e., Janet Leigh's shower murder, Anthony Perkins' mother's attack on the private detective, and the revelation of the dead mother. There were moments of laughter followed by unexpected shock.

Elvira's murder is completely shocking. Davis' impersonation of Crawford is hysterically funny (even though she really lip-synchs Crawford's voice).

Psycho deals with ordinary, real people (outside of Perkins), whereas no one in *Jane* seems normal or real, except the housekeeper.

Davis had often played characters who are transformed, most apparently in *Now, Voyager*, an ugly duckling story, but here she never has a transformation because she is so far gone to begin with. In her last scene, she has become completely childlike, dancing on the beach with two ice cream cones in her hands. She physically looks and acts like a child. She is once more Baby Jane.

It is an error to say, as others have, that Davis had not experienced successes, critically or commercially, since 1950's *All About Eve*. This 1962 film was preceded by the popular *A Pocketful of Miracles*, and earlier by *The Catered Affair* and *The Virgin Queen*. She had also returned to the Broadway stage in 1962 in Tennessee Williams' New York Drama Critics Circle Award-winning play *The Night of the Iguana* prior to this film. Irene Selznick wanted Davis for the lead in *A Streetcar Named Desire*, but she was under contract to Warner Brothers and couldn't do the play. When *The Glass Menagerie* was to be filmed, Producer Charles Feldman approached her to play the mother, but Jack Warner wouldn't even consider her return to the lot after their acrimonious split. When *Iguana* was filmed, Ava Gardner played Davis' role.

Davis returned to Hollywood, disillusioned with Broadway, and saw this offer as a means to regain a foothold in Los Angeles. It was a box office bonanza, and she did receive a series of film offers after its release. However, that year she lost the Oscar to Anne Bancroft, star of *The Miracle Worker*, a role Davis could easily have played in her younger years.

Crawford brought the novel to Aldrich to produce and direct, and wanted Davis to play Jane, which was obviously the showier role, the total bitch, something Crawford never was willing to do. Davis relished the role, and Aldrich relished having her to work with and let her pull out all the stops. The screenplay was by Lukas Heller, based on Henry Farrell's novel. This is a horror film with gallows humor. One is shocked when Jane serves Blanche a dead rat for dinner on a silver tray, under a silver cover. But when Blanche raises the lid and screams, in the outside hallway Jane breaks into raucous laughter — and the whole audience, having just gasped and screamed, breaks into hilarious laughter along with Jane.

On seeing this film, in which she had a small part as a neighbor's daughter, Barbara Merrill, née Sherry (Davis' real-life daughter), said this time her mother had gone too far! Well, maybe she did, if she cared about how she looked on screen — plain ugly — but Davis really didn't care. What she cared about was expressing the character of Jane, and that she did in spades. She delighted in playing such a bitch. When producers were asked to finance the project, they said, "Who wants to see a picture with those two old broads." Well, plenty of people wanted to see it, and it was a smash hit. Davis reclaimed her box-office status. In *People Will Talk*, John Kobel declares, "*Baby Jane* launched Bette Davis on a renewed starring career, but it proved to be a clouded dawn for Crawford. Davis was a more flexible, adaptable actress who played *Gothic Guignol* with a relish that let one see she was laughing."[3] However, it wasn't until 1964, when she made four films, that she

Jane (Davis) in a childlike state as she dances on Malibu beach in the final scene of *What Ever Happened to Baby Jane?* (Photofest).

reclaimed her status as a Hollywood star. Thereafter she did her best work in TV movies.

It's hard to watch *Jane* today without viewing it as camp, but when it first appeared camp hadn't been "invented" yet. Audiences responded to the horror as frightening, and only laughed at the intentionally funny parts. Today audiences go to see Davis and Crawford as those movie stars, not as Blanche and Jane.

When Davis viewed the completed film for the first time at the Cannes Film Festival with Robert Aldrich at her side, she broke down in tears and asked him, "Do I really look that awful?" One can only hope Aldrich's reply was a firm, "No, but Jane does, and you as an actress were willing to show that."

Charles Higham quoted Robert Aldrich in *The Celluloid Muse*:

> The two stars didn't fight at all on *Baby Jane*. I think it's proper to say they really detested each other, but they behaved absolutely perfectly. There was never an abrasive word in public, and not once did they try to upstage each other. Nor did Miss Davis allow her enmity with Miss Crawford to color her playing of the scenes in which she was supposed to torment her.... They both behaved in a wonderfully professional manner.
>
> Miss Davis was wonderful in it, too. She ... decided on her Baby Jane makeup, that ugly chalky mask.
>
> Miss Davis is a strange lady. She's been misled so many times and placed her confidence so many times in situations and/or people that didn't pay off, that she's naturally terribly hesitant to trust anybody. Once she trusts you, however, she's marvelous.
>
> ...*Baby Jane* ... was such a bravura, all-out Gothic eye-catcher that everybody thought it superior to *Hush ... Hush, Sweet Charlotte*.[4]

The mask is the key to Davis' bravura performance in this film. In silent films, Lon Chaney was the master of facial masks through make-up and prosthetics. Classically, masks derive from the Greeks. The actors all used masks with built-in miniature megaphones. Rudy Vallee, a popular singer in the twenties, used a megaphone, even when he started appearing on radio. Masks were, and still are, a vital part of Kabuki Theater in Japan. Masks can help focus a character or hide a character, or, even more so, hide the actual performer.

Davis used "masks" throughout her career. She changed her facial looks in films such as *Of Human Bondage* and the two Elizabethan movies as the queen, and, most particularly (over the objections of her producers and director), as the aged, disease-disfigured Fanny Skeffington.

William Wyler objected strenuously when Davis appeared as Regina Giddens in *The Little Foxes*. Davis and Perc Westmore had come up with a period-appropriate white calamine lotion face, with eyes narrowed by mascara, and Davis' small mouth not overly extended (as was usual for her lip line). It caused Wyler and Gregg Toland, his cameraman, to readjust their whole lighting plan for the movie.

Davis never really hid behind her masks to the extent Lon Chaney, or even Paul Muni, had done. She was aware that the public appreciated her foray into the use of make-up, but they wanted to know that Davis, the star, was there behind the mask and visible to a degree.

For Baby Jane, she developed the mask totally by herself. She said she wanted Jane to appear as though she never really washed her face, but just added more make-up each day. She loved the blonde corkscrew curls Norma Koch suggested for Jane. She cackled, "It's the nuts!"

As always, she placed great emphasis on the physicality of her performance. Just the way she shuffles along, scuffing her slippers, tells everyone what a slovenly person she is.

Throughout much of the film Davis' voice is harsh, angry and in a low register. Even when she is supposedly nice to Elvira, when she gives her the day off, she uses her sloppy enunciation and speaks in a dismissive tone.

However, when she is confronted by Elvira later she reverts to a childlike little girl voice, as she does when she sees herself as an old hag in the music room mirror. Lastly, when she has completely reverted to childhood at the beach, she asks for two ice cream cones, strawberry, from the vendor and acts like a young girl.

The mask, however, is not all there is to her performance. It is the factor which allows Davis to bring out the hidden, piteous person behind the mask, the woman who never grew up, the woman who never had the love she wanted. In using the mask, she becomes all the more vulnerable, one who inspires sympathy as well as horror with what she does.

Davis manages to do what Lon Chaney did so often. She brings humanity to her gothic monster. Her final scene with Crawford demonstrates the kind of relationship she really wanted with Blanche. Blanche, dying, reveals her responsibility for the 1930s car accident. Jane replies with a sweetness of voice, "All these years we could have been friends." The irony is that she has become completely demented. She's speaking in childish terms, not as an adult. As a child, she goes to get an ice cream cone for her sister, another childish act. Blanche is dying because of her actions. Both are victims, victims of their past. Neither of them can let go of that past which has brought them to their destruction.

In real life, Davis had just come off a very unpleasant experience on Broadway, playing in Tennessee Williams' *The Night of the Iguana*. Although it received critical recognition, Davis' part was the minor role of Maxine. She continually fought with her director and was virtually on non-speaking terms with her co-stars, Margaret Leighton and Patrick O'Neil. The performances were not of a professional ensemble with Davis ostracized. She even had the director legally barred from the playhouse before it opened. Her entrance continually stopped the play because of overwhelming applause, to the point where she had to break character and acknowledge it. They tried to resolve this by delaying her entrance so that the scene had already begun before she entered, but she was still met with an ovation. When she left the play in April of 1962, it continued running with her replacement, Shelley Winters. However, attendance dropped off immediately. Davis was the star draw.

It was while she was in this play that *Jane* was offered to her. She really jumped at the opportunity, not just because of the role, but because she needed the salary. She had planned on the long run of *Iguana*. She also released her autobiography which became a best-seller.

Before *Jane* was released she did something most people thought was a desperate call for work. She took out a job-wanted ad in *The Hollywood Reporter*. She said it was tongue-in-cheek. But the fact that no job offers came in speaks much more clearly.

As it turned out, *Jane* was block-booked to open all over the U.S. on the same day. Within two weeks, it had earned back its cost. Davis and Crawford, working for a salary *and* a percentage of the gross, made tidy sums from this picture.

Much to Crawford's displeasure, Davis, and not she, was nominated for an Oscar. Davis desperately wanted to be the first female actor to win a third Oscar. Both were presenters at the ceremony. Davis, along with Patty Duke for *The Miracle Worker*, had won gold medals from *Look* magazine for their performances, along with James Stewart and Josephine Hull for *Harvey*.

Crawford had gone to all the female nominees, other than Davis, to say she would accept their Oscar if they couldn't be present for the ceremony, Katharine Hepburn (always a no-show), Geraldine Page, Lee Remick and Anne Bancroft.

Davis sat backstage with her supportive friend, Olivia de Havilland. When Bancroft won for *The Miracle Worker*, Crawford swept by them, saying, "Excuse me, I have an award to accept." She took it east to present to Bancroft, who was playing in Bertolt Brecht's *Mother Courage*.

Two years later, Davis and Crawford were signed to be reunited in *Hush ... Hush, Sweet Charlotte*, but after less than two weeks, due to "illness," Crawford was replaced by Olivia de Havilland. Davis had another hit, another gothic thriller.

In *Confessions of a Cultist*, auteur theorist Andrew Sarris voiced:

> ...Lacking genuine suspense or horror, *Baby Jane* is sustained by outrageous humor, curiously self-enclosed lyricism, and above all, intelligent professionalism. Aldrich had a job to do and he did it. He realized that Bette Davis was a more gifted actress than Joan Crawford. So he allowed Bette to shock everyone with ludicrous makeup and then break through with a performance of emotional intensity.
> The world has not made the Hudson sisters what they are. They did it all to themselves.[5]

Jeff Simon, in the *Buffalo News,* April 25, 2006, simply labeled *What Ever Happened to Baby Jane?* "a brilliant movie."[6]

Cast: Jane Hudson — Bette Davis; Blanche Hudson — Joan Crawford; Edwin Flagg — Victor Buono; Della Flagg — Marjorie Bennett; Elvira Stitt — Maidie Norman; Mrs. Bates — Anna Lee; Liza Bates — Barbara Merrill; Baby Jane — Julie Allred; Young Blanche — Gina Gillespie; Ray Hudson — Dave Willock; Cora Hudson — Anne Barton.

Production: Kenneth Hyman — Producer; Robert Aldrich — Associate Producer and Director; Lukas Heller — Screenplay; Henry Farrell — Based on his novel; Ernest Haller — Cinematographer; Frank De Vol — Musical Score; Norma Koch — Costumer; William Glasgow — Art Director; Michael Luciano — Editor; 1962; Running time: 132 minutes.

7

A Piano for Mrs. Cimino (1982)

A Concerto for Davis

> *"Bette's performance ranks with some of her finest screen work."*[1]
> — Christopher Nickens

A Piano for Mrs. Cimino begins with Davis, screaming. However, this time it's an elderly lady, afraid for her life because of a legitimate medical crisis. Davis spent much of the 1970s and '80s making movies for TV. It was a period in which she played complex, interesting characters in well-written teleplays, directed by more than competent directors, such as Ron Howard and George Schaefer.

A Piano for Mrs. Cimino was her fourth TV movie in a row, and arguably the best of the lot. She won the International Television Festival Award for Best Actress in Monte Carlo.

Ironically, as with several of her roles, this character was a mirror of what would occur to Davis herself in a few years. Actually playing her own age, 72, in the present-day role of Mrs. Esther Cimino, Davis excels as a multifaceted person. Mrs. Cimino is an elderly woman whose husband recently died when they were on a Caribbean cruise. She has become confused and disoriented to the point where neighbors called 911 for an ambulance.

It has been said that Davis could not play a normal, regular person. This movie refutes that opinion. Esther Cimino is a housewife and mother who gave up her piano playing to support her husband, a musician and music store owner, and to raise two sons. When, in later life, her husband decides to slow down, they take a cruise to Argentina. On the cruise, he has a fatal heart attack.

The film concerns Mrs. Cimino and what happens to her as a result of an emotional breakdown, attributed to the encroachment of senility. As the movie opens, Davis is strapped on a stretcher, screaming for help as she is taken away. At the hospital, she is diagnosed with the onset of senility, the loss of brain cells. When her two sons come to visit she is confused about where she is and can't hear or see well because she does not have her eyeglasses or hearing aid. She thinks she is in a hotel in Argentina. She has her arms strapped to the side rails of the bed.

Davis looks confused, her eyes blinking at times, staring at other times. She cannot answer a nurse's question as to where she is or what day it is. Her voice is frightened and questioning. At her first, brief competency hearing, the judge asks her the president's name. Esther hesitantly replies, "Juan Peron?"

After the hospital stay, her two sons, George (George Hearn) and Harold (LeRoy Schultz), and her doctor decide the best course is to put her in a convalescent/nursing home. They also decide to place a power of attorney with her banker, Edward Leach (Graham Jarvis). Mrs. Cimino is a well-off, middle class person who owns her own home and a music store, and has a modest stock portfolio.

Her sons decide on the institution to which they plan to transfer their mother. However, her granddaughter, Karen (Alexa Kenin), objects and finds a better place, St. Hills, more home-like and also cheaper by half, at $45.00 a day.

When Mrs. Cimino first arrives at the new facility she is again confused, thinking she is in a hotel, and doesn't have her hearing aid turned up enough to hear well.

Mrs. Cimino's granddaughter tells the nursing home administrator, Mrs. Polanski (Penny Fuller), that her grandmother hasn't been the same since her grandfather's death on the cruise.

The caring Mrs. Polanski and support staff insist that Esther follow the house rules, be dressed properly for breakfast, and repeat what she is learning and remembering, all in a loving but firm way. When she learns that she is paying $45.00 a day and does not have power of attorney, she experiences a definite set back. She really doesn't even remember the brief court hearing at which all the decisions were made.

Mrs. Cimino acts confused and slow. At St. Hill's, her progress is tentative and hesitant but she steadily improves. At a birthday party in the home, she approaches a piano and starts to play. She is on the road to recovery.

Her granddaughter visits and tells her of the loss of her house and furnishings. Esther is surprised and angry. She goes to her room, unhappy and confused.

However, the next day she returns to her dinner table companions, and starts and continues a normal conversation. She also contacts her young lawyer, Philip Ryan (Christopher Guest), who applies for a second competency hearing to restore Esther's rights.

At the hearing, she is deliberate and clear in her answers to the judge's questions and is therefore granted release from the nursing home, although the bank retains power of attorney. Davis reveals Mrs. Cimino's fear but also her determination to restore her independence.

She is able, with her own lawyer, to convince the judge she is mentally competent to make decisions about herself. She moves out of the convalescent facility to an independent resident facility in Santa Monica, a great distance from Oregon.

Once in Santa Monica, Esther resumes her independent life. She is smartly dressed and walks with pride in her step. While walking one morning from the bank where she has deposited money in a new account, she is accosted by a "purse snatcher," and helped by a man who retrieves her purse and then proceeds to con her in a scam, pretending he is an FBI agent. She returns to withdraw $500 from her account that the "agent" says he'll mark in order to trap a suspected teller. Fortunately, the teller calls the manager, who explains to Esther that she has become a victim of a scam. Again, Davis shows Esther in total confusion, and declares herself stupid for believing the con man. She asks the manager, "Do you think I'm competent?" There is fear and pleading in her voice. The manager reassures her that con men are very clever, and she, indeed, is a competent person.

While living at this residence, two other significant events occur. One, her banker appointee, Mr. Leach, refuses to grant her $200 for Christmas gift buying, sending her only $100. She sits in the hotel lobby to read the letter from Mr. Leach. Angered, she puts the check in her handbag and crushes the letter, putting it in an ashtray. She no longer doubts herself, knowing she is a competent woman. At a New Year's Eve celebration at her complex, Esther dances with a fellow resident and surprisingly recognizes the band's clarinetist, Barney Fellman (Keenan Wynn), an old musician friend of her late husband. They reminisce.

Later Esther and Barney go to his small Santa Monica house where she spends the night. They realize this could be more than a friendship. Barney suggests that the two of them could perform together for people their age. Esther is quite hesitant, but agrees.

At her hotel residence, Esther, in a slip, views herself in a mirror and says, "Esther, you're an old lady." She smoothes her slip, looks at herself sideways, and amends, "Not bad for 72." She smiles. Later Barney wants her to stay with him, declaring he loves her.

Esther receives news from Karen that there will be a third competency hearing to enable her to regain total independence. She is elated.

Soon thereafter, she goes to the hearing in Oregon to regain control of all her assets and resume her normal life. With her lawyer's help and the support of her family, particularly her granddaughter, the incompetence of her banker (who holds her power of attorney) becomes apparent. He was also responsible for the mishandling of the music store. The judge's decision grants her wishes, but also reflects his concern for her future welfare, saying her stock portfolio must be placed in the hands of a power of attorney, of her choice, in case of later need.

Esther Cimino (Davis) is perplexed but listening and learning during a group therapy session in *A Piano for Mrs. Cimino* (Photofest).

During the hearing, the opposition's lawyer questions her behavior with Barney, stating she was consorting with a younger man, not knowing Barney was near her age and a friend of forty years. Both he and the banker are shown to be incompetent, even unprofessional.

Even though the result of the hearing is positive, Esther realizes she has always lived with her family and wishes to return to them. So she rejects Barney's offer. To celebrate, she goes to her son George's (George Hearn) highrise luxury apartment for dinner. Both sons, their wives and her granddaughter are there. She notes her old bone china, her silver flatware and the tea service being used. Her two sons weakly state that they did the best they could for her, following the doctor's and the banker's advice.

Esther exhibits small surprise at their comments and suggestion that she

Bernie Fellman (Keenan Wynn) receives a massage from Esther (Davis) in *A Piano for Mrs. Cimino* (Photofest).

will have a small apartment nearby. They offer the fact that they have repurchased her old piano for her.

When Karen's date, Philip Ryan (Christopher Guest), who is also her grandmother's lawyer, arrives to pick up Karen, it registers with Esther that she has choices also. Calmly, Esther rises from the dining table and excuses herself.

Her son, George, asks where she is going. At first, she answers, "I don't know." She walks a few steps toward the door, hesitates, then turns to the table and declares, "No, that's not true. I do know where I am going, and it's a good idea." She leaves. Davis handles all this calmly and deliberately, just as her character dictates.

She returns to Malibu and her old clarinetist friend, Barney.

Her return is quiet and slow, as she slips onto the piano bench, joining Bernie in a jazz riff. There is an expression of relief and love on Wynn's face, returned by Davis as she continues joining him musically.

What is so remarkable (and wonderful) about this movie and Davis' performance is that she plays a modern woman her own age, not some grotesque or theatrical person. She is an everywoman who faces the serious problem of old age. Davis plays it subtly, quietly and gives a lovely performance.

At her first collapse, she is confused and afraid, not living in the real world. As she begins to recover at the convalescent home, she is still tentative, but starts to relearn how to live and act like a competent individual. She has her first real confrontation when she tries to go to breakfast improperly attired in her nightclothes and a robe. Acting in character, Davis quietly acquiesces with strength and ultimately understanding of how it's necessary to accept some things in order to be considered adult and competent. No histrionics are necessary.

As she become healthier and more reasoning, she plainly shows her gratitude to those who help her, and in turn is pleasant and gracious to others. She even starts playing the piano again, and well.

Davis plays her reacquaintance with Wynn in a very low-key manner, enjoying him and the musical talent they share. But as you would expect Mrs. Cimino to do, she firmly rejects his offer to marry, thinking she must return to her old life of family. Here is a woman who had given up everything to raise her family.

It is only after she sees her sons' lack of caring, and her granddaughter's independence with her boyfriend, that she realizes she deserves the same and leaves for Malibu. It's a quiet, strong decision. Davis plays it perfectly.

The reconciliation with Wynn is sweetly accomplished as she arrives while he is playing his clarinet. He doesn't notice her enter. She slides onto the piano bench and starts accompanying him. The song completed, they stand and embrace.

Keenan Wynn, Penny Fuller, Paul Roebling, Christopher Guest and all the other cast members, especially the granddaughter, Alexa Kenin, are well cast and professional.

The film is straightforward in dealing with the aging issue, nursing homes, family relationships, the various emotions of those related to Esther, and the medical and legal world with which the elderly must deal.

7. A Piano for Mrs. Cimino *(1982)*

It isn't the first time Davis played a normal person. She didn't always play aristocrats, queens or murderesses. Her roles in *Payment on Demand, The Man Who Came to Dinner, The Corn Is Green*, and her Emmy-award winning performance with Gena Rowlands in *Strangers: The Story of a Mother and Daughter* are all normal people. At any rate, it is difficult to imagine what critics mean when they criticize her for not being able to play normal or regular people. Half of her 23 movies from 1938 to 1949 at Warners had Davis in a sympathetic role. Dramatists don't usually write plays or screenplays about "regular" or "normal" people, whatever that means. Dramas are written about people who have dramatic problems or lives, as evidenced by the work of Shakespeare, Ibsen, Chekhov, Williams and even Sam Shepherd. The last playwright writes about lower working class people, but are they "normal" or "regular?" I don't think so.

The fault lies in the material. The regular, normal people that Davis played were, for the most part, uninteresting and undramatic, as in *Storm Center*, where she was a librarian fighting censorship.

Human relationship is the key to understanding the impact of *A Piano for Mrs. Cimino*. The film centers on Davis' performance as an elderly woman, Esther Cimino, and her life-changing relationships with family and all the people she comes in contact with after suffering a breakdown because of the death of her husband — medical caretakers, nursing home administrators and personnel, financial advisors, lawyers — all the people one has to interact with as one gets older, particularly if judgments are made concerning one's competence. It is not an easy road to travel in the modern society known as the U.S.A.

Davis carefully winds her way through all the emotional ups and downs of Esther. Each relationship is different and worthy of investigation. Davis clearly understands her character's plight.

Esther has devoted her life to her family, her musician husband and her two sons. When she is first placed in a hospital because of her breakdown, her sons are the first two family members to come see her, but their visit is extremely brief, even though Esther asks for their help in having her wrists untied from the hospital bedside bars and returning her eyeglasses and hearing aid. She is understandably confused and unable to clearly see or hear the questions posed to her. Davis shows the fright and confusion clearly on her face.

The doctor glibly diagnoses her condition as advanced senility and recommends an in-house court hearing to give her sons power of attorney. When the hospital attendants come to take Esther to the hearing, she greets them with confusion. They frighten her and do nothing to alleviate her fears, but physically remove her to a wheelchair while she calls for the police.

As Esther is brought to the hearing room, a hospital storeroom, she is strapped in her chair, with a look of total confusion on her face. The judge takes no recognition of her condition except to ask her questions she cannot answer in her present condition. These people, the judge, the doctor, the hospital attendants, have all treated her with disinterest. There is no reason she should trust them.

Her two sons seem totally resigned to accepting the doctor's quick assessments, and do as he suggests. They rule out taking her into their homes because there isn't room and it would require expenditures for a nurse, etc.

Only her granddaughter, Karen, has any clear feeling for her grandmother. It is she who arranges for Esther to be placed in a caring convalescent hospital, St. Hill's, and she who takes her grandmother there. She is the only family member who seems to care to see if her grandmother can get well.

At St. Hill's, the staff and programs show the dedicated purpose they have toward assisting their patients toward recovery and dismissal. In the first home the son looked at it was obvious the staff only cared to sedate and create a quiet atmosphere where the patients merely stagnated.

Davis plays her entrance to St. Hill's with an understandable hesitancy, but she thoroughly reads the items on a common bulletin board and responds to the head administrator's positive requests in an intelligent way. She is still confused and unsure of where she is, which Davis expresses fully in her hesitancy, her facial expressions, and her unsure responses to initial requests.

The administrator makes it clear to Esther that she is expected to respond positively to programs and learn to socialize with her fellow patients. Davis slowly tries to participate, first at a meal, then in group therapy. But she's still unsure of her competency. Davis lets us see that it is not easy to become sure of oneself after suffering unpleasant events, but she also shows us her willingness to improve her behavior. The patients, the staff and particularly her granddaughter encourage her efforts and improvement. She can trust them.

Esther's banker, in charge of her finances through power of attorney, decides to sell her home and furnishings without consulting Esther. It appears the two sons did not discuss it with her either. Once more Esther is undervalued by her family and the financial advisor. Only Karen reveals the facts to her, along with the hospital's administrator.

Esther is devastated, and breaks down in tears over the lack of caring displayed by her two sons. Davis plays the scene while sitting at a table listening intently to Karen. When she realizes the extent of the damage, she cries, but that's all. She has become surer of herself and decides to see her own lawyer.

Karen takes her to the law office, and, for once, a professional is willing to help her regain her competency status. However, he's firm in stating that they must only ask for one thing, not a removal of all the restrictions. The judge watches Esther and listens to her answers. Davis appears as a careful, competent woman, one who even has a sense of humor as she lectures the judge about getting a hearing aid for himself.

Davis displays the character's acquired competence, and reveals that she will reside in a resident hotel in Santa Monica which a relative of her lawyer owns, a place for older people. When the judge grants her request, Esther and Karen are elated.

After her move, Esther has a run-in with a scam artist which throws her in an awkward situation with her new bank. She worries about her competency, but here she meets a caring institution in the bank and its personnel, who calmly reassure her and warn her of the cleverness of such people. Davis reacts with a worried face, but increasingly calms down when she realizes she's okay and that the banker is someone to be trusted.

Beyond this, Esther has a court session at which her erstwhile banker, who had ineptly administered her finances, and an inept lawyer, who tries to impugn her behavior, are proven by her lawyer to be incompetent. But the judge is reasonable and, in the interest of justice, gives Esther full release from her prior restrictions on her funds, apart from placing her stock portfolio into a power of attorney of her choice.

Davis plainly and simply shows us how every situation has to be assessed, one at a time. She shows us the anxiety caused by different people and institutions, even family. Also, we know all relationships change over time.

The hardest thing for Esther to accept is that her relationship with her sons has changed. It is her granddaughter who liberates her. Just as children must grow and change, and grow independent of their families, parents have to let go of their children and retain or regain their own lives.

Davis certainly had the life experience to be able to relate to this theme. Over her many years as a Hollywood star, she was the financial support, plus emotional support, for both her mother and her sister. Even though both married and remarried, they both came to completely rely on Davis for their well-being.

Davis had an overly close relationship with her mother, always feeling she owed her everything for the success she had attained as an actor. Yet she also realized her mother took advantage of the situation by actually living a more expensive lifestyle than her daughter. It was not always a smooth relationship. Davis also had to pay financially and emotionally for a sister who couldn't achieve the success Davis had gained. She was more than once confined to mental health facilities, at Davis' expense.

Davis was also privy to the experience of putting her trust in someone or some project, only to have it turn out badly. Her career ended badly at

Warners for that very reason. She was "forced" to accept properties that were far below her abilities and unsuitable for her in the late forties, ending with her disastrous miscasting in *Beyond the Forest.*

She basically felt her career had been ruined. Both *All About Eve* and *Payment on Demand* proved this to be wrong, but the rest of her career was not easy, as it included an array of projects which did her little good (e.g., *Two's Company* on Broadway and *Bunny O'Hare*, a movie).

Her matrimonial affairs all failed, and even her relationship with her children changed as they grew older and became independent. It wasn't until 1985, however, that her older daughter wrote a scathing autobiography.

In *A Piano for Mrs. Cimino* there was a happy ending for Esther Cimino. Davis was superbly able to show all the facets of this woman's character as she responded to people, caretakers, institutions, and environment, and, most importantly, how she was able to assess herself.

Her director on *A Piano for Mrs. Cimino*, George Schaefer, who later directed her with James Stewart in *Right of Way*, told me, "She was a pussy-cat to work with."

In *Pieces of Time*, Gary Fishgall believed:

> ...[O]ne of her [Bette Davis'] most successful projects, 1982's *A Piano for Mrs. Cimino*, had been directed by George Schaefer...
>
> [In *Right of Way*], given their similar ways of working and their love of acting, [James] Stewart and Davis ... got along beautifully.
>
> "I've never had a more delightful experience," Bette told one reporter thereafter. "We were both in practically every scene, and if we hadn't liked each other, we would have made it, but it wouldn't have been nearly as special an occasion. I just found him heaven."
>
> Returning the compliment, Stewart said, "Bette is absolutely amazing. Professional just isn't ... it's more than that. She's a master of craft. When she's there, she's there."
>
> Schaefer said, "Well, they're both likeable people and both big stars who had a greater heyday than this. So they could look back on the past and the record..."[2]

The *New York Times* reviewer observed, "Miss Davis plays Mrs. Cimino with reserve, intelligence and suitable irascibility, and her initial senility is convincing too."[3]

Charles Nickens, in *Bette Davis, a Biography in Photos*, sums it up by saying, "[H]er fourth TV movie [is] a sensitive study about the ignorance and confusion surrounding the conditions of senility. ...Bette's performance ranks ... with some of her finest work. She brings a proper mix of vagueness and determination to her character."[4]

Mrs. Cimino finds apparent happiness in her life ahead with Barney, which was not always the way things ended in other Davis movies.

Cast: Esther Cimino — Bette Davis; Barney Fellman — Keenan Wynn;

7. A Piano for Mrs. Cimino *(1982)*

Mrs. Polanski — Penny Fuller; Karen Cimino — Alexa Kenin; George Cimino — George Hearn; Philip Ryan — Christopher Guest; Edward Leach — Graham Jarvis; Roger Desmond — Paul Roebling; Harold Cimino — LeRoy Schultz; Dr. Mitchell — Walter Marsh.

Production: Roger Gimbel and Tony Converse — Executive Producers; George Schaefer — Producer and Director; John Gay — Teleplay; Robert Oliphant — Based on his book; Edward R. Brown — Cinematographer; Graeme Murray and Fred Price — Art Direction; James Horner — Music; Rita Roland — Editor; 1982; Running time: approximately 100 minutes.

8

The Old Maid (1939)

THE 19TH CENTURY AND ILLEGITIMACY

> *"The Old Maid ... is a superb romantic drama with a demonical, bittersweet, love-hate quality and a sweeping dramatic élan that few pictures before or since can match."*[1]
> —Lawrence Quirk

Self-sacrifice is shown over and over again by Charlotte Lovell (Davis) as she lives only for her daughter's welfare in *The Old Maid*. Made in 1939, a year in which Davis made four films (three of them costume dramas), it was filmed between *Juarez*, an historical film of the Mexican revolution in which Davis played the Empress Carlotta (and in which scenes of her were cut in deference to Paul Muni, the lead), and *The Private Lives of Elizabeth and Essex*, in which she played Elizabeth I.

All four scripts were well-written and the directors (Goulding, Curtiz, Dieterle) excellent, but in Zoe Akins' Pulitzer Prize-winning play *The Old Maid*, Davis, not for the first time, nor the last, plays a sympathetic role, that of a Philadelphia belle who has a child out of wedlock with her cousin's rejected suitor, Clem Spender (George Brent). The two cousins, Delia Lovell (Miriam Hopkins) and Charlotte Lovell, are the center of the drama.

In *Mother Goddam*, Whitney Stine states, "Davis had never co-starred with a female before and looked forward to an opportunity to particularly meaningful chemistry. But Hopkins made life on the set unendurable. A fine actress in a fine part, she was not above engaging in such unnecessary amateur shenanigans as upstaging."[2]

Davis said she respected Hopkins' talent as an actress, but she detested her as a person, and her unprofessionalism. Hopkins was prone to try to upstage any actor by fussing with her costume, etc. while the focus should have been on the other actor. Once again, though, the director, Edmund Goulding, prized superior performances from both actresses. Their relationship and acting ring true.

Never one of Davis' favorite films, *The Old Maid* is a fine example of a drama which allowed Davis to shine as a sacrificing woman. It was a very popular film. To make four superior pictures in one year was really quite a feat.

The Old Maid is mainly about sacrifice, a sacrifice necessitated by the times (prior to and after the Civil War). The Lovell cousins come from a well-to-do family in Philadelphia. Yet when the film opens, Delia's wedding to Jim Ralston (James Stephenson) is taking place in the Ralston home. Apparently, Delia and her cousin, Charlotte, have been living with their grandmother (Cecilia Loftus). Grandmother Lovell is in her downstairs parlor where her doctor (Donald Crisp) is telling her she cannot attend her granddaughter's wedding ceremony because it would be too much of a strain on her heart.

Charlotte is a bridesmaid for Delia. She is upstairs helping her elder cousin get dressed for the wedding. As Charlotte, Davis exemplifies the giddy happiness she feels as her cousin Delia as she prepares for her wedding day. Charlotte bounds into the dressing room, all smiles and glittering eyes, wishing happiness for her cousin's marriage, dressed in a beautiful antebellum gown with a flowered bonnet. Her corkscrew curls bounce as she twirls one way, then another. Charlotte admits, "I wish it was me." Dr. Lanskell tells her she's "very pretty," and she is. It is not explained why neither the wedding nor the reception are in the grandmother's home, nor why it is that neither cousin appears to have any parents available. Later we learn that the Lovells are prone to weak lungs. So perhaps they had tuberculosis, but this is never divulged.

While the cousins are dressing, a telegram arrives from Clement Spender, Delia's former fiancé. He says he is arriving that day to reunite with Delia. However, Delia, having waited two years while he went to Boston to make a financial success, has decided instead to marry Jim Ralston, a wealthy local banker. She is afraid Clem will show up to disrupt the wedding, but Charlotte offers to go to the train station to ward him off.

In her conversation with Delia, prior to her going to the train station, Charlotte shows disbelief in Delia's actions towards Clem, not understanding why she didn't wait for him. At the station she is sympathetic towards Clem and tries to dissuade him from going to Delia.

Charlotte returns to the Ralston house in time to warn Delia that Clem is at the outside back door. Clem appears in the dressing room and, in front of Charlotte, expresses his hurt and dismay that Delia has not waited for him. Clem tells Delia she'll be "condemned to a life of elegant boredom," and that she has a "consuming passion for the First National Bank." He also bestows on her a blue-stoned necklace which he had bought for her. Before she descends the stairs, she puts the necklace on: something blue.

When Charlotte sees Delia and Clem together, she shows her recognition of how Clem has been treated, and of her hidden feelings toward Clem. When the wedding procession begins to go downstairs, Charlotte leaves to find Clem.

Clem and Charlotte do not return to the Lovell house until late evening, where a maid is awaiting her. Charlotte tells Clem, "If I could do anything..." She looks down, away from his face.

"You have. You've been sweet."

"Sweet little Charlotte," she replies.

"You mean more to me than anything. Don't laugh at me." Clem embraces her.

Some time passes before Charlotte and Delia bid Clem farewell as he, a lieutenant, and his unit leaves for the Civil War. He promises to try to return to Charlotte. The loving care shows on Charlotte's face. It is noticeable that Delia still cares for Clem, and is wearing the necklace he gave her. Clem dies in battle in 1864.

Several years pass. The war is over. Using her money from her deceased grandmother, Charlotte opens a nursery. She is running an orphanage for war orphans. There is a foundling, Tina (Marlene Burnett), with whom she is particularly concerned. She hasn't seen her cousin Delia for a while, but Delia shows up while Dr. Lanskell is at the orphanage to examine Tina. Tina takes an immediate liking to Delia, who expresses maternal care toward her. In the intervening years Delia has had two children, a boy and a girl.

She tells Charlotte, "You've changed. Ever since you went out west."

"Changed? I don't understand you. How?"

"Morose and distant."

"I've heard all this before. I'm not giving up the nursery. I believe Joe Ralston [Jerome Cowan] is different. That's why I'm marrying him."

Then Charlotte breaks into a smile and asks Delia to stay and have a cup of tea.

"You know, Delia, you'd like to rule the world, wouldn't you?" she laughs.

When Tina comes into the room to see Delia, Charlotte tells Delia that Tina is a foundling. Dr. Lanskell gives Charlotte a knowing look.

Delia's brother-in-law, Joe, has been courting Charlotte. Both Delia and her husband, Jim, are concerned about Charlotte running an orphanage. Charlotte is determined to keep the orphanage, against the Ralston wishes and she believes Joe is independent and man enough to buck the Ralston desires.

What no one except Dr. Lanskell knows is that Tina is Charlotte's daughter by Clem. She went west for the birth, with everyone thinking she had gone because of a lung problem.

Prior to Charlotte's wedding in the Ralston house, Delia begs her to give up the nursery. Finally, with agony written across her face, Charlotte replies, "I can't give up my baby." She asks Delia to help her, as she reveals the truth of her relationship with Clem; Tina's full name is Clementine.

Delia says Charlotte must tell Joe the truth.

"I do love Joe," Charlotte sincerely replies.

However, Delia deceives Joe into believing Charlotte has had a recurrence of TB and can't marry anyone. Under this false assumption, Joe goes to Charlotte, saying he releases her. Charlotte believes the reason is her illegitimate child. Sadness and confusion cross Charlotte's face as she looks away from Joe.

A few months later, Charlotte receives a letter notifying her that Delia's husband, Jim, has had a serious horseback riding accident. Charlotte goes to comfort Delia. When she arrives, Joe, who has returned from Boston, where he has married, greets her. He asks about her health. Charlotte realizes Delia had lied about her condition to prevent the marriage. Realizing Delia's deception, she turns to leave, just as Delia comes downstairs. Charlotte confronts her, very quietly but determined. Her voice only rises once, when she declares, "It was wicked of you!"

Just then, Dr. Lanskell comes downstairs to inform Delia that Jim has died. Charlotte turns away and leaves.

The following Christmas, Charlotte and Tina come to spend the night at the Ralstons. Charlotte has given up her orphanage but retained her "foundling." Tina loves being with Delia's two children, and mimics them when they say goodnight to "Mommie." As they are being tucked in, Tina again mimics the other two children when they say goodnight to "Aunt Charlotte."

Delia asks Charlotte and Tina to come live with her so that Tina can have companionship and a privileged upbringing. Charlotte answers with a definite no. Delia argues, "You'll have to tell Tina the truth, sooner or later."

"But I want to take care of her myself," Charlotte replies.

Charlotte acquiesces for Tina's sake.

Fifteen years pass. Once again there is a wedding in the Ralston house. The groom is Delia's son, John (DeWolf Hopper). Although only in middle age, Charlotte has become rigid and gray-haired, with a hardness in her face. She is compulsive in requiring Tina (Jane Bryan), now near 19, to behave in a strict way, and is constantly critical of her behavior. Charlotte is precise and uncompromising, for she feels Tina is too much like Clem, wild and adventuresome, the very traits which she loved in him. Tina realizes Delia isn't her mother, but loves her as if she were, and is clearly treated as a daughter by Delia. Tina has also become critical of and nasty toward Charlotte.

At John's wedding, Tina even belittles Charlotte in front of Dr. Lanskell, saying she's never been loved, nor can she dance. Dr. Lanskell asks Charlotte to dance.

"You heard what Tina said. I don't dance. I never have danced."

She slowly climbs the stairs, going to her bedchamber. She lifts her right arm in a rhythmic motion in time to the music below and turns, "dancing" toward her settee. She looks at the fire, sits on the settee and quietly leans forward and says, "Oh! Clem."

When Tina and Lanning (William Lundigan) return from a winter ball, Charlotte is waiting for them in a darkened library. She hears their talk as Lanning is partially explaining why his family objects to Tina. He is going away because his parents feel she is a nobody, not a Ralston, not of their station. As Charlotte moves to confront them, Delia descends the stairs to inquire of their lateness at getting home. She holds Lanning accountable, but Charlotte speaks up and says it is not him to blame but Tina. He admits he is going away and that he will not return.

There is a confrontation among the three women, and Tina is sent upstairs. In the debate between Charlotte and Delia, the former says she's been wrong all these years. "I've deliberately made Tina think I'm an old maid." She will take Tina away to where people won't know of her illegitimacy, but Delia pleads with her to think of Tina's welfare and offers to adopt her. Charlotte sacrifices her feelings once again for Tina's well-being.

After their discussion, Charlotte sends Delia to bed, returns to the library and sits before the fire. She speaks aloud of her love for Tina and her concerns, all with easy humor, love and feeling. Then she continues speaking aloud her thoughts to Tina, but in a fierce, unkind tone, making herself appear unloving and rigid.

Another Ralston wedding, this one between Tina and Lanning. Charlotte has taken care of all the arrangements, right down to the last doily. When Lanning leaves the evening before the wedding, she tells Delia that tonight she will tell Tina of her origins because for once, this night, she wants Tina to call her "Mommie." Delia tries to dissuade her.

Charlotte states, "The word between us is revenge. You thought of him [Clem] all the time. I am her mother."

Delia answers, "We'll see which one of us is her mother. You're wicked."

"No, I could never do what you've done to me."

Charlotte mounts the stairs and enters Tina's room.

Tina is beside herself with happiness. When Charlotte expresses her sorrow at being so strict with her at times, Tina allows as how she has not meant the mean things she has said to her over the years. She also reveals she knows Delia is not her mother, but doesn't care because she loves her so. Charlotte then wishes her goodnight and god bless.

When Delia sees Charlotte, Charlotte tells her she couldn't reveal the truth because, "She never really belonged to me. Her father never belonged to me, either. They're both yours."

Delia goes to Tina. She tells her how Charlotte wouldn't marry years ago because she would have had to give Tina up. She also asks Tina to save her last goodbye the next day for her Aunt Charlotte, which she does.

When Tina and her husband leave, Tina calls her aunt. She gives her last goodbye kiss to Charlotte. Charlotte's face softens as she walks toward the departing carriage and leans a hand on a tree. With her right hand she touches her cheek where Tina kissed her. She turns and puts her arm around Delia's waist. Then, arm-in-arm, they reenter the Ralston house.

Lawrence Quirk, the author of *The Great Romantic Films*, opines, "This film showcased another Davis — the actress of sweeping range threading with infinite art the odd vagaries of love and hate, bitterness and idealism, aspirations and frustration."[3]

Even though this is a movie about self-sacrifice, Davis shows the determined strength of her character, determined to do "what's best" for her illegitimate daughter. She is also a forgiving person. Delia basically ruined her chance at marriage with Joe Ralston by lying to him. In one brief scene, when Delia loses her husband, Davis had to show her anger at the deception, yet be able to reason and feel the grief Delia must feel when she learns of her husband's demise.

Davis delineates a range of emotions, from her entry as the giddily happy young girl at her cousin's wedding to the concern and love for Clem as he leaves for war. Her total acceptance of usefulness and "motherhood" at the orphanage, her consuming concern for her daughter's well-being, and her deliberate choice to become a strict, dour old maid all add up to Charlotte's devotion to her daughter's happiness.

Even at the end, the two cousins sharing the remainder of their lives will not be easy, even though both have Tina's best interests at heart.

The movie is a thorough depiction of the life and times of women in that mid-nineteenth century era. No woman today, especially in the aristocracy (if there is such a thing now), would ever consider such a life of self-

Charlotte Lovell (Davis) in a confrontation with her cousin, Delia Ralston (Miriam Hopkins), in *The Old Maid* (Photofest).

sacrifice. Society no longer demands it. There are many single-parent homes, and even in upper-middle class society, divorces are acceptable, as are abortions. Among the upper class, abortions were always an option, but perhaps not before twentieth century medicine.

Certainly the upper class society which Edith Wharton depicted so well allowed men to make mistakes. It was the women who had to pay for men's indiscretions.

Edmund Goulding helped Davis deliver a touching, restrained performance, as he did in *Dark Victory*. In *Star Acting*, Charles Affron affirms, "The processes of self-understanding Davis undergoes in *Dark Victory* are further articulated in *The Old Maid*.... [L]imited to a few rooms and a short time span, he [Goulding] finds the kind of concentration that is richly focused..."[4]

Just as importantly, Goulding kept Miriam Hopkins under restraint. She wasn't allowed to get away with her usual scene-stealing tactics, but had to perform in a credible way to maintain the relationship needed between the two cousins.

Some critics have called this a romantic film, but I think that's incorrect. Romantic films generally end up with a man and a woman's requited love. Not in this picture. This is a film of mother love and familial love. It's a woman's picture, if you define a woman's picture as a movie with strong appeal for women.

It's a film about women, lost love, and another, higher, love — maternal love. In fact, both women in *The Old Maid* raise children without a father's presence, unless one construes Davis as becoming the father figure. That would be stretching it considerably, as neither Wharton nor Zoe Akins was suggesting this.

Affron asserts, "From *Dark Victory* until her departure from Warner Brothers in 1949, Davis portrayed the courageous, long-suffering, and essentially sympathetic heroine in roughly half of her twenty-three films."

It was with great enthusiasm that Davis looked forward to acting with Miriam Hopkins in *The Old Maid*. It wasn't that she hadn't worked with other actresses at Warners. She had. Early on she had been in supporting roles for Ruth Chatterton, Barbara Stanwyck and later with Joan Blondell but for the most part, her co-stars were male, Henry Fonda, Edward G. Robinson and Leslie Howard.

She had also known Hopkins when they were both in George Cukor's stock company in Rochester, New York, in the late 1920s. That is not to say they were friends, however. For Davis, it had been an unpleasant experience because Cukor fired her during her second season.

Hopkins had achieved great success in Hollywood, mostly at Paramount where she made *Design for Living*, *Becky Sharp* (the first Technicolor feature), and *The Story of Temple Drake*, an adaptation of William Faulkner's novel *Sanctuary*. She was a skilful, talented actor, but she also acquired a reputation for temperament and upstaging other actors.

When filming began, Hopkins showed up in an exact copy of a dress Davis had previously worn in *Jezebel*. This did not sit well with Davis. As filming progressed, Davis and her director, Goulding, noted her attempts to upstage Davis during their scenes together, where she'd try to maneuver Davis out of the light or fidget with her costume or hands when Davis was in a two-shot, distracting the audience to pay attention to her rather than the speaker. What finally irked Davis more than anything was that as the film progressed and the characters aged, Hopkins started looking younger and younger. Finally, Hal Wallis, at Jack Warner's orders, had the make-up artist check Hopkins' make-up each morning on the set to make sure it was correct. (One might presume that Hopkins resented the fact that she played the older cousin, and also had the lesser of the two roles.)

Having noted all this, it is the remarkable ability of Davis that allowed her to use it all in her delineation of Charlotte Lovell. The two characters, although loving cousins at the beginning of the story, actually are rivals in a way that deeply affects both their roles and their interplay as actresses.

The incident that starts the chain of events that brings the two together at the end of the film is Delia's rejection of her true love, Clem Spender, to marry Jim Ralston. She marries Jim partially for spite. Therefore, when Charlotte responds favorably to Clem and sympathizes with him over his rejected status, Delia is actually jealous of Charlotte's conquest.

Hopkins is all spite, dismissive in her portrayal, allowing Davis to be caring, kind and sympathetic toward Brent.

In the orphanage scene where Dr. Lanskell checks out Charlotte's special little girl, Delia arrives and is overly concerned about Charlotte's health and work. She proceeds to heap affection on Tina. The overreaction again gives Davis the ability to show her the concern for the child's well-being.

Hopkins' projection of false concern and affection for both Tina and Charlotte allows Davis to exert her stronger character and true human feelings whenever Hopkins fails to restrain her emotions, which is often.

Charlotte only accepts the offer and pleadings of Delia because of her deep concern for her illegitimate child's needs and future.

Delia is actually sanctimonious and self-righteous, but she does offer Charlotte a secure place and family in which to raise her child.

The only time Charlotte expresses her repressed anger with Delia is when she discovers that Delia had lied to her fiancé, Joe Ralston. The Davis eyes flash, and you can see her deep-set anger and hurt. Hopkins' response is almost immediately mitigated by the announced death of her husband.

The only scene where Davis and Hopkins really get to play against each other for any length is when Charlotte finally decides she will reveal herself as Tina's real mother the night before Tina's wedding. Charlotte is determined that Tina know her real mother's identity so Charlotte can finally receive the love from her that she has striven to avoid by being so strict and critical of

Tina over the years. Charlotte wants that maternal recognition, and Davis is forceful in her reasoning as to why she wants it. Delia reacts sincerely, begging Charlotte not to disillusion Tina, even though Tina knows Delia is not her real mother. Charlotte's determination carries her to her daughter's room where, for the first time, she apologizes to Tina for her behavior and shows her love for Tina.

It's all quiet and sincere, but Tina's acceptance and expressed love for Delia as a mother causes Charlotte to renege on her threat. Across Davis' face comes a look of resignation and acceptance of her role as the old maid, for she realizes Tina does love her, but for all these years Tina has been Delia's child, not hers.

Throughout the film Davis shows her capacity for maternal love, for self-sacrifice. She willingly, in the end, accepts both the loss of Clem, to death, and her daughter, to Delia. Davis proved again that she did not need to be highly dramatic to succeed in a role. She definitely could express the sympathetic emotions of womanhood.

In all her scenes, she is obviously committed to her character and, as she always was, willing to change from a delightfully pretty young woman to an aged, stiff-structured, middle-aged spinster with gray hair and dark eyes and an unsmiling countenance.

Both Davis and Hopkins were guided by one of the finest directors of the day, Edmund Goulding, a very kind and considerate person who often helped with the screenwriting of a film. He was aware of the possible contentions between the two women and therefore was able to avert any real problems. He listened well to both. The stars were greatly supported by an excellent script based on Zoe Akins' play and Edith Wharton's novel. The sets were all accurate to the period, as well as the costumes for both men and women. This was another picture that most likely would have benefited tremendously if it had been made in color.

The supporting players were of the best caliber, starting with Donald Crisp as Dr. Lanskell, Cecilia Loftus as the grandmother, George Brent as Clem and Jane Bryan as Tina. As in other pictures, Davis really praised Jane Bryan, her protégée, for whom she saw great success. But Bryan gave up her profession to marry, and remained a lifelong friend of Davis.

No expense was spared on the details of the sets, nor on the use of extras in wedding scenes, railroad scenes or at the orphanage. It was definitely a quality production.

Graham Greene stated:

> Great actresses choose odd mediums and perhaps Miss Davis is a great actress. Her performance ... is of extraordinary virtuosity — as the young girl, as the secret mother and as the harsh, prim middle-aged woman. Goulding keeps her scenes so that her moral self-reproach never turns into self-indulgent masochism.[5]

Easter time on the set of *The Old Maid* with Davis and Marlene Burnett (Young Tina) (Photofest).

In two other films (*The Virgin Queen* and *The Private Lives of Elizabeth and Essex*) Davis would again deliver a performance of self-sacrifice but not for maternal reasons.

Cast: Charlotte Lovell — Bette Davis; Delia Lovell — Miriam Hopkins; Clem Spender — George Brent; Dr. Lanskell — Donald Crisp; Tina — Jane

8. The Old Maid *(1939)*

Bryan; Dora — Louise Fazenda; Jim Ralston — James Stephenson; Joe Ralston — Jerome Cowan; Lanning Halsey — William Lundigan; Jim — Rand Brooks; Grandmother Lovell — Cecilia Loftus; Dee — Janet Shaw; John — DeWolf Hopper; Tina as a child — Marlene Burnett.

Production: Hal B. Wallis — Producer; Henry Blanke — Associate Producer; Edmund Goulding — Director; Casey Robinson — Screenwriter; Based on Zoe Atkins' play, adapted from Edith Wharton's novel; Tony Gaudio — Cinematographer; Max Steiner — Music Composer; Leo F. Forbstein — Music Director; Orry-Kelly — Costumes; Robert Haas — Art Director; George Amy — Editor; 1939; Running time, 96 min.

9

The Virgin Queen (1955)

AGAIN, A QUEEN

> "I think Bette Davis would probably have been burned as a witch had she lived two or three hundred years ago. She gives the curious feeling of being charged with power which can find no ordinary outlet."[1]
> —E. Arnot Robertson

For the second time, Davis explored the life of Queen Elizabeth I. In this instance the title *The Virgin Queen* cannot be taken literally, but is accurate historically because Elizabeth never married. The state, or rather colony, of Virginia was named in her honor. *The Virgin Queen* was ostensibly a vehicle for Richard Todd as Sir Walter Raleigh but once Davis signed on to play Elizabeth I, both her character and persona as an actress took over the production. Sixteen years after her first queenly incarnation, in *The Private Lives of Elizabeth and Essex*, she was rightfully more mature to handle the role and actually had a better, more literate script from which to work. She had been off the screen for over two years, and, at 47, she looked older than her years, especially with the "Elizabeth" make-up, high forehead and orange wig. Regardless of the opulent costumes and jewels, she was no longer the beauty she had once been in her Warner Brothers years.

Sir Walter Raleigh's (Richard Todd) presentation at the court of Queen Elizabeth I, toward the beginning of the movie, is precipitated by a chance encounter with Lord Leicester (Herbert Marshall). The lord's carriage becomes mired in mud and a large pothole while he is traveling in a rainstorm to court one night. At a nearby inn, the lord asks for help from men

9. The Virgin Queen *(1955)*

Davis in her *Virgin Queen* nightcap when she presented the 1954 Best Actor Oscar to Marlon Brando for *On the Waterfront*.

at the tavern. It is only through the intervention of Raleigh, who has just returned from an English attack on Ireland, that men are recruited to rescue the stuck coach. Lord Leicester promises to secure an audience with the queen for Raleigh after Leicester learns that he knew Raleigh's father.

While waiting for his presentation to the queen, Raleigh observes and listens to the courtiers. It becomes obvious to him that the court is full of intrigue, with everyone currying the queen's favor. When the queen arrives and Raleigh is formally presented to her, he is honest with her about his desire for three ships to sail to the New World in order to gather gold and spices for England. He wins her favor, but no promises are made concerning his request.

Raleigh is appointed captain of the queen's palace guards, a role he resents.

Raleigh also catches the eye of Beth Throgmorton (Joan Collins), who surmises that Raleigh will become one of the queen's lap dogs, sitting on a large, green-striped cushion at the queen's feet. Beth warns him that this will not lead to new ships. Her prediction comes true at a bow and arrow hunt when she sees him sitting at the queen's feet.

Later, at the Queen's Council, Sir Christopher (Robert Douglas) questions and attacks Raleigh verbally. Raleigh storms from the chamber after quarreling with the queen. When he leaves, the queen follows him out to the larger court room and berates him for his disrespect to her, his queen.

Beth hears of Raleigh's banishment and goes to his chamber to support him. They then perform an informal vow of marriage.

The queen sends for Raleigh at this point. The queen is in her bedchamber, having been taken somewhat ill after her confrontation with Raleigh. She has just been presented with a handsome sword from the French ambassador (Romney Brent). The ambassador has been continually trying, on the queen of France's behalf, to arrange a marriage between Elizabeth I and a member of Catherine d'Medici's court.

Elizabeth sets aside the differences between Raleigh and herself because he respects her and loves England. He has been honest and truthful with her. She acknowledges this by knighting him with her new sword, and promises him one ship. He is then announced to the court as Sir Walter Raleigh.

Raleigh travels to Plymouth to oversee the building of the vessel, but Beth has deserted him, for she believes he has betrayed her with the queen. The queen announces that she is sending her four ladies-in-waiting to the French court for an indefinite stay. She expects France to reciprocate with four gentlemen. The ladies are given leave to go to their respective family houses to prepare for their journey.

Word soon passes that Beth has fainted in the chapel and is not well. In truth, she is with child and planning not to go to France. When Raleigh hears of this turn of events, he travels to the Throgmorton estate and declares his love for Beth. They are then legally married.

Elizabeth sends word to Raleigh of her impatience with waiting to hear from him. She wonders when the ship will be ready. At court she tells everyone that Raleigh will remain in her court rather than sail to America. She also sends her scarf to him.

When Raleigh learns of her plan, he and Lord Derry (Dan O'Herlihy) plan to speed up the completion of the shipbuilding in order to sail for America with Beth. A double bed is built for the captain's quarters. When word of these events reaches the queen, she executes an order for Raleigh's arrest. In trying to escape with Beth, Lord Derry is killed. Beth is captured and taken to court.

Raleigh is in the tower, awaiting execution. Beth steals into the queen's bedchamber to plead her case with Elizabeth. The queen does not relent, but realizes she can't execute Beth until after the birth of her child, seven months hence.

The queen goes to Raleigh in the tower prison to confront him as a traitor, but is surprised when Raleigh only pleads that she let the ship go to America to secure treasure for England. He also asks to see Beth, but never pleads for himself.

While leaving his cell, the queen stops and returns, admiring his continuing honesty and truthfulness and loyalty to England. She also realizes he is the only one she wants to captain the ship. The last scene shows the queen watching the ship sail from London on the Thames, Raleigh and Beth at the rail, and the queen's scarf flying from the mast.

The Virgin Queen's screenplay was taken from Mindret Lord's biography of Sir Walter Raleigh and his quest to garner three ships from the queen to sail from England to the New World.

A subplot concerns the romance of Raleigh and one of the queen's ladies-in-waiting, Beth Throgmorton, which is the least interesting part of the film. If the queen demands total loyalty from Raleigh, and has a controversial attachment to him, it's obviously not possible that there would be a physical relationship. Queen Elizabeth is far too old and ravaged by the effects of smallpox, which she suffered as a child. The dialogue provided Davis is authentic, taken from Lord's book, and Davis plays it for all it's worth, from her anger over Raleigh's deception to her piteous revelation concerning her physical appearance. Richard Todd is, perhaps, at his best in this picture, where he rises to the acting bar set by Davis.

The obvious comparison must be made with Davis' previous attempt in 1939 at performing the same role, vis à vis Errol Flynn, who played Essex. Both films were in color, but the earlier picture was not in CinemaScope and had a darkened palate very reminiscent of Rembrandt paintings, as did the costumes. The prior film was based on Maxwell Anderson's play, a typical polemic in verse that he was fond of writing—a message for the pre–World War II era. The blank verse also was not Shakespearean. In its favor, the film offered a greater range of emotions for Davis to express, which she delivered in a rather fidgety style but also with humor.

The later film finds her just as imperious, but minus the distracting mannerisms, such as clutching and unclutching her hands. She is true to the feelings of the queen as expressed in the dialogue, and there is a great humor. The director, Henry Koster, had the technical virtuosity to handle CinemaScope with subtlety, as far as light and shadow and focus went. Every corner of the wide screen is lit for visibility of detail. What could have been nothing more than a costume, action picture revolving around a love story between Raleigh and Throgmorton became an historical drama of Tudor England with Elizabeth I at its center.

There is swordplay in a fight between Raleigh and Sir Christopher, but, more important, one sees the court maneuvers and intrigue, and the control and intelligence the queen has to exert in order to rule her great empire. One also sees the queen's non-public persona. Davis has a field day showing us the queen in her aged grandeur, her imperiousness, her knowledge of the workings of the court and foreign intrigue, her skepticism in dealing with her courtiers, her weariness in dealing with governing, her humor in one-upmanship with the French ambassador, and finally her acceptance and sorrow at being a queen rather than a woman.

Dressed in regal gowns, full at the bottom, with large lace stiff collars, one watches Davis rocking side to side as she walks with authority. She displays moods and feelings through her face and eyes.

Her face is dominated by her orange wig, with a high forehead, white make-up, a small rouged mouth, and her head sometimes crowned with a coronet.

In her first meeting with Raleigh, the interest and intrigue she has in her smile and eyes is evident as she listens to Raleigh's request for ships. She looks directly at him, assessing his truthfulness, honesty and worth.

She expresses anger with her flashing eyes and clenching hands when she learns of an Irishman (Lord Denny) in her palace guard — treachery, from her viewpoint.

When the queen, in her bedchamber, commands Raleigh's presence, he arrives just after her encounter with the French ambassador. She has let the ambassador see her without "make-up," in her bedclothes and a peaked nightcap. He will think her quite ill. She knows he will report this to his queen, Catherine D'Medici. When the ambassador leaves, Davis falls back upon her pillows with great laughter, knowing she put one over on him.

Upon Raleigh's entrance, the queen returns to her wounded anger at his betrayal. When he won't back down, and she again realizes his loyalty, relief sweeps over her face, and also the wish for his love, not personal, but love for the queen which he shows as he kisses her hand. She then knights him with a sword. Davis falls upon her pillows with a wistful look as he leaves.

Perhaps the most telling scene in the film is the confrontation between the queen and Lady Raleigh when the latter pleads for her husband's release from the tower. Immensely angry with Sir Walter for betraying her, and the revelation that he married one of her ladies-in-waiting, Davis spews her venom from her bed at Collins. Lady Raleigh is adamant that the queen won't be able to execute her because she is pregnant and due in seven months. Still angry, the queen reveals her inability to have children because she had smallpox as a child, and she forces Lady Raleigh to see her as she is physically, without her nightcap and make-up — a basically bald old lady without any youthful attraction. What she has had to rely on is her power and her steadfast love for England. When she finishes exposing herself emotionally and physically, she screams, "Take the strumpet out." As Lady Raleigh is removed from the chamber, the queen lurches forward and crumples on the bed, her hands covering her face as she chokes out a sob.

All her pride and sorrows have been revealed in this one emotion-filled scene. The camera rises slowly from her broken body. The price she has paid to be queen has been exacted.

In her final confrontation with Raleigh in the tower cell, Davis shows her intelligence, her vulnerability, and finally her unhappy resignation with the fact of Raleigh's own loyalty to the Queen and England. She states her basis for his pardon. She couldn't stand the thought of hearing a bawling brat, seven months hence because she had once been that bawling brat herself.

Aside from Davis and Todd, the surrounding cast, including Jay Robinson, Herbert Marshall and, of course, Joan Collins, are all more than competent and add the required British flavor to the picture.

This is a sumptuous period film filled with court rooms, throne rooms, taverns, and wars, all in color. The level of lighting is excellent in all scenes, whether it is a tavern at night or outdoors in an open field. Darkness prevails in the Queen's bedchamber when Collins arrives to plead her case. The widescreen ratio is handled well throughout the film.

Davis was nervous about appearing in the movie after nearly three years off the screen, but, of course, she needn't have been. She dominates the entire picture, giving a sincerely royal, believable performance.

At this time, the entire industry was in flux, and 20th Century–Fox was the leader in CinemaScope productions (principally historical romances such as *The Robe*, and *Prince Valiant*, a comic-strip adventure movie). When this movie turned out to be about the queen and Raleigh, not the Todd-Collins romance, they didn't know what to do with it, nor how to sell it. So they threw it away.

Davis as Queen Elizabeth I, with her lady-in-waiting Beth Throgmorton (Joan Collins), in *The Virgin Queen* (Photofest).

Reviews were mixed. Very few critics analyzed Davis' rounded performance. Contrarily, Alexander Walker, in *Stardom*, viewed Davis' performance as follows:

> Her exercise of pure power is ... served in the two films about Elizabeth Tudor....The court setting parallels a film studio. Both royal films ... give full reign to ... the star's inherent characteristics. This is her sarcasm, her talent for public rebuke ... those two institutionalize it in the person of a Tudor queen who is by protocol... "unanswerable."[2]

In 1953, while performing on Broadway in *Two's Company*, Davis suffered a case of osteomyeletis of the jaw, which required oral surgery. In March, she left the show for surgery. She then went to recuperate at her new home in Cape Elizabeth, Maine, with her husband Gary Merrill and their three children.

Between 1953 and 1955, 20th Century–Fox developed CinemaScope, a widescreen projection of film requiring an anamorphic lens. Developed to give audiences a larger picture than TV, it proved very successful. Darryl F. Zanuck, production head of 20th Century–Fox, who held the same position during the filming of *All About Eve*, had developed a script from Mindret Lord's book *Sir Walter Raleigh* for his contract player Richard Burton, the Welsh actor, who had been a great success in *The Robe*, the initial CinemaScope film. Zanuck, knowing Davis from her Warner Brothers years when he had been executive producer for a while in the 1930s, and from her successful portrayal in *The Private Lives of Elizabeth and Essex*, thought Davis the only one suitable to portray Elizabeth. He'd also been pleased with her two recent 20th Century–Fox films, *All About Eve* and *The Star*, both of which garnered her Oscar nominations.

Davis was less than pleased with the script submitted to her because her part was obviously not the dominant character. When Burton backed out of the movie, the script was refashioned to suit Richard Todd, a very competent young English actor who had experienced success with *The Hasty Heart* and Hitchcock's *Stage Fright*, both Warner Brothers films.

Davis agreed to sign because she loved playing Queen Elizabeth, and the final script favored her role. It would have been fascinating to see her play opposite Burton, who was critically feted at the time. He eventually was miscast in *Who's Afraid of Virginia Woolf?* with his then-wife Elizabeth Taylor, the film Davis desperately wanted to make opposite James Mason.

Davis wasn't just worried about the script of *The Virgin Queen*, but was nervous because she had been off the screen for over two years. She had required much time to recuperate from her surgery, plus she and her husband had become heartbreakingly aware that their daughter, Margot, had suffered brain damage, apparently at birth, and would require institutional care for the remainder of her life. Both the physical and emotional tolls affected Davis. She had gained weight and aged quite a bit, looking even older than her 47 years. It was not a stretch for her to look Elizabeth's age.

To her relief, her portrayal only required eleven shooting days. Every day she had to have the front half of her scalp shaved, and the Elizabethan make-up and wig applied. Contracted for three weeks, she was delighted with the speed of the production.

As was her way, Davis had memorized the entire script, and delivered the literate dialogue by Harry Brown and the book's author, Mindret Lord, in her clipped "British" accent with great efficiency. Her vocal authority served the monarch well, and Davis effectively expressed her character's moods, whether in a queenly mode or, most affectingly, when she voices her womanly concerns about her physical appearance and lack of any loving relationship. One sees the vulnerable old woman under the queenly stature and posture.

Davis still had the power, the energy and concentration to ignite the screen with her presence. For instance, one can see the relish with which she played the scene in which, leaving the castle, she encounters a running stream of street water. When she hesitates to cross it because she would have to step in it, Sir Walter thrusts his new sable cape over the water for her to step on. At first, she defers, but then laughs, with a glint in her eye and, with the help of Sir Walter's arm, crosses the stream by stepping on his cloak, making a caustic remark to the other members of her court who had offered no assistance. She then turns and contemptuously commands him to retrieve his cloak, which he does. Of course, it is ruined. The queen moves on.

No one could be more queenly than Davis. She not only knew and understood the royalty of Elizabeth I, but relished her power, just as she relished the power she had had herself when she was the queen of the Warner Brothers lot.

The studios were certainly like fiefdoms, as Joe Mankiewicz remarked. The executive producers, such as Jack Warner and Darryl Zanuck, acted like kings and ruled their studios by treating their employees, especially the actors, as so much chattel. It wasn't until the middle forties that Olivia de Havilland's court case in California prevented the studios from adding time to an actor's seven-year contracts when he had gone on suspension rather than accept a weak script. Actors, like Davis and Cagney, suffered many a suspension for their unwillingness to perform in what they regarded as junk.

This became a moot point as the late forties and fifties saw studios divest themselves of contract players. Actors became free agents and contracted to play roles on a film-by-film basis, with salaries negotiated by their high-powered agents. Some actors even formed their own production companies.

In *The Great Movie Stars*, David Shipman says, "Her dialogue was a brilliant pastiche of Elizabeth's letters and speeches, and she was even better than she had been in 1939."[3] Both films about Elizabethan England hinge on the queen's relationship with strong knights of her court, but the two actors, Richard Todd and Errol Flynn, were worlds apart, as were the Hollywood years of 1939 and 1955.

Cast: Elizabeth I — Bette Davis; Sir Walter Raleigh — Richard Todd; Beth Throgmorton — Joan Collins; Chadwick — Jay Robinson; Earl of Leicester — Herbert Marshall; Lord Derry — Dan O'Herlihy; Sir Christopher — Robert Douglas; Ambassador from France — Romney Brent.

Production: Charles Brackett — Producer; Henry Koster — Director; Harry Brown and Mindret Lord — Screenwriters; Charles G. Clarke — Cinematographer; Leonard Doss — Color Consultant; Franz Waxman — Musical Score; Mary Wills — Costumes; Lyle Wheeler and Leland Fuller — Art Direction; Robert Simpson — Editor; 1955; Running time — 92 minutes.

10

The Private Lives of Elizabeth and Essex (1939) (aka *Elizabeth the Queen*)

First and Forever a Queen

"Go hang yourself."[1]
— Jack L. Warner

"Never stop daring to hang yourself, Bette."[2]
— Charles Laughton

Davis' fourth film in 1939 for her home studio, Warner Brothers, offered her a role she coveted, even though she was only 31 at the time. In *The Stars*, Richard Schickel, eminent critic for *Time* magazine, allows, "No one has ever been better than Davis at her best on the screen."[3] The simple reason why *The Virgin Queen* is listed at number nine in this book — above *The Private Lives of Elizabeth and Essex*— is the matter of the written work. Maxwell Anderson's play *Elizabeth the Queen* was written in blank verse (unfortunately, not of Shakespearean caliber), and much of the dialogue is polemic in nature.

The silly title, *The Private Lives of Elizabeth and Essex*, was just a case of star power and ego massage. Errol Flynn felt slighted by *Elizabeth the Queen*. Interestingly, Davis wanted Laurence Olivier for the part because of his expertness with poetics, but, as was his wont, he turned it down. In retrospect, Flynn is credible and not as foolish a choice as Davis thought, but he's not quite up to the dramatic challenge of Davis and the script. Ultimately, he hurts the film by refusing to respond to Davis.

This film was made in 1939, a year extolled for the sheer number of excellent films it produced. *Elizabeth* was Davis' first picture in color. In fact, her next color film would be *The Virgin Queen* in 1955. Consider her 1939 list: *Dark Victory, Juarez, The Old Maid,* and *Elizabeth*. She narrowly lost the Oscar for her performance in *Dark Victory* to Vivien Leigh, who won for *Gone with the Wind.* Davis was the official runner-up for the New York Film Critic's Circle Award.

Elizabeth was a role Davis felt destined to play. She had seen Lynn Fontanne in the role on Broadway. She admired Alfred Lunt and Fontanne tremendously. But she obviously made the role her own for the film. Her characterization is fully-rounded, full of royalty, intelligence, humor and even love for the man she must have executed, Essex.

However, what makes this film almost unbearable to watch for admirers of Davis is the extent to which she is allowed to use unnecessary mannerisms, specifically her hands. They never seem to be at rest. She continuously clutches and unclutches her fingers, wrings her hands or drums her fingers on chair arms. It adds nothing to the characterization of the queen unless the queen was a major arthritic. Her facial expressions and body language are perfect, but director Michael Curtiz did nothing to still her nervous hands.

A telling scene concerning the queen's age and appearance occurs toward the beginning of the film as Elizabeth is surrounded by her servants and ladies-in-waiting. She is out-of-sorts, waiting for Essex to return from Cadiz. After spoiling a game of chess with Lady Penelope (Olivia de Havilland), she begs for some entertainment.

Lady Penelope and Lady Margaret (Nanette Fabares, later Fabray) play and sing a new song concerning the love of a man for an older woman. As she listens, the queen realizes it is about her. In her anger she smashes her looking glass and another mirror in the room and bans all mirrors from the palace.

With the aid of pasty white make-up, no eyebrows and a high brow, she did look much older than her 31 years, but not unattractive. Davis was a stickler for authentic detail. She and her costume designer, Orry-Kelly, designed two sets of costumes because the executives didn't want the authentic large size of the stiff lace collars and neck pieces. In costume tests, she wore the smaller sizes, but in the actual filming she wore the authentic larger size. The dresses range in beauty from pure white, to red, to multi-brocaded black in her final scene before Essex's execution.

The costumes are beautiful, but Davis doesn't allow them to overwhelm her performances. To her, they are just the queen's clothes.

10. The Private Lives of Elizabeth and Essex *(1939)*

Beautiful as the color is, particularly in the costumes and the dark Rembrandt-like scenes, it should be secondary to the scenario. For much of the first half of the picture the sets and costumes are the primary source of entertainment. It isn't until Essex's return from Cadiz, defeated but rebellious against the crown, that the movie actually comes alive. The action is powerful, and the drama between Elizabeth and Essex seems real. From here to the execution of Essex the movie holds one's interest. Elizabeth and Essex are both believable.

This is a story in which an officer returns from a qualified success at fighting the Spanish at Cadiz to confront the queen at her court, which includes Sir Walter Raleigh, and which is, of course, full of political intrigue. Essex's popularity with the masses is apparent. He rightly believes he was undercut in battle by the lack of support from the court and the queen, because he returned without treasure.

It is obvious that he is the queen's lover. Elizabeth I can't wait for his return, although her primary role in life is being the Queen of England and the protector of England and its people.

The queen welcomes Essex's (Errol Flynn) return, although she views his battle at Cadiz a failure. They reconcile their differences and privately acknowledge their love for one another.

Essex agrees to serve on the Queen's Council, and promises not to react to machinations by others to involve him in troubles in Ireland. When the council meets, however, Essex can't ignore Lord Burghley's (Henry Stephenson) taunting challenges to Essex's manliness and competence as a leader in war. It is proposed that Essex and Raleigh (Vincent Price) be co-leaders in the attack on Ireland. Essex rises to the bait, insisting he alone can defeat the Earl of Tyrone (Alan Hale). Elizabeth reluctantly accedes to the council's determination to send Essex to Ireland.

As is to be expected, once Essex is in Ireland with his army, he becomes bogged down, literally and figuratively, not because of lack of skill, but because he does not receive logistical support from the queen. Unbeknownst to him, and to the queen, their correspondence is intercepted by court deceivers, and each blames the other for the lack of communication. Only Francis Bacon (Donald Crisp) learns of the deception, and, upon threat of death, he is bound not to reveal the truth to the queen. Naturally, Elizabeth recalls Essex. Essex is so angered that he mounts one last attack to try to defeat Tyrone which is impossible. In fact, Tyrone offers a white flag of truce to demonstrate Essex's futility. The truce allows Essex to return to England along with the remains of his army.

When they arrive at Whitehall, Essex has his army surround the palace. He means to take over the throne. However, Elizabeth knows of his action

Errol Flynn, as Lord Essex, having a private moment with the queen (Davis) in *The Private Lives of Elizabeth and Essex* (Photofest).

and his popularity. She commands that Essex be allowed to enter without resistance.

In their confrontation, they both realize how their communiqués have been thwarted. They also realize they still love each other. Elizabeth is willing to have Essex as her consort, at her side, but not as king.

Essex wants the power to share in ruling the land, but in the end he accedes to her insistence that she remain queen alone. He dismisses his soldiers from the palace and from the exterior. The queen determines from him that if she calls for her guard, her men, not his, would appear as they do. With that she has Essex arrested and sent to the Tower to await execution as a traitor.

Prior to Essex's departure for Ireland, the queen presented him with a ring she received from her father, King Henry VIII. If, at any time, Essex would wish to ask her forgiveness, all he has to do is send her the ring.

Days pass, and the queen takes up residence in the tower apartments. Still there is no communication from Essex. Torn between her duty as a queen and her love for Essex, at last, minutes before his execution, she sends for him.

Through their emotional confrontation, Essex reveals he couldn't send the ring, for she wouldn't believe his sincerity in wanting forgiveness. They both realize he would have fought, probably with popular support, to take over the throne. She reveals that winning wars is not the point of her reign, but protecting England and her people is her *raison d'etre*. With this mutual understanding, he elects to submit to his execution. Elizabeth collapses upon her throne, fully realizing her role in life won't ever allow her personal happiness.

Throughout the film, Davis realizes the royalty of her character and expresses the range of emotions the queen must go through. She acts resolutely in protecting her throne and her country. She understands the constant court intrigue. She commands as a man on her council. She allows herself moments of love, vulnerability and humor in private with Essex.

The queen struggles as she converses with her only honest courtier, Francis Bacon, when trying to understand the lack of communication from Essex in Ireland. As a queen, she must remain skeptical, even of Bacon, as she struggles with the political and personal ramifications of the situation. Her face expresses confusion and yet determination to ascertain the truth.

When Essex returns from Ireland, he is a threat to Elizabeth's court. Davis plays it all very calmly and deliberately, especially after she realizes the truth about the intercepted letters, and the truth about Essex's undeniable ambition for the throne.

It obviously kills Elizabeth to have Essex arrested, but she also acknowledges her necessary resoluteness to carry through as a queen. She shows no mercy, but one can tell she's vulnerable inside.

Later, Lady Penelope acknowledges her role as a conduit in the deception of the queen, giving the queen some reason to save Essex. Davis expresses, with ease, her realization of this information, but also shows how she must remain in charge, the queen.

When the two protagonists meet, the sadness in her eyes belies the necessity to let Essex go to his death which is her personal death also. As she says, her greatest love is and must be England.

In the last scene Elizabeth finally, desperately, relents, calling after Essex to come back, that she'll give up everything, even the throne, for him. Essex continues down the stairs, however, realizing she could never do that.

Davis falls back onto the throne, grips the arms and leans forward, with a pained look on her face. She stares ahead, with her eyes almost crossed as she absorbs and displays the knowledge that her personal happiness will never be.

Davis, as Elizabeth I, quizzes her lady-in-waiting Penelope (Olivia de Havilland) (Photofest).

When one compares this film to the later *The Virgin Queen*, one must acknowledge the age of Davis when she played the two roles. At 31 for *The Private Lives of Elizabeth and Essex*, even with a shaved forehead, no eyelashes, bags under her eyes and a small lip line, she looked older than her years but still becoming. One could imagine Essex's love for her and not just her power. When Davis was close to the right age of Elizabeth in 1955, at 47, she had aged quite a bit. With the same sort of make-up she easily looked as Elizabeth might have looked, but by this time she was not physically attractive.

There is no way the latter film's Raleigh could be personally in love with her. The script makes it clear that he loves the queen as a symbol, not Elizabeth. There is no physical romance between them, as there is in *The Private Lives of Elizabeth and Essex*. Simply put, 1955, for Davis, was not 1939.

Davis sets her characterization early in *Elizabeth*. In the first scene, we do not see her initially. She is dressing, or rather being dressed behind a folding screen. One hears her voice and sees her shadow. The voice tells it all. Davis has deepened her voice to a contralto to give it a more authoritative, almost masculine tone, one suitable for a king, such as her father.

Throughout her "quality" years, 1938–1950, Davis often used different

10. The Private Lives of Elizabeth and Essex *(1939)*

gradations of voice levels to help define her characters, as she was always concerned with the total acting effect of her physical attributes. Most people comment on her make-up for this film, her shaved head, the carrot-red wig, her pasty white make-up, all used to good effect in an effort to make her look more Tudorish.

Charles Affron, in *Star Acting*, writes:

> As another monarch,* in *The Private Lives of Elizabeth and Essex* (1939), she has a different manner, and this one of the best examples of her vocal bravura. The range of her tonal colorations matches the range of her roles during her peak years. Her diction, no longer from the acting school of communication, is unmistakably Davis, whether as baritone Elizabeth [or a] mezzo soprano modern woman in *Dark Victory*....Whatever her accent, Davis finds a sound for the role that bridges portrayal and person....She itches and fidgets through most of *The Private Lives of Elizabeth and Essex*, but her voice, weighted to her toes, gives a firm base to her flailing.[4]

Toward the end of her first scene, the camera divulges the queen, feet first, finally rising to the full portrait of her majesty, an effect often used in Davis' films.

Upon visiting the set, Charles Laughton, who had won an Oscar portraying King Henry VIII in 1933, told his "daughter" Davis, "Never stop daring to hang yourself, Bette." This was in response to her demurring, "I certainly have nerve trying to play Elizabeth I, at my age." Davis took his advice as her credo for years to come.

It is interesting to note that Laughton's advice wasn't much different from Jack Warner's warning to Davis when he finally allowed her to go to RKO for *Of Human Bondage*. He said, "Go hang yourself!"

In *5001 Nights at the Movies*, Pauline Kael, the major critic for *The New Yorker*, commented on this film:

> Bette Davis, well-painted and dressed for the role of the shrewd old queen, looks the part and gives a magnetic, tough performance, but an impossible task was set for her, since in Essex, Errol Flynn couldn't come halfway to meet her.... Davis' performance is bound to suffer from a comparison with Glenda Jackson's multifaceted Elizabeth on television, but Davis' Elizabeth is a precursor for the Jackson portrait.[5]

Alexander Walker, in *Bette Davis: A Celebration,* sums it up with: "Watchful, proud, devious, distrustful, ruthless, her Tudor monarch maintains her absolutism in ways that had obvious affinities with Davis' own experience of how treacherous human relations could be. For queen and star, work was a sense of satisfaction..."[6]

Davis had earlier that year played Empress Carlotta in Juarez.

Cast: Elizabeth I — Bette Davis; Earl of Essex — Errol Flynn; Lady Penelope — Olivia de Havilland; Francis Bacon — Donald Crisp; Sir Walter Raleigh — Vincent Price; Earl of Tyrone — Alan Hale; Lord Burghley — Henry Stephenson; Sir Thomas Egerton — James Stephenson; Sir Robert Cecil — Henry Daniell; Sir Edmond Coke — Leo G. Carroll; Mistress Margaret Radcliffe — Nanette Fabares; Lord Knolleys — Ralph Forbes; Lord Mountjoy — Robert Warwick; Lord Charles Howard — Guy Bellis.

Production: Hal B. Wallis — Producer; Robert Lord — Associate Producer; Michael Curtiz — Director; Norman Reilly Raine and Aeneas MacKenzie — Screenwriters; Maxwell Anderson — Based on his play; Sol Polito — Cinematographer; Natalie Kalmus — Technicolor; Erich Wolfgang Korngold — Musical Score; Leo F. Forbstein — Musical Direction; Orry-Kelly — Costume Designer; Anton Grot — Art Director; 1939; Running time: 106 minutes.

11

The Whales of August (1987)

THE GREATEST STAR AND THE GREATEST STAR

> *"In a way [director] Lindsay [Anderson] found Bette more intriguing. They were both confrontational ... were mirror images of each other."*[1]
> —Jocelyn Herbert

> *"Bette, [is] still the consummate if egomaniacal professional."*[2]
> —Mike Kaplan

Two queens of the silver screen acted together, for the first time, in their last completed film, *The Whales of August*. They again proved themselves to be the exemplary actors they always were in all the movies in which they appeared. Vincent Canby, film critic for *The New York Times*, wrote, "...Miss Gish and Miss Davis ... together exemplify American films from 1914 to the present."[3]

Chekhovian in nature, this closet drama goes nowhere at considerable length, with a trenchant script and careful direction by a master director, Briton Lindsay Anderson, who was known for much different comedy-satires, such as *If*. The film opens in black and white with a scene on the coast of Maine: the ocean, the coastline of an island, and a summer cottage atop an embankment. Three young women appear at a cottage window and a door as they laughingly go out to look for the annual passing of the whales in August. The young women, dressed in early twentieth century clothing, are two sisters, Sarah (Mary Steenburgen) and Libby (Margaret Ladd), and their good friend, Tisha (Tisha Sterling). They look out to sea to observe the whales through a pair of binoculars. The camera then focuses on a buoy, its bell ringing. The scene changes to color and forty-some years later.

An elderly man, Mr. Maranov (Vincent Price), is being deposited on the beach via rowboat, to do some fishing. He looks up and spots Sarah Webber (Lillian Gish). He says hello. She has been hanging laundry on an outdoor line. She returns to the cottage and calls out for her sister, Libby Strong (Davis), to come from her bedroom for her breakfast. She then returns to the outdoors to cut some flowers, and converses with Mr. Maranov about his fishing and the day.

This is the story of two sisters, one cantankerous and demanding, the other seemingly a caretaker who is kindly and forgiving, but in her own way passive-aggressive. Libby, who is blind but has substantial funds, controls the purse strings, whereas her sister, Sarah, has to take care of the real-world demands, the demands of caring not only for Libby, but for the upkeep of their oceanfront summer cottage, in Maine, where they grew up as young girls at the turn of the twentieth century.

In the cottage, a first floor bedroom door opens. Libby appears in her nightgown. She calls out for Sarah, to no avail. Then, as she is blind, she feels her way over to her accustomed chair and side table on which her breakfast has been set. She pours herself a cup of tea and then sits down.

When Sarah returns, she chides Libby to eat her breakfast, which Libby refuses to do. Initially, Sarah appears to be a concerned, quiet woman, while Libby is a cantankerous soul.

The sisters live in Philadelphia during the winter in Libby's house, and in the summer in the cottage their aunt built fifty years ago. The present must be the 1940s. They listen to Arthur Godfrey on the radio, Truman is apparently president and Eleanor Roosevelt still writes her newspaper column. There is no mention of the Cold War, but they talk about the danger of submarines being on the coast, which happened during World War II.

Sarah's husband apparently died in World War I, for there is a photo of him in uniform. She is celebrating their forty-sixth wedding anniversary. Libby talks of the time she and her husband, Mark, looked after Sarah when her husband was killed.

The issue is whether or not to install a picture window in the cottage, with Libby opposed to the idea because they are old and don't need new things. However, Sarah would like it and talks with the repairman, Mr. Brackett (Harry Carey, Jr.). A neighbor, their old friend, Tisha Doughty (Ann Sothern), tries to mediate, and introduces the sisters to the visiting émigré, Mr. Maranov, whom Sarah invites for dinner.

What is really at issue is that they both realize they are very old. Libby says, "Time is short." Libby seems more than belligerent when she tells Mr. Maranov that he will not find refuge in their cottage because he has lost his benefactress to death. Sarah apologizes for Libby's behavior, but Maranov recognizes the truth in Libby's statement, and knows she will not take him in.

Libby's rudeness upsets Sarah considerably. She feels she must find another place for Libby, who is estranged from her daughter in Philly. Also, Sarah feels Libby's daughter should help find a place for her mother.

Upon their disagreement over Maranov and the picture window, Libby goes to bed and has a nightmare. She awakes, calling out for Sarah. She even comes from her bedroom seeking Sarah, who has been sitting, reminiscing about her long-dead husband on what would have been their 46th anniversary.

Libby finds Sarah and, frightened, she reveals her nightmare, a fear of losing Sarah's care. Sarah calms her and sends her back to bed.

The next morning, Libby apologizes to Sarah and asks if she has been too much to care for. She tells her they know each other so well, and that they are both strong women. They reunite and grasp each other's hands. Libby asks Sarah to take her to the overlook point where as young girls they watched for the long-gone whales.

Arm-in-arm they slowly traverse the landscape. Libby asks, "Are there any whales?"

Sarah answers, "No, they're all gone."

Libby replies, "You never know."

The underlying fascination in watching *The Whales of August*, an excellent movie, comes from seeing virtually the entire history of the movies unfold before your eyes in the persons of the silent era's greatest player, Lillian Gish, and the sound era's counterpart, Bette Davis. In reality, Gish was in her 90s and Davis 79. Foster Hirsch, in *Acting Hollywood Style*, asserts, "Age as antimask: Lillian Gish and Bette Davis act their age, truthfully and beautifully in *The Whales of August* (1987)."[4] Both actresses had suffered over the years, with Gish rebounding better than Davis. The latter had had a series of strokes, as well as breast cancer, but they were both still forceful actors. Gish's best scene involves the recollection of her long-dead husband. She reminisces all alone with a glass of wine and a rose. It's subdued and lovely.

Throughout the film, Libby is always questioning and making demands on Sarah. She likes to pester Sarah, always questioning her busyness and being contrary, such as refusing to eat her breakfast. Even though she's blind, Libby continually wonders if her hair is still beautiful, if it is as white as their mother's hair. She shows her complete dependence on Sarah. By always being shrill and demanding, Davis gives Gish something to act with and against. Oth-

Lillian Gish and Bette Davis as the two sisters (Sarah and Libby) in *The Whales of August* (Photofest).

erwise, Gish would have seemed a simple romantic fool. As Foster Hirsch says, "As Davis' astringency brushes against Gish's sentimentality, the film's slight story is elevated by the gift of their presence."[5]

Each actress is given opportunities to express the range of their characters. Notably, Gish's scene of reminiscence over her late husband's photo and a vase with a red and white rose (red for passion and white for truth) is poignant as she speaks aloud of their 46th wedding anniversary while drinking a glass of wine and singing "The Rose of Piccardy."

Davis' evocative scene comes when she sits in her bedroom chair and pulls a lock of her hair from an envelope. She brushes it against her face, regretting her lost youth. Gish does a similar thing with her red rose, but the regret is her lost husband.

Gavin Lambert feels:

> He [Anderson] also brought a similar ironic elegiac mood to *The Whales of August*, especially in two almost silent scenes where the sisters are alone with themselves and their pasts....Libby clings to a very different memento, and reacts very differently....The touch of lost youth brings a look of terrible rancor to her face, and explains why Sarah as she tells Tisha (Ann Sothern) is afraid that Libby has "given up on life."[6]

11. The Whales of August *(1987)*

Davis, in character as Libby Strong, listens for the whales (Photofest).

In addition to those of Gish and Davis, *The Whales of August* features two other strong performances given by Ann Sothern as their best friend since childhood, and Vincent Price as the Russian émigré.

Tisha sees Libby as cantankerous and bitter. Yet in a scene with the three of them she regales Sarah and Libby with island gossip, and receives sympathy from both for her humiliating loss of her driver's license.

It is Maranov who sees the truth in Libby's appraisal of him when she calls him an old fraud. He confides to Sarah the truth of Libby's statement, even though Sarah is appalled by Libby's rudeness.

Harry Carey, Jr., as Joshua, the repairman, offers insight about both sisters, and also provides comic relief as he hammers away on parts of the cottage he's repairing. At the end, when Libby has apologized to Sarah, Joshua comes looking for a lost tool. Libby stops him and says, "Mr. Brackett, we've decided to have you install a picture window." The key word is *we've*, of course. She includes her sister; they will always do things together.

Although Gish made the transition to sound movies with ease, her type of Victorian heroine was passé. Her few sound movies came when she was past her prime. She was essentially a character actress, with her best sound role coming in Charles Laughton's *The Night of the Hunter*.

Davis entered sound movies from the stage in 1931, with her halcyon days being from 1938 (*Jezebel*) to 1946, plus 1950's *All About Eve*. After *Eve*, although she continued to star in theatrical movies and movies made for TV, she had few roles worthy of her talent. She returned to the stage four times, first in a revue, *Two's Company*, then in a successfully dramatized reading of poetry in *The World of Carl Sandburg*, and in a secondary role in Tennessee Williams' prize-winning play, *The Night of the Iguana*. A musical based on Emlyn Williams' *The Corn Is Green*, called *Miss Moffat*, never made it to Broadway because of her back problem.

Davis, according to reliable sources, was very temperamental on the *Whales* set and not friendly towards Gish or anyone else. But when all was said and done, Lindsay Anderson allowed that, even though she fought everything and was difficult, she probably needed this dynamic in order to perform, and that he'd rather fight and work with her than the "too cooperative" Gish. In the end, he enjoyed Davis. She said to the crew on the set one day, "I must be slipping. I've given in to the director three times today!"

The elderly are all individuals, and, as Maranov puts it, all of one's time in life is their time of life, even old age.

Anderson produced a beautiful film with well-developed performances from his entire cast. It is a real tribute to two legends: believable, complex individuals facing old age with two highly developed characterizations delivered by great actors, not just movie stars, allowing everyone to starkly see old age.

Alexander Walker feels that for Davis, Libby is

> ...the ultimate part. Appropriately, *The Whales of August* wasn't only about friendship: it was about mortality. It mixed the wistful with nostalgia of a film like *On Golden Pond* with the terminal clarities of *The Cherry Orchard*. Like the leviathans of the title, the whales that used to arrive off the coast of Maine to spout joyously among the waves and have become rare events in these waters, players like Davis and Gish were links with the time when the cinema itself was in the making.
> In Davis' final performance, one can discuss her evolutionary past. Once the epitome of battling womanhood, her independence assailed by professional combat and marital strife, she now played a proud, blind, embittered woman living with her sister in a cliff top cottage and sardonically putting down her sibling's dedication to sweetness and light...
> ...The film ends with a close-up of hands of Davis and Gish clasped in a final bond of sisterly sympathy. It is a moment that also united two of the greatest icons that American cinema has produced.[7]

Afterward, in interviews, Davis declared that Anderson was too "macho," an interesting comment about the gay Anderson. One wonders if she felt the same way about Edmund Goulding, one of her best directors, who was also gay.

11. The Whales of August *(1987)*

Vincent Canby, in *The New York Times*, lauded the "...two beautiful, very different, very characteristic performances by Miss Gish and Miss Davis ... not to be underrated. Miss Davis is more than up to the competition which comes to look like harmony ... cuts through the stasis, not to overwhelm Miss Gish but to give her something to act with *and* against."[8] Davis really ended her career in Lindsay Anderson's last film, *The Whales of August*, with a rounded characterization worthy of any of her other major character achievements.

More than any other of her later films, whether theatrical or for TV, this movie, with its superior script, stands as a fitting cap to Davis' career. Based on a David Berry play, *The Whales of August* was considered as a Gish vehicle several years before it was made. Davis, before she had her stroke, had rejected it, but after script rewritings, it was again offered to her with her complete knowledge of Gish's casting. She readily accepted.

At this point, Davis was still really fighting cancer, a circumstance that is often overlooked. Additionally, she was still suffering complications as a result of her stroke, including a slurred speech pattern and a mouth that drooped on the left side. Also, her movement was jerky because of her impaired left leg. In a way, one could say the energy had been drained from her via the illnesses.

Her remaining asset, and what an asset, was her brain. Davis was an intelligent woman. She knew what her physical condition was, but she didn't want pity. She wanted to act and to be respected for her talent. She wanted to make one more great movie, one great theatrical movie, before she died. Most likely, she knew this film was it.

Davis had a lot to be proud of— her halcyon days provided her with a dozen films or more that were worth her talent. Many of these films, however, were not first offered to her. She had to fight to get them made.

There were projects that never came to fruition, times when promises were made only to be broken, and opportunities missed. She was alert to this and realized she was a difficult actor, but all that became part of her acting dynamic. If it isn't worth fighting for, it isn't worth doing. But she had always had the energy, a driven energy, to succeed. That energy provided her the means to realize her ambition to become a great actress.

At this point, a little energy was about all she had left, and it took all of it to surmount her physical difficulties in order to perform. One way to become energetic or to get the adrenaline flowing is to become angry with anything, major or minor, that might impede the energy she needed to perform.

Consequently, without Kathryn Sermack, her personal assistant who was unavailable on this shoot, Davis had to fend for herself. She had to feel she was not only competent to act with Gish, but that she was superior, the top star. Gish had the fuller, more sympathetic role, so Davis had to be her better, not her equal. If this meant belittling Gish, so be it. Such an attitude provided the constant dynamic in her performance of Libby vs. Sarah. As much as she seemingly disliked Gish, however, Davis would remark to her director on how well Gish played a scene, as if she and Anderson were in cahoots to elicit a performance from Gish.

When Davis was acting and fighting suggestions or angered over some idiotic slight, she was pumping herself full of energy, the energy she needed to act.

Never one to watch dailies, she went to every evening's dailies on this movie. She didn't want to miss a scene. Why? It all goes back to her conversation with Joe Mankiewicz. No one but she would be the horse's ass up there on the big screen when the movie was released, and she still firmly believed that.

What Davis and Gish did so well together was to enact what they were, without any deception, two old ladies who were professional actors. They showed it all on the screen. These were the marks of age with nothing to hide behind. They exposed their characters, Sarah and Libby, but more than that, they exposed themselves, two old venerable actors giving all they had learned over their considerable careers and exposing it for one to behold in all its rawness.

When filming was nearing completion, Davis became friendlier with her director, the crew and other actors. She realized she had made it through the grueling making of a movie. Making it was a victory for her.

She really didn't want it to end. She loved acting and loved making movies. She didn't want it to end because then her career, her life, would be over. And with this film, her career and life basically *were* over.

She made one more attempt at filmmaking, and it was a disaster. She saw in the dailies how horrible she looked and sounded. She quit and went to New York. Thereafter, she only appeared at celebrations of her life and career at Lincoln Center and in Spain.

Her epitaph on her tombstone says it all: "She did it the hard way." It was yet another remark from Joe Mankiewicz.

Cast: Libby Strong — Bette Davis; Sarah Webber — Lillian Gish; Mr. Maranov — Vincent Price; Tisha Doughty — Ann Sothern; Joshua Brackett — Harry Carey, Jr.; Mr. Beckwith — Frank Grimes; Old Randall — Frank Pitkin; Young Randall — Mike Bush; Young Libby — Margaret Ladd; Young Tisha — Tisha Sterling (Ann Sothern's daughter); Young Sarah — Mary Steenburgen.

Production: Carolyn Pfeiffer and Mike Kaplan — Producers; Shep Gor-

11. The Whales of August *(1987)*

don — Associate Producer; Lindsay Anderson — Director; David Berry — Screenwriter, based on his play; Mike Fash — Cinematographer; Alan Price — Music Score; K.C. Fox and Bob Fox — Art Direction; Jocelyn Herbert — Production Design; Nicolas Gaster — Editor; 1987; Running time — 90 minutes.

12

Jezebel (1938)

THE LEGEND BEGUN

> *"Gone Before the Wind"*[1]
> —Time magazine

For the first time in Davis' career, a literate script (thanks in part to John Huston), major production values, and, most significantly, a master taskmaster as a director (William Wyler) came together to allow Davis to become a first-rate actor and a major movie star. It was here she became Warners' fourth "brother," a star with major box office clout, a status that lasted for eight solid years. William Wyler took Davis, the actress, and, according to her autobiography, made her the star that was to endure.

Jezebel had been an unsuccessful play on Broadway with Miriam Hopkins, who took over from Tallulah Bankhead in the title role. The southern Civil War–era drama features Davis as strong-willed Julie Marsden, who loves Preston Dillard (Henry Fonda) but enjoys being the manipulative flirt who plays her beaus against one another, even causing a duel between two of them. She appears at a cotillion wearing a red dress, flying in the face of the traditional, virginal white. The embarrassing episode causes Pres to leave her. He goes north to work in banking and subsequently marries a northern girl. When he returns to New Orleans, Julie begs his forgiveness, unaware of his marriage. Of course, she is devastated but thinks she can still win him back. An epidemic of malaria is sweeping across Louisiana and Pres contracts it. Julie then begs his wife, Amy (Margaret Lindsay), to let her accompany Pres to the island where they are isolating the victims, to care for him, which she is allowed to do.

12. Jezebel (1938)

The film opens with a tracking shot of a street in New Orleans, showing the vibrant life of the city in the 1850s. Vendors are selling various wares and food, carriages are pulled by horse through the street, and crowds of people meander through the bazaar-like atmosphere. It is a bright sunny scene. The Lafayette bar is where Buck Cantrell (George Brent) and his young friend, Ted Dillard (Richard Cromwell), react to a slur upon Julie Marsden's reputation. Buck is calm and all southern tradition as he reprimands the speaker, while Ted is impetuous and wants to challenge the man to a duel. Their characters are set in the well-lighted, elegant gentlemen's bar.

The use of light is telling in every respect as the film moves along its course, from the "bright" years prior to the Civil War and the malaria epidemic to the very dark film noir look at the latter part of the film. After the epidemic has begun, until the final scene as Julie escorts the sickened Pres through a bonfire-lit city night, the lighting is noteworthy.

In Davis' first scene, Julie arrives on horseback at the portico of her southern country plantation, "Halcyon," which she shares with her aunt, Belle Massey (Fay Bainter). She dismounts, hands the reins over to a groom, and strides into an already-in-progress afternoon party. She whips her riding habit skirt aside with her riding crop to make a dramatic entrance, unsuitably dressed. She astounds her aunt by her lateness and her mode of dress. Her character is set.

Davis creates a willful, strong character, immediately setting the tone for the scene and the

Davis, beautiful in white crinoline in the antebellum-set *Jezebel* (Photoplay).

movie. She is overtly gracious and welcoming to her guests, knowingly ignoring their questioning looks and sub rosa comments, and showing her complete disregard for tradition and manners. Because of her obvious social position, she is allowed to get away with it.

Here is a privileged, spoiled young woman, a Southern belle, cutting a fiery swath through society. With William Wyler's strong guidance, Davis never performed better. Her nervous mannerisms were diminished; she did not play every scene at top dramatic range, but allowed her character to develop into a multi-faceted person. She has quiet, forceful moments.

The matching of Wyler with Davis at this particular point was perfect timing. He was a taskmaster, at times requiring thirty to forty takes, a perfectionist. Sometimes he didn't even seem to know what he was looking for from his actors, but said he knew it when he got it. This was not always good for film actors who seemed to give their all on the first take and became less and less effective in subsequent takes. However, Davis was also a perfectionist, and would do anything she could to improve her performance for take after take, even though it might exhaust her. To be truthful, many times the first take was the best and was printed. But Davis and Wyler developed a high regard for each other's professionalism.

Julie is engaged to Pres, a young Southern banker. At the same time, she flirts with other beaus, notably Buck Cantrell (George Brent), an adventurous, strong-willed southerner who adheres to tradition. Pres is taken aback by Julie's willfulness, but loves her, and does not anticipate the lengths to which she will go to revolt against tradition.

At her dressmaker's, Julie is on a raised platform having her cotillion ball gown fitted. She is a humorous, alive, vital young woman. When the white gown is removed, Julie is seen sitting on a tall stool, in her undergarments, with a large bell hoop attached to her waist which gives the ball gown its fullness. It is a startling, funny moment.

A strapless red gown catches her eye and her attention. She demands it be fitted to her for the cotillion. Her aunt and the dressmaker are aghast. No one has ever worn anything but white to the ball.

When Pres arrives to take Julie to the ball, both he and her aunt are astounded when she comes down the stairs in her red gown. Julie is adamant about going to the ball dressed as she is. Pres grimly helps her into her cloak and escorts her out the door.

When they arrive at the ball, Pres removes Julie's cloak and gives it to a servant. As the crowd begins to see Julie, they move away from her. Julie finally realizes the enormity of her insult and asks Pres to take her home.

He insists they dance and moves with her to the dance floor. As they begin dancing, the crowd thins until they are the only couple on the floor.

12. Jezebel (1938) 143

The orchestra stops. Pres demands the conductor continue the tune, and Pres and Julie continue to dance until the end. Completely humiliated, Julie begs Pres to take her home which he eventually does.

He also breaks their engagement and travels north to manage a bank. Yellow Jack progresses, affecting New Orleans. Julie and her aunt remove themselves to Halcyon to be away from the yellow fever, malaria, which is infecting and killing many in the New Orleans area.

Over this period of a year, Julie isolates herself from society, but eventually decides to have a dinner at her country plantation when she hears Pres is returning to the South.

Pres arrives, coming home to the southland where he will support the South in the Civil War. He is invited by Aunt Belle to spend his time at Julie's country home. He and his wife, Amy, accept the invitation.

Julie does not realize Pres has married. She dons her white ball gown, meets him in a first floor drawing room, at which point she humbles herself, dropping to the floor to beg his forgiveness and ask him to accept her love. Embarrassed, he pulls Julie to her feet. Still believing Pres loves her, Julie rises on her toes and gives Pres a deliberate kiss, which he rejects by pushing her away as Amy enters the room. Pres introduces Julie to his wife. Julie immediately thinks he's joking, but quickly realizes she is wrong. She acts politely but coldly toward Amy. Davis, quietly and with complete stillness, only expresses her emotion through her eyes. The look on her face, even though she tries to hide it, is one of complete disbelief. She even says, "You're funnin' me, aren't you?" When Pres says no, Julie uses all her strength to congratulate them.

By herself, Julie swears to win back Pres from his northern wife because she believes Pres belongs to the South and to her as a southern woman. At dinner, she instigates a conflict over the coming war between Buck Cantrell and Pres. After dinner, Pres goes outside alone to sit on a garden bench. When Julie finds him she implores him to accept her love. Rejected, she then returns to Buck to say that her honor has been compromised by Pres. Cantrell rises to the bait. Pres' brother, Ted, challenges Cantrell to a duel.

Everyone is shocked. Even Julie realizes she has gone too far. She tries to dissuade Cantrell, to no avail. The next dawn, the families hear the shots. Pres' brother, Ted, arrives with the news that Buck is dead.

Pres has returned to New Orleans to complete pressing banking business. While there, he collapses from fever: malaria. The news reaches Julie's country house. She travels with a black servant through back woods to retrieve Pres, to take him to her town house.

Julie persuades Amy to let her take Pres to the isolated Lazarette Island where yellow-fever victims are being quarantined. At last, Julie seeks redemption for her previous behavior, intending to sacrifice herself in order to care for Pres and prevent Amy's exposure to the illness.

In *Star Acting*, Charles Affron declares:

> Davis pleads with Lindsay to be allowed to accompany fever-stricken Fonda in quarantine. The star's face, exposed by a coiffure that has evidently not been abetted by curlers and mirror and brooks no frivolity, is now relieved of Julie's initial mindlessness.
>
> The various camera positions relentlessly root the sloping planes in a will that is no longer willful and we are grateful to melodrama for providing patterns so worthy of a star's belief and fortitude.
>
> Her face resumes her centrality on her way to Lazarette Island; first, in gratitude, as she sweeps out of the door, then riding in the cart with Fonda's head cradled in her lap. The face of a star matches the blaze of a bonfire.[2]

What could have been very soap opera-ish is validated through superior acting and direction of a literate script.

This film really was a Scarlett-type film, made one year prior to *Gone with the Wind*. Even David O. Selznick was furious because he thought *Jezebel* would undermine his production of *GWTW*. However, even with *Jezebel*'s critical acclaim and popularity, it couldn't compare with *GWTW*. If it had been photographed in color, as it should have been, it probably would have been even more successful.

Jack Warner had had an option to buy *GWTW* the previous year for Davis. However, when she left Warners to go to Britain to make two films, she ended up in a court battle which she lost. She also lost "Scarlett."

Davis' popularity was such, at the time, that the U.S. public, in polls, expected her to play Scarlett. She and Errol Flynn were offered to David O. Selznick, the newly independent producer. But the public also expected/demanded Clark Gable for the role of Rhett, a role he did not want. Selznick wanted him also, which provided a distribution deal through MGM. MGM received distribution and subsequent release rights and profits thereafter.

Davis desperately sought the role of Scarlett, but Selznick never even asked her to test for the part. Instead, he went for an unknown, with Katharine Hepburn as a backup, even though he thought Hepburn lacked sex appeal. Filming had already started when Selznick's brother, agent Myron Selznick, brought Vivien Leigh to see the filming of Atlanta burning. He uttered the famous line, "Here's your Scarlett O'Hara." And she was.

In *Matinee Idylls*, Richard Schickel states "*Jezebel* is a much better movie [than *GWTW*]—darker, meatier, much more tightly wound. Moreover, it brought Davis her second Oscar and forever established her feverish screen character.... [I]t offered a shrewd reading and projection of her essential nature."[3]

12. Jezebel (1938)

In *A Talent for Trouble*, Jim Herman believes, "Davis learned how to modulate her performance and tone down her mannerisms ... she didn't mind because her own professionalism demanded excellence at any cost. Wyler had met his match as a perfectionist."[4]

It was a film in which she never looked more beautiful, and in which she gained star quality from the camera. Molly Haskill, in *From Reverence to Rape*, comes at Davis from a different angle:

> The super female is an actress by nature ... coquetry is an art and Davis exalted in the artistry. In *Jezebel*, she captivates her beaux.... Her charm, like her beauty, is something willed into being. It is not a question of whether she is inside or outside the part (for obviously she is both) but of the intensity of her convictions, a sense of character in the old-fashioned sense of "moral fiber." Through her driving guts she turns herself into a flower of the old South, and in that one determined gesture reveals the bedrock toughness of the superfemale....
>
> William Wyler was her toughest director.[5]

Davis won her second, well-deserved Oscar for *Jezebel*, playing the bitch who finally seeks redemption.

At the 1938 Oscars, Jack L. Warner congratulates Fay Bainter and Davis for their winning performances in *Jezebel* (Photofest).

During filming, she and Wyler fell in love, and the affair lasted until the completion of the movie. He married another. Davis, as much as she loved him, was afraid of being dominated by him, and therefore lost him to Margaret Tallichet, another actor. Davis always kept the large portrait of herself as Jezebel well-displayed in her houses.

The critics welcomed the picture and Davis' performance with accolades as well as heaping praise on Fay Bainter, who played her aunt and her conscience, a restraint to Julie's willfulness.

More than any other Davis film, *Jezebel* exhibits the difference a superior director makes to a talented star's performance. William Wyler, the most honored director in Hollywood history, was the third director considered for *Jezebel*. The other two were Edmund Goulding and Michael Curtiz, both of whom had garnered superior Davis performances before in *That Certain Woman* and *Cabin in the Cotton*. Goulding had treated Davis like a star and had given her the star treatment. He would guide her in several more films. Curtiz would never work with Davis after *The Private Lives of Elizabeth and Essex* in 1939. He was not Davis' favorite, even though she later said she looked forward to working with him on *Life with Father*, a picture she lost to Irene Dunne in 1948.

Davis had met Wyler only once before, when she was an ingénue at Universal. She went to a screen test for him, wearing a low-cut dress supplied by wardrobe. Upon seeing her, he remarked, "What do you think about dames who show their chest to get a job?" Davis was so embarrassed and mortified that she never forgot it.

She reminded him of the incident when they met for *Jezebel*. The wily Wyler said, "I've grown up a lot since then." That broke the proverbial ice.

Their first day on the set was the dressmaker's scene wherein Julie espies the notorious scarlet gown. Wyler demanded and got 128 takes before he was satisfied. Again Davis was embarrassed. She had never had more than two or three takes on a film.

As the picture progressed, Davis became more and more concerned because Wyler never complimented her for a scene well-done. Finally, she could stand it no more. She approached him and said she, as an actress, needed to know if he was pleased or not when a scene was shot.

Thereafter, Wyler complimented her after every take, "Miss Davis, that's marvelous ... marvelous." After two or three takes of this nature, Davis, getting the point, asked him to stop and revert to his old ways, which he did immediately. Wyler really never told an actor how to play a scene, for he wanted to let the actor show his or her creativity. If an actor didn't measure up to his expectations, then Wyler would speak to him or her.

Unfortunately, he usually had a scapegoat on every picture who had to

12. Jezebel (1938)

bear his tough criticism. On this picture it was Henry Fonda, who never accepted such an approach. So there were confrontations, but then Fonda would go on to become known as a very difficult actor with whom to work, whether one was a director or another actor. He, like Wyler and Davis, sought perfection.

Jezebel made Davis a major star, lauded by both the critics and the moviegoing public.

What worried the screenwriter and producer, Hal Wallis, was that Julie was not a heroine, but rather a bitch with whom women could not or would not identify. The problem was solved by Julie's redemption at the end of the movie. The character sacrifices her well-being to care for Pres. But more importantly, Davis' performance allowed the audience to identify with this contrary southern belle because of her intense, full-bodied, flirtatious persona.

Thanks to the sumptuous costumes, the period hairdressing and the charming rich southern customs, Julie cuts a swath that women envied and adored. She is a woman at whose feet men fought. She is irresistible.

So not only does Davis appear as a beauty in this film, but Wyler helped her craft a performance as she had never done before. Most critics point out the fact that he was able to get Davis to drop the mannerisms which adversely affected many of her earlier performances, the busy hands and the constant dramatic high-pitched vocalizations. Most importantly, he harnessed this woman's talent so that she wasn't playing everything in one key. There were scenes in which Davis is very quiet in her delivery, with the internality of the scene coming from her emotional restraint.

When Pres arrives to take Julie to the debutante ball, he is horrified that she is wearing a red dress. As an actor, Davis could have responded in an angry, loud way, defiantly expressing her will, but she is quiet yet determined, making her playing that much more effective opposite Pres' anger. Later, when Julie learns of Pres' marriage to Amy, she again reacts in a very quiet way, even suggesting it's a joke. It is only through her eyes, not her voice, that one sees she is devastated and vulnerable.

More than these "corrections," Wyler should be credited with the total inspiration he gave to Davis to elicit a fully developed performance. He was a director who knew the script backward and forward, a director who knew exactly what he wanted the total picture to look like, and what he wanted thematically.

He inspired Davis to be a perfectionist, to develop into a fully rounded, complicated woman. He inspired her to be creative, not to rely on technique or mannerisms, but to allow herself to express her characters' emotions through risk by showing her true inner self.

Wyler had Davis' total trust. Not only that, but as in the case of many actors, Davis fell in love with him and he with her. Davis always believed love enhanced her performance. Here, it certainly did. One can see how the relationship between a director and star can lead to a superior performance and a superior film.

This isn't a perfect movie, but it is an excellent one because its director, Wyler, knew how to shoot and construct a completely believable story. Davis learned how to turn a character into a believable woman, not a heroine per se, but a woman who, in the end, one believes has experienced a transformation, and one who throughout the movie can elicit sympathy even when she is doing her best to cause trouble. One likes her spunk, her small rebellion, her liveliness.

Julie is a person who hates convention and loves to control or manipulate situations and people, a person who wants and almost always has gotten her own way. Yet she also wants to be controlled, and wants someone to love her whom she respects enough to submit to. She realizes too late that Pres is that person.

Davis said that in real life Wyler was the love of her life, but she was afraid to submit herself to his control, because, in the final analysis, she did not want anyone to control her. She thought all men wanted complete control of women. She pushed her men to the point where they did react as predicted. A split would occur and the men would leave her just as her father had left her mother.

Davis and *Jezebel* were, indeed, made for each other, and the movie-going public was the beneficiary in 1938 and for years to come until her death in 1989, after sixty years of watching an actor develop into an icon.

James Shelley Hamilton, in *National Board of Review* magazine, called *Jezebel* "...a penetrating study of character.... At the center is Bette Davis, growing into an artistic maturity that is one of the wonders of Hollywood."[6] Henceforth and throughout her career, and particularly through *All About Eve*, Davis maintained her singularity as the one film actor who could fully develop a screen character while still letting the Davis persona shine through. Because of her status she was, in essence, an "auteur" as well, for the films were Davis films, not just a director's film; she was a consummate artist.

A Davis film is a Davis film just as surely as a Picasso painting is a Picasso. You cannot divorce the work from the artist.

Cast: Julie Marsden — Bette Davis; Preston Dillard — Henry Fonda; Buck Cantrell — George Brent; Dr. Livingstone — Donald Crisp; Aunt Belle Massey — Fay Bainter; Amy Bradford Dillard — Margaret Lindsay; General Bogardus — Henry O'Neill; Jean La Cour — John Litel; Dick Allen — Gordon Oliver; Mrs. Kendrick — Spring Byington; Stephanie Kendrick — Margaret Early; Ted Dillard — Richard Cromwell; Zetté — Theresa Harris; Molly Allen — Janet Shaw; Huger — Irving Pichel; Gros Bat — Eddie Anderson.

Production: Hal B. Wallis — Executive Producer; Henry Blanke — Associate Producer; William Wyler — Director; Clements Ripley, Abem Finkel and John Huston — Screenwriters; Robert Buckner — Screenplay Contributer; Owen Davis, Sr. — Original Play; Ernest Haller — Cinematographer; Robert Haas — Art Director; Max Steiner — Music Score; Leo F. Forbstein — Music Director; Orry-Kelly — Costume Designer; Warren Low — Editor; 1938; Running time — 100 minutes.

The Second Tier

"Like a handful of other great Hollywood personalities, including Chaplin, Wayne and Cooper, Bette Davis is/was/is the exemplar of 20th century discipline for which she set many of the standards."[1]
— Vincent Canby

"Davis' face possesses something beyond beauty; it has grandeur and wit."[2]
— Peter Travers

13

Not to Be Overlooked: Twelve Other Significant Performances in Not Always Significant Films

> *"The skeleton of your acting is in your head, your brain, and that comes out in your eyes. What comes out of your eyes is caring, but it's also being the person you're trying to be. You'd better be thinking every minute* something.*"*
> —John Calhaune on Bette Davis
> The New York Times, *1980*[1]

As with other great actors of their time (i.e., Eleonora Duse and Sarah Bernhardt), Davis gave life, energy and significance to roles in films with less than great screenplays. Some would be rated as junk, even by her, but because she gave her full talent to whatever character she played, the performances became fully-realized characterizations and worthy of note.

The following twelve movies are listed in random order, with an eye towards variety rather than a list of bests to better or least good. It provides a chance to view the range of her ability, in a range of roles in a range of screen material.

Of Human Bondage (1934)

In viewing *Of Human Bondage* again, Davis' performance undeniably still holds up after all these seventy-some years. Her performance blew the critics away, particularly James Agee, who called it, in 1934, "probably the best performance ever recorded on the screen by a U.S. actress."[2]

Over the years, there may have been other superior performances, even by Davis herself, but this particular one stands out for a number of reasons.

Davis had to fight to get this role, which no female star of the time would even approach because of the character's vileness. In the film, Mildred Rogers (Davis) almost succeeds in ruining Philip Carey's (Leslie Howard) medical career.

Director John Cromwell wanted Davis, who, in turn, badgered her boss, Jack L. Warner, to loan her to RKO. After she completed *Bordertown*, Warner, tired of her constant haranguing, told her to "Go hang yourself" and granted the loan-out.

An adaptation of W. Somerset Maugham's semi-autobiographical novel, the picture received favorable reviews across America, particularly for Davis' acting as a completely self-centered bitch, her break-through role. It opened at Radio City Music Hall in New York City.

"You disgust me," says Philip Carey, late in the film when, once again, Mildred is trying to seduce her way back into his favor. Dressed in a flimsy negligee, her well-made up face alluring, Mildred rises from the arm of Philip's chair, turns on him and lets fly a searing diatribe.

"I disgust you? You disgust me! I only let you kiss me because you begged me. And when I kissed you, I wiped my mouth!... WIPED MY MOUTH!" she shouts as she wipes her arm across her mouth.

Davis let her anger loose, flailing her arms at Philip, angrily denouncing him, her peroxide hair flying outward as she finally declares what she's felt all along. She calls him a cripple as she slams her way out of the sitting room. This absolute slut has finally realized she's gone too far. He only has pity for her, not love. She is completely destroyed by his severance.

Charles Affron states, "No one could play Mildred as Davis does."[3]

This is the climactic moment of the screenplay. Davis has saved and planned for this dramatic moment. In her thorough characterization, she proved the worth of her approach toward a screenplay. She always memorized the entire script. As George Arliss had told her years before, always know what came before a particular scene and what was to come after, because films are mostly made out of sequence.

In *Of Human Bondage* Philip Carey is a young failed artist who leaves Paris to return to London to pursue a rocky road in his quest to become a doctor. The pursuit becomes difficult and is interrupted because of Philip's overwhelming, passionate lust for Mildred Rogers, a waitress in a restaurant frequented by fellow students and other men who are out for an evening of pleasure.

Leslie Howard (Philip Carey), the focus of those Bette Davis eyes (Mildred Rogers), in *Of Human Bondage* (Photofest).

In her first scene with Philip, Mildred is dressed in a black and white waitress uniform (black dress, high white collar, white apron and white peaked cap). She is very officious, surly even, with Carey, holding her pad and pencil at the ready, barely looking at him. When Carey tries to be friendly with her, Mildred basically ignores him, looking away from him and even turning her back to him rather than meet his eye.

Just prior to taking Philip's order, she has been flirting with another male customer, smiling, laughing and lingering over Miller's (Alan Hale) banter and jokes. With Philip, she barely speaks. When she returns with his check, Philip persists in asking her for a date. He offers her a sketch he has drawn of her.

Mildred finally says, "I don't mind," in a surly tone.

All the while Mildred is engaged with Miller she is relaxed and flirtatious. With Philip, she stands tall and is strictly business.

It's the first time one hears her speak in her low Cockney accent, a voice filled with disdain. Her whole body moves in a dismissive way. Her not looking at Philip emphasizes her disregard. One sees her bitchy character immediately. Even with her physical attractiveness, she negates it through her voice and manner toward Philip.

They agree to meet at Victoria Station for the dinner date. Through no fault of Philip's, he can't find Mildred at the station. She has deliberately gone to the wrong waiting room. When Philip does find her, she is instantly angry and berates him. She completely takes control of the situation, causing Philip to apologize for his behavior. She exerts her power over a man.

Sitting across from one another at dinner, Mildred lets her character show a modicum of appreciation when Philip pours her some champagne. Looking up from the edge of her champagne glass while drinking, she gives Philip a flirtatious, seductive look — those Bette Davis eyes — as she says, "You really are a gentleman. Champagne!" The look promises more than Mildred is willing to deliver to Philip, which is part of Mildred's manipulative nature.

When Philip escorts Mildred home, she stands on the stoop and brushes off Philip's attempt to kiss her with the tired expression, "What kind of girl do you think I am?" One knows what kind of girl she is from her behavior toward Miller and her shoddiness toward Philip.

With her Cockney accent and deliberate flirtiness and bitchiness, Davis was stealing the picture. All the British cast, most particularly Leslie Howard, the ostensible lead, realized her power. His energy level observedly increased in his performance, particularly in his scenes with Davis. All the other British actors realized her worth. Davis is not in a majority of scenes in this movie, yet she is the catalyst for all the action.

Even after fellow students question his relationship with Mildred, Philip invites her to attend a symphony. When he picks up the tickets, he runs into Miller, who tells him he is too aesthetic and should be more manly. Mildred stands him up. He goes looking for her and finds her with Miller. Upon finding her, she immediately takes the upper hand, accusing Philip of spying on her.

Still infatuated with Mildred, Philip takes her to dinner again to offer her marriage and a ring. Before he can tell her his surprise, she tells him she's going to marry Miller. She admires Philip's ring, all the while smiling, with no regard for his feelings. He is completely devastated.

Philip does begin a relationship with an honest, caring woman, Norah (Kay Johnson), who encourages him in his studies.

Out for a walk one evening, Philip returns to find Mildred waiting for him in his apartment. She has been jilted by the married Miller. "I'm going to have a baby," Mildred whines to Philip. She displays all her abject feelings, piteously trying to worm her way back into Philip's favor. He offers her an apartment of her own, and warm support. He falls again for her charm, her flirting. She even bats her eyes at him, saying, "You were the only one who cared for me, Philip."

Philip confesses his love for Mildred to Norah.

After the baby is born, Mildred tells Philip from now on things will be different, but she subsequently gives the baby girl to an older woman to care for.

One evening, Philip and Mildred, along with a fellow student, Harry (Reginald Denny), go out to a restaurant for dinner. All through dinner, Mildred unabashedly flirts with Harry, ignoring Philip, much as she had done with Miller when Philip first met her.

The next day, Philip confronts Harry, who claims absolutely no interest in Mildred. When Philip tells Mildred this, she produces a love note from Harry, to Philip's astonishment. She treats him disdainfully, as of old, and tells him, "I can't help it if I love someone else, can I?" She leaves him to go to Harry. Harry later throws her out and calls the police. He sees Philip at the hospital and informs him that he and Mildred are through.

Philip is interning at the hospital when he administers to an elderly man, an artist. After his recuperation, the elderly man invites Philip to his home for dinner. Over time a romance ensues between the man's daughter, Sally (Frances Dee), and Philip. Completing his internship, Philip learns from Harry that Mildred is back in town. Philip, still caring for her, goes to see her.

Mildred butters him up, and he takes her and the baby girl to his apartment to live. He neglects Sally but tells Mildred he's just helping her out of friendship.

While he's out, Mildred looks through his travel brochures and steams open a letter containing bonds from his uncle so that he can finish medical school. When he returns, Mildred tries to seduce him and fails, with the ensuing climactic scene. Before she leaves the next morning, she slashes his "salacious" nude paintings and burns his bonds.

Philip has to leave medical school, but Sally comes to him. She and her family offer him a job in the family department store. At the hospital, doctors offer to operate on his club foot and he is cured.

He goes to see Mildred. Her baby girl has died, and she is obviously sick with TB and can't stop coughing. Even so, she begs Philip to stay. He doesn't.

He has accepted a position on a cruise ship. He and Sally know they'll be parted for two years. He is able to go back to the hospital because of his inheritance from his uncle. When he arrives at the hospital, he hears of a case that the other interns are discussing. Mildred, in a harrowing scene, has been found by interns at her tenement room after the landlady called for help. Mildred is lying beside her bed in her nightgown, her emaciated appearance, gaunt face, deep-sunken eyes and unkempt hair indicating she is near death. The interns try to prevent Philip from entering her hospital room, but he does. However, she has died.

Philip cancels his cruise ship ticket, with Sally at his side. She tells him, "You're free." Oblivious to the city traffic, they cross a street to get into a cab.

When the film began shooting, the basically British cast had little respect for this impertinent American actress daring to try to play a Cockney. However, after a few days, Howard realized Davis was not only stealing scenes, but also the picture. His usual lackluster British subdued playing became energized, something one can detect in his response to Davis' acting challenge. Howard and Davis played together in several films, notably *The Petrified Forest* and *It's Love I'm After*. Howard never underestimated her again.

Of course, it isn't just the climactic scene that plays well. Davis built the character piece-by-piece: the dog-tired waitress who accepts crude jokes and flirts with apparently well-off men, and her almost-but-not-quite revulsion toward the soft-spoken, club-footed Howard. She barely looks at him when taking his order, even after he has succeeded in taking her out on a dinner date.

No actress of the day had ever let herself look so ugly on the screen. Davis was adamant in her desire to realistically portray this TB (actually syphilis) ravaged woman. There is nothing glamorous in her death. She no longer has her pride; she has nothing.

As admired as her performance was by critics, the public and her fellow workers, she was not nominated for an Academy Award by her peers. The three nominees were Claudette Colbert for *It Happened One Night* (the winner—a role Frank Capra wanted Davis to play), Norma Shearer for *The Barretts of Wimpole Street* and Grace Moore for *One Night of Love*.

There was a public outcry, but those were the early years when studios nominated and voted for their contract players. Since Davis wasn't an RKO star, neither her home studio, Warner Brothers, nor RKO would nominate her. The Academy allowed a write-in vote, but Davis still came in a poor second. In the early years, the Academy published the resultant vote. This was but one of many Oscars she lost, and not through any lack of talent. What the movie did show was her ability as an actress, but it still took Warners four more years to recognize and reward her with better roles.

In *Movie Star*, Ethan Mordden opines that *Of Human Bondage* made her fascinating as an actress, maybe even a little scary, and launched her reputation as the kind of person you have to go to the movies to see.

Davis was often asked where she got the wherewithal to portray the bitchy Mildred. She would laugh her signature guffaw and proclaim she didn't know, that her husband and her mother were dumbfounded that she could play such a character. This façade deserves skepticism. For it was even readily admitted by Davis that in her early career when the studio was forcing her to play simpering ingénues, she was bored out of her skull at having to be pleasant and nice all day long at the studio. When she arrived home at night, she vented her pent-up anger in spades at both her mother and her husband. Really, Mildred was a character right up her alley.

Movie history is full of screenplays adapted from other sources. Particularly in the thirties and forties, popular novels and plays were brought to the screen. Over the years, works by W. Somerset Maugham were repeatedly used. *The Letter* was a silent film with Jeanne Eagels in the twenties; *The Painted Veil* starred Greta Garbo; *Of Human Bondage* was remade twice after the 1934 version; *Quartet* and *Trio* were two films made from Maugham short stories in the forties; *The Moon and Sixpence* was made in the thirties.

Maugham's work included short stories, novels and plays. As recently as 2006 a film was remade of *The Painted Veil*, beautifully shot in China. His plays are produced continually throughout the world.

In the case of novels, many critics used to think they were perfect material for motion pictures because Hollywood films, until the sixties, were predominantly plot-driven. The problem was always that films were basically limited to 90 minutes or less, with rare exceptions like *Gone with the Wind*. Therefore, adaptations were rarely as good as an excellent novel. Where films excelled was in adapting mediocre novels, condensing them and making many into fine pictures. The best example of a superior adaptation is the filming of James Jones' *From Here to Eternity*. A good but verbose novel turned out to be perfect fodder for an excellent screenplay.

Maugham served cinema well because his work was highly melodramatic, a term some think of as demeaning. The two Maugham properties Davis essayed served *her* very well, *Of Human Bondage* and *The Letter*.

Of Human Bondage was made a few years after the introduction of sound. Sophisticated sound equipment was really not available yet. Often times the actors seem to be declaiming, as if on stage, rather than simply speaking. Another negative factor was the imposition of the Production Code, which really became overbearingly applied in 1934.

Of Human Bondage just barely got by the censors, largely because Mildred dies at the end of the movie. She is punished. But notice she ostensibly has TB rather than a sexual disease (obviously syphilis). Consequently, it was incumbent upon the writers, director and actor to convey the unspoken about Mildred's "occupation" and her death.

After twenty-one films, this was the first picture which really challenged Davis on a whole new level. Among those previous movies are a few of interest for her performances, such as *The Man Who Played God*, *Cabin in the Cotton* and *20,000 Years in Sing-Sing*. For the most part, the films were, at best, mediocre properties with little to recommend them, even though Davis and her co-stars gave interesting performances in them.

Warners probably didn't know what to do with Davis. At the time, they were more interested in making *au courant* gangster films and Busby Berkeley musicals. Davis even got cast in *Fashions of 1934*, a Berkeley "epic," in which she was so overly made-up with mascara, lipstick and a platinum blonde wig that she was basically unrecognizable. It was ludicrous.

RKO, at the time, had hit a streak of luck with several Katharine Hepburn movies, *Morning Glory*, *Little Women* and *Alice Adams*. Hepburn was getting quality scripts with top directors, such as George Cukor and George Stevens.

John Cromwell wanted Davis for *Of Human Bondage*. It took much persuasion and constant bombardment by Davis to get Warners to agree to the loan. The result astounded everyone, even Davis. She had never had such a challenging role, and she did what she always did, she internalized her character to the point where it became a part of her being.

Of Human Bondage was the only movie (prior to videotape and DVDs) of which she owned a print. She was that proud of her performance. This film enabled Davis to show her specific capability to play a woman of the lower working class, a basically vile, ignorant being, a person incapable of any growth outside her self-centered being. She was even clueless as to how she was taken advantage of by men other than Philip. She had no desire to be around a good person but abused him over and over for his kindness toward her. She had no appreciation for his prior work as an artist, nor any concept of his needs for progression in the field of medicine. She was completely trapped in her lower class values and had no desire to improve herself as a human being. She simply lived for pleasure and what money could provide her in terms of instant gratification. She was doomed to a life of failure. Her nature almost causes Philip's failure also.

Davis made Mildred's character explicit in every way. She is coquettish, manipulative, demeaning, nasty and unremittingly self-centered throughout her relationship with Miller, Philip and Harry. And she is ultimately incapable of being any kind of mother to her illegitimate daughter. She loves no one, least of all herself.

Much of what Davis expresses about Mildred is enhanced by her costumes—severe waitress uniform, her "pretty" but unremarkable dress she wears to go out with Philip, her beret, and later her slatternly negligee and nightgown. She is careless with her appearance around Philip, even when she thinks she's being enticing. Her tone of voice belies her true feelings, even when she begs Philip to take her back after leaving him. She obviously has no regard for Philip or any man.

The men she seduces react to her as she actually expects them to. They, with the exception of Philip, mistreat and mislead her. However, that is obviously expected and causes the men to behave in such a dismissive way because of the way she treats them. That is her expectation.

Unfortunately (though hardly ever referred to), this is similar to the behavior Davis herself exhibited toward the men in her life. In fact, she displayed such behavior with her first husband, Harmon O. Nelson. She became more and more resentful that she was the primary breadwinner in the family. She came to view Nelson as a failure and treated him with contempt.

It was at this time that Davis had an abortion. She, and her mother, decided having a baby would damage her career. According to later reports, Nelson wasn't even consulted in the matter.

Artists, such as Davis, usually reach a point in their careers when their artistic ambitions become paramount. Their art is their life, their very being. Davis would later reiterate this thought, her life was her work which was the most satisfying part of her life. Nothing stands in the way of the art — nothing or, more tellingly, no one.

From this point forward, nothing could stand in her way of becoming a great actress. She even risked her career by leaving Warners because of the poor scripts they were offering her. She went to England in 1936 for the purpose of making two movies for an English producer. Warners took her to court and she lost the battle. But, remarkably, she won the war. Warners took her back, paid her court costs, and finally recognized her unique ability. They offered her better scripts and top directors. By 1938, she was at the top of her profession and had shed husband number one. Actually, he divorced her.

Of Human Bondage gave her the resolve to succeed.

Cast: Philip Carey — Leslie Howard; Mildred Rogers — Bette Davis; Sally — Frances Dee; Norah — Kay Johnson; Harry — Reginald Denny; Miller — Alan Hale; Athelny — Reginald Owen.

Production: John Cromwell — Director; Pandro S. Berman — Producer; Lester Cohen — Screenwriter; Based on a novel by W. Somerset Maugham; Henry W. Gerrard — Cinematographer; Max Steiner — Musical Score and Direction; Van Nest Polglase and Carroll Clark — Art directors; William Morgan — Editor; 1934; Running Time — 83 minutes.

The Catered Affair (1956)

The Catered Affair was written by Paddy Chayefsky, the famed playwright of the '50s era whose early TV play was turned into a surprise movie hit, *Marty*. The naturalistic drama, in black and white, went on to win an Oscar for best picture and for best actor, Ernest Borgnine. One of the secrets of its success was the marketing, which targeted the small art house theaters prevalent during the '50s and '60s. Good reviews and word-of-mouth created its popular appeal.

M-G-M, the largest of the old movie studios, bought the film rights to the TV play *The Catered Affair*, hired an excellent director in Richard Brooks, and chose a competent cast, Ernest Borgnine, Bette Davis, Debbie Reynolds and Barry Fitzgerald. The earlier TV play starred Thelma Ritter, who had appeared with Davis in *All About Eve*. The film version's screenplay was an adaptation by Gore Vidal, which seems a strange choice to deal with Chayefsky material, but Vidal was having a run of screenplays at the time. Titled *Wedding Breakfast* in Great Britain, the film received great reviews and garnered a large following.

In the USA, M-G-M booked the movie in its large city Loew's theaters with barely any publicity. The reviews were respectable but not ecstatic for either the film or for Davis. Why M-G-M did not treat this picture as an art film and book it in art houses is a mystery. Perhaps they thought Borgnine, the recent Oscar winner, along with Davis and their ever-popular ingénue, Debbie Reynolds, could pull in the large audience needed to fill their large theaters. They were wrong.

The cast worked beautifully together as the Bronx-Irish family, consisting of taxi driver, Tom (Borgnine), his wife, Aggie (Davis), and their daughter, Jane (Reynolds). Jane and her fiancé, Ralph (Rod Taylor), decide on a simple marriage ceremony to take place quickly so they can take advantage of a financial offer to drive a friend's car across the country and have a honeymoon. Tom Hurley and his taxi partner, Sam (Jay Adler), have just learned of a licensed taxi that will be up for sale. They decide to buy it together for $8000 to fulfill a lifetime wish to own their own cab. The problem is Aggie's wish: to provide her daughter with a proper wedding reception, something Jane will remember for the rest of her life. Tom is less than enthusiastic because of his cab deal. From the beginning, one sees the animosity between Tom and Aggie. Their marriage has become one of endurance, not love and kindness.

Jane and Ralph want a small, family-only wedding. Aggie's brother, Uncle Jack Conlon (Barry Fitzgerald), who lives with them, is offended that he won't be invited to the small family affair.

When Ralph's parents, Mary and Joe Halloran (Madge Kennedy and Robert Simon), come to the Hurleys' for dinner, Mrs. Halloran expounds about the fine wedding they gave their daughter. At the end of the evening, Aggie feels compelled to provide Jane with an equally classy affair.

Aggie gets Tom to agree, and they decide to go to a professional caterer,

Debbie Reynolds, as Jane Hurley, listens to her mother's (Davis) marital advice in *The Catered Affair* (Photofest).

where Tom realizes the cost will wipe out his savings. He won't be able to buy the cab. Aggie, however, is insistent. Meanwhile, Jane, on her own, has seen what a hardship it will be for her best friend, Alice (Joan Camden), to be her matron-of-honor because she cannot afford the dress (her husband has lost his job).

By 1956, Davis was really not making many movies, and this was a major departure from what one would expect of a Davis movie. She is heavy, looks her age, is dressed in off-the-rack housedresses, and wears oxford-type shoes. She affects a Bronx accent, dropping her usual precise enunciation of words and syllables. It may not be a pure Bronx accent, but it certainly sounds as if Davis learned a lot from working with Thelma Ritter in *All About Eve*.

Barry Fitzgerald, Aggie's brother, has his very distinctive Irish brough, while the children, Jane and Eddie (Ray Stricklyn), are essentially American.

Davis' performance is consistent with her character, and with Borgnine's playing. Here is a woman who has been in a loveless marriage her whole adult life, struggling to keep her family together and live within the tenement apartment which accommodates her family, including her brother, Jack.

She tells her daughter, Jane, how she wants her to have something to remember when the hard times come, that marriage isn't a bed of roses. Davis plays this scene with Reynolds while she is cooking breakfast, standing over a stove, frying eggs. The tenement kitchen has several electrical cords plugged into one socket. There's a small wooden table and chair. Davis, paying attention to the eggs, manages to convey her message to Reynolds and make her understand why she wants her daughter to have a wedding reception. Reynolds listens and accepts her mother's advice, but reminds her why she and Ralph want a small wedding.

What Jane comes to realize is that her mother is trying to make up for the sad wedding she had as a young girl. She doesn't want to disappoint her mother, but she also realizes her father can't afford a catered affair, that it will wipe out his savings.

When Tom and Jane agree that the large affair isn't what Jane and Ralph want nor feel the need for, Aggie is defeated. Aggie's total disappointment is expressed in her face, but she holds her emotion in check. She slowly walks down the hall to her bedroom, enters and closes the door, then collapses on the bed, covers her face and desperately sobs, her whole body shaking. She's not crying for Jane, but at the memory of her own plain wedding ceremony. She has had to let go of that experience to accommodate her husband's and daughter's wishes. She finally realizes the source of her misplaced resentment.

We realize she's crying for her whole life, the life she wished she had had, and crying because she'll now be alone with just Tom. She's not crying over a wedding breakfast for Jane.

When Tom comes in, he asks, "You all right now?"

Aggie takes off her dress and says, "I cried. So what?"

When Jane later comes in to apologize, Aggie and Tom tell her to leave. Tom says, "What about me? Just me you have left in your old age. I can't afford a big wedding. Why can't you sympathize with that instead of everyone else?"

The next morning in the kitchen Aggie says to Jane, "It's funny. We were never alone. We never talked together. Nobody's ever movin' in again. Something new, your pa and me together."

Aggie has a glow and displays caring behavior toward Tom on the morning of the wedding. She has had a transformation, and Davis shows it through her actions and looks toward Tom and Jane.

Aggie is at peace with herself. She realizes she does love her husband; they've been together all these years. As the sunlight wakes Tom, he's upset it's so late, but Aggie assures him it will be all right. She has accepted her life and values it.

As they leave the apartment building, they encounter Sam (Jay Adler) waiting in their new cab, much to Tom's surprise. Aggie has arranged it. Tom is flabbergasted, goes to get in the cab, then turns to open the door for Aggie, who lifts her head and lets out a raucous laugh, then smiles and enters the cab.

It was not second nature for Davis to play this role. In fact, the producers were not sure they wanted her for Aggie. Her reputation in recent roles, i.e., Queen Elizabeth I in *The Virgin Queen*, and *The Star*, did not indicate her ability to master Aggie Hurley's character. It was Richard Brooks, the director, who argued for her.

Even in Hollywood, executives have short memories. M-G-M executives could have viewed her career easily and realized she had proved her worth in such films as *Three on a Match, 20,000 Years in Sing Sing, The Girl from Tenth Avenue*, and especially *That Certain Woman*.

Davis, herself, when she was just starting out, had lived an uncertain financial life when she, her mother and sister moved from place to place in New Jersey and New York City, while her mother found work as a housekeeper. Bette had also waited tables to help pay for her tuition at a girls' school.

Davis loved working on this film, and liked working with Borgnine. It was while they were filming that he won his Oscar for *Marty*. They worked together once more in a disaster of a film, *Bunny O'Hare*. Davis went to court to try to prevent its release. She detested it but not Borgnine.

Besides Davis' and Borgnine's, other gem-like performances grace this film, not least of which is Barry Fitzgerald's turn as Uncle Jack, Aggie's brother. His scenes with theater actor Dorothy Stickney, as a widow, were charming and amusing as she gently lets him convince himself that he shouldn't be living alone. He then proposes to her.

All the supporting cast was well-chosen and shine in their various roles. Ray Stricklyn as Eddie, Tom and Aggie's son, is just right as the young man eager to leave home to join the Army. So is Joan Camden as Alice, Jane's close friend, who is totally embarrassed that she can't afford a bridesmaid gown to participate in the wedding. It is surprising how U.S. critics were dismissive of this film, while English critics extolled its virtues.

Throughout the picture, Davis played her role of a Bronx housewife with suppressed emotion. There are no histrionics, no melodrama. Her emotions are read through her eyes, as usual. Davis was rather heavy in this movie, and she underlined this with off-the-rack clothes and unappealing hair, creating a rather frowzy look. Even when she is dressed up for her daughter's wedding, there is a plainness to her clothes, a small fur piece, a dark, ordinary hat, and sensible oxfords. Aggie was a role most people would consider beyond Davis' range, but that is a complete underestimation of her talent. If you didn't know who Bette Davis was when you watched this movie, you would entirely accept her as a great character actress.

In the scene in which the Hurleys have Ralph's family over for supper, Davis is mostly quiet, but very engaged in listening and watching everyone, smoothing over some of Tom's awkward moments and, most importantly, assessing what she hears about the wedding the Hallorans gave their daughter. Davis sits quietly in a side chair, watching the total picture of the two families. Her gestures and demeanor tell us she is not ashamed of her family's circumstances, but she is internally embarrassed to think they can't do something special for their own daughter. After the Hallorans leave, Aggie expresses her feelings to Jane and Tom. She does want to measure up to the Hallorans. Underlying her desire is her unhappy memory of her own lack of a proper wedding when she married Tom.

Unlike the English critics who found much to admire both in the production and in Davis, American critics were unfavorable and virtually unkind in their assessment of Davis' performance.

Brooks' direction is valid throughout and is underappreciated.

Even Reynolds gives a touching portrayal as the daughter. She later noted what a help Davis was on the film.

As Philip K. Sheurer concluded, "Miss Davis, required to be realistic in a role that is alien to her — from the dumpy figure to the dropped g's of her speech — summoned all her admirable resources to meet the challenge."[4]

Cast: Agnes Hurley — Bette Davis; Tom Hurley — Ernest Borgnine; Jane Hurley — Debbie Reynolds.; Uncle Jack Conlon — Barry Fitzgerald; Ralph Halloran — Rod Taylor; Joe Halloran — Robert Simon; Mary Halloran — Madge Kennedy; Mrs. Rafferty — Dorothy Stickney; Mrs. Casey — Carol Veazie; Alice — Joan Camden; Eddie Hurley — Ray Stricklyn; Sam Leiter — Jay Adler; Hotel Caterer — Dan Tobin; Bill — Paul Denton; Mrs. Musso — Augusta Merighi.

Production: Sam Zimbalist — Producer; Richard Brooks — Director; Gore Vidal — Screenwriter; Paddy Chayefsky — Based on his TV play; John Alton — Cinematographer; Andre Previn — Musical Score; Cedric Gibbons and Paul Groesse — Art Directors; Gene Ruggiero and Frank Santillo — Editors; 1956; Running Time — 92 minutes.

Bordertown (1935)

Marie Roark (Davis) is helped by a jail matron into a courtroom where Johnny Ramirez (Paul Muni) is on trial for complicity in the murder of Marie's husband, Charlie (Eugene Pallette). She is hesitant, and walks slowly toward the witness stand. She appears disoriented. When she is asked to swear on the Bible, she is so inaudible with her answer that the judge asks her to speak louder. Again, she utters a barely audible, "Yes." Her face is rather blank, framed by her very blonde hair. She has a vacant stare.

Grilled on the witness stand, Marie is barely able to answer the prosecutor's questions with a yes or no. After four questions, she reaches to her head and desperately, quietly repeats, "I'm Mrs. Charlie Roark. I'm Mrs. Charlie Roark." Her eyes are frantic, but she's unable to do anything but repeat herself. The matron leads her away. She is obviously, heart-wrenchingly, insane. The trial is declared a mistrial because Marie, as the only witness to the murder, is incompetent to testify.

Davis fought with *Bordertown*'s director, Archie Mayo, about how to play this scene. As was typical in those days, the director thought the way to play it was for Marie to be completely hysterical, screaming and yelling and throwing herself about. Davis won her battle when she was allowed to play it in her quiet way, and Mayo saw how much more effective the scene was. Of course, this was neither the first nor the last time that Davis questioned a director's viewpoint.

Davis made this film before 1934's *Of Human Bondage*, but it wasn't released until 1935. Warners actually wanted to capitalize on the critical success of *Bondage*. In *Bordertown*, one can see the range Davis had to offer in the better role, Mildred in *Bondage*. Here she is a driven woman also, out to manipulate a man and fulfill her desires.

A Paul Muni vehicle, the film is the story of a Mexican-American, a working class man's struggle to improve his status by becoming a lawyer through attending night school. Muni is heavily made up, sports dark, greasy hair, and affects a "Mexican" accent. Johnny Ramirez (Muni) had been a rough gang boy who worked diligently to proudly graduate at the head of his law class, pleasing his mother and neighborhood padre (Robert Barrat).

Experiencing very little success as a lawyer, he finally gets a case, a fellow Mexican-American whose vegetable truck has been severely damaged by a drunken driver, an L.A. socialite named Dale Elwell (Margaret Lindsay). However, *her* lawyer, Brook Manville (Gavin Gordon), proves too knowledgeable for Ramirez, who hasn't properly prepared his case. When the case is dismissed, Manville makes a derisive remark about Ramirez's ethnicity, which results in a fistfight. Ramirez is subsequently disbarred.

He wanders south of the border and becomes a bouncer for casino owner Charlie Roark (Eugene Pallette). He is so efficient and hardworking that Roark soon promotes him to manager. When a syndicate offers to buy the joint for $3500, Johnny advises Charlie to decline the offer, which he does. Roark then offers Ramirez a partnership. They go to Charlie's home to discuss the proposition with Charlie's wife, Marie.

Charlie thinks anything Marie has to say is the height of humor, even when she is actually mocking him. However, she agrees wholeheartedly with the partnership idea. To celebrate, Charlie goes to their kitchen to make flapjacks. Marie takes the opportunity to flirt openly with Johnny, who rejects her advances.

One night at the club, Charlie is commiserating with his cronies about his ailments. They tell him it's a dental problem, that he ought to go to L.A. to get a set of dentures. Charlie drives home and wakes Marie to get her to go to L.A. with him, but she declines. She even warns him not to come home with any rattling teeth. He laughs and leaves.

Marie turns around in bed and eyes the clock, then gets up with a determined look on her face. Very soon, there is a click at the front door and Johnny enters the living room and turns on the lights. He is bringing the night's receipts to the Roarks' home safe. When the lights go on, Marie is seen standing seductively, dressed in a negligee, by the opposite doorway. Johnny is surprised, deposits the money in the hall safe and apologizes for the intrusion. Marie dismisses his apologies and moves toward him to openly seduce him. Johnny protests that he and Charlie are partners, but he succumbs to her wiles.

After Charlie's return from L.A., he and Marie, and another couple, go to the club to celebrate his successful dental work. Bottle after bottle of champagne arrives at the table, and Charlie proceeds to get very drunk. Finally, Marie decides it's time to go home. Johnny offers to drive them, but Marie insists she can handle Charlie. She wishes the other couple's wife luck with her husband, saying Johnny could drive them home.

On arriving home, Marie drives the car between the two posts which contain the newly installed electric eye that opens the garage door. Once inside, she gets out to try to retrieve the passed-out Charlie from the back seat. He is drunk and beneath her contempt. She's barely able to get him to speak, let alone move. Disgusted, she lets him stay in the back seat, returns to the front seat and starts to reach for the ignition key. Suddenly, she looks in the rear-view mirror. Her body stiffens. Her eyes stare. As she hesitates, her face gives way to another thought. She leaves the car running. Closing the doors of the open-top car, she walks deliberately out of the garage to the drive, to the electric eye posts. She pauses for the briefest moment, then, with a look of determination on her face, she crosses the line. The garage door descends. She knows what the outcome will be. She walks through the light, sealing Charlie's fate and her own.

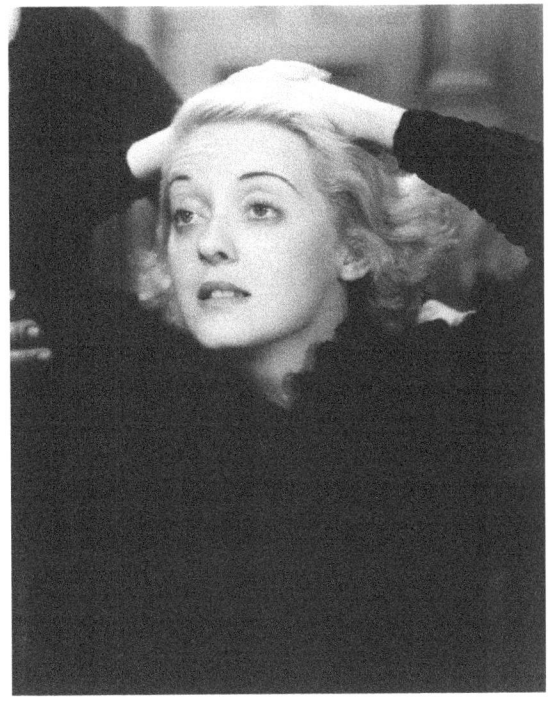

Marie Roark (Davis) loses her sanity in the *Bordertown* courtroom scene (Photofest).

At the coroner's inquisition, Marie quietly, with a stricken look, explains the accidental death. She says Charlie must have awakened at some point and turned on the ignition and then fallen back asleep. The authorities accept her explanation.

At a hearing with her insurance agent to learn of her legacy from Charlie, everyone agrees that the successful Johnny's advice to deposit her money in a U.S. bank is the best idea. Later at her house, Marie tells Johnny, "Anything you do is okay with me, you know that." She also gives him the house key. They decide to build a larger casino.

Johnny throws all his energy and time into the new construction, to the point of neglecting Marie. She has gradually become frightened of, and openly abusive toward, her houseboy, even thinking he is Charlie. Desperate, she gets a taxi to take her to the casino. She tells Johnny she needs to see him once in a while. When he drives her home, he disregards her telling him to stop the car before entering the driveway. She becomes hysterical, and when she gets out of the car, she reveals her fear.

After much pressure from Johnny, the new casino opens. He is glad-handing everyone, forgetting that Marie is waiting for him to pick her up.

Two of the arrivals are Dale and her lawyer friend, Manville, who caused Johnny's disbarment. He welcomes them and joins their table, where he takes an inordinate interest in Dale. Dale and Johnny go to be alone on the terrace.

Meanwhile, Marie has become hysterical waiting alone at home. She abusively orders the houseboy to call her a cab. When she arrives at the club she spots Johnny and Dale on the terrace. Marie informs Dale that she and Johnny are partners in every way. Dale leaves, and Johnny takes Marie to his offices where he berates her for her actions, saying he was talking to a lady.

Marie fires back, "I made you rich. You're riff-raff and so am I. I committed murder to get you!"

She is out of control, feeling more and more betrayed by Johnny, but still attempting to control herself to keep her hold on Johnny. Johnny replies, "It makes me sick, even to look at you. I warn you. Stay away or you'll end up with Charlie!"

He goes to find Dale in L.A. She tries to brush him off, but he is persistent and drives her about in his new car.

Back at the casino, Johnny and Marie confront each other again. He tells her he intends to marry Dale. With barely controlled speech, Marie finally congratulates him. When he leaves for L.A. again, Marie desperately calls the D.A.'s office to say she was forced to murder Charlie at Johnny's urging.

When Johnny returns he is arrested. In jail, he writes a love letter to Dale.

Exonerated, he goes to see Dale again. She tries to rebuff him, but he insists on driving her to her family dinner. He pulls to the side of the busy highway to press his case, to ask her to marry him. Dale rejects his offer, but he hotly continues and she gets out of the car. When he comes around to her, she says he must recognize he is from a different tribe. His anger causes her to rush out into the road where she is killed by an oncoming car.

Johnny subsequently sells the casino for $235,000 and takes the money to build a school in L.A. for Mexican-American children. He tells his mother and his padre that he is back where he belongs, with his own people.

Already acclaimed for *Of Human Bondage*, Davis was placed in this Paul Muni vehicle. It was he who suggested the property to Hal Wallis. As was his style, Muni submerged himself in an ethnic role. To this famous Jewish actor, the best roles were those that allowed him to completely hide himself behind or within a character, such as Louis Pasteur, Benito Juarez, Scarface or the Chinese man in *The Good Earth*. He was Warners' prestige star in the 1930s. He was given $50,000 per film, story approval, script approval, sole star billing and permission to appear in stage plays. Unfortunately, his continual "hiding" in his character tended to obscure Paul Muni, the actor, and his acting became very mannered and declamatory. Basically, he didn't essay enough roles whereby the public could identify with him.

While he and Davis worked well together in *Bordertown*, in the later *Juarez* he had the power to remove scenes from the overlong picture, which displayed Davis as Empress Carlotta and Brian Aherne as the Emperor Maximilian.

For Davis, *Bordertown* was really a step backward compared with *Bondage*, but a giant leap forward compared with *Housewife*, the first picture she was forced to do after returning to Warners after *Bondage*.

Bordertown provided her with another total bitch role. (In the novel, Marie was a prostitute.) She is a seductress of the first order, and unfaithful to her husband, who completely, unbelievably, can't see through her. As strong a character as Marie is, however, she is undone by the murder she commits. Killing her husband, which she did cold-bloodedly, does not seem to affect her initially because she believes she has Johnny for a mate. What she doesn't realize is that he holds her in contempt and yearns for the riches of life and an equally immoral upper crust woman in L.A., Dale Elwell. When Marie realizes this, she is not only jealous but threatened. Ultimately, she is unable to handle the fact that she killed her husband for nothing.

It is then that she begins falling apart. She has no one, and she knows it. When she finally confronts Johnny with the fact that they are both riff-raff, and that she killed her husband for him, Johnny finally discards her and drives to L.A. to find Dale.

Marie is openly hysterical when she informs the police of Johnny's implication in Charlie's murder, but we also realize she knows he is not to blame for her actions. She has lost control of her life. But by this time he is on trial and she is put on the witness stand. She has gone over the edge and can barely speak, let alone testify. For lack of a credible witness, Johnny is freed.

It is only then that he returns to his people, his family, to help the downtrodden Mexican-Americans improve their lot. Such a denouement seems very farfetched, and was most likely imposed by the newly-enforced Production Code.

No one is really likeable in this movie. Johnny is a self-centered, shallow man; money is his god. Dale and Manville are irresponsible, high-living socialites. She was responsible for the car accident involving a Mexican-American's truck, the case Johnny ineptly prosecuted. Even Johnny's mother and padre are foolish stereotypes, mouthing platitudes about life.

Marie is the only character of interest, and ninety percent of this comes from Davis' portrayal. She gives Marie life and vitality — energy. Frankly, she just outsmarts herself, and Davis makes her believable.

Davis again received below-the-title billing, but she is what gave the film its electricity, its spark. She is carefully dressed in alluring evening clothes, with her peroxide hair becomingly surrounding her well-made-up face. The expensive clothing displays her wealth (bounty from the gambling business her husband runs), and is in excellent contrast to how she looks when in jail. When she appears in court, there is basically no make-up. Her face is pale, and her outfit is simple and plain. She is still attractive, but not in a gaudy way as before. Because of her simplicity of appearance and behavior, she does elicit sympathy for her demented character.

Davis is completely believable throughout, adroitly expressing her various emotions of disdain, humor, sexual allure and finally dementia, making Marie a complex, rounded human being, albeit an opportunistic bitch.

"Miss Davis plays the part with the ugly, sadistic and utterly convincing sense of reality,"[5] ventured Andre Sennwald in *The New York Times*.

Cast: Johnny Ramirez — Paul Muni; Marie Roark — Bette Davis; Dale Elwell — Margaret Lindsay; Brook Manville — Gavin Gordon; Manuel Diego — Arthur Stone; Padre — Robert Barrat; Mrs. Ramirez — Soledad Jiménez; Charlie Roark — Eugene Pallette; Doc Carter — William B. Davidson; Harry, the drunk — Hobart Cavanaugh; Mrs. Garner — Vivian Tobin.

Production: Jack L. Warner — Executive Producer; Robert Lord — Producer; Archie Mayo — Director; Laird Doyle and Wallace Smith — Screenwriters; Robert Lord — Adaptation; Carroll Graham — Based on his novel; Tony Gaudio — Cinematographer; Bernard Kaun — Musical Score; Jack Okey — Art Director; Thomas Richards — Editor; 1935; Running time — 80 minutes.

All This and Heaven Too (1940)

Charles Affron notes of Davis' performance in *All This and Heaven Too*, "Without sighs, tears, or breast-heaving, she exudes a grandiose self-assurance and a knowledge that she is deeply loved."[6] Even so, it must be admitted Davis sheds quite a few tears in what could be called a soap opera — but for the fact that the movie was based on a novel by Rachel Field about a true, scandalous French case of the nineteenth century, and for the A-plus acting from the entire cast, consisting of Davis, Charles Boyer, Barbara O'Neil, and four extremely talented child actors, June Lockhart, Virginia Weidler, Ann Todd and Richard Nichols.

All This and Heaven Too is proof positive that Davis could play a sympathetic role, not just bitches, and give a full characterization as a loving tutor. Her most telling scenes are with the children. In one, which could be a frightening scene for children, both as viewer and participant, all four youngsters are in a wooded area at night on All Hallow's Eve. The two older girls, Isabelle (June Lockhart) and Louise (Virginia Weidler) are hiding from the others under a large pile of leaves. Holding the hand of Berthe (Ann Todd) and Reynald (Richard Nichols), Mlle. Desportes (Davis) calls out for the other two children as they walk through the dark woods, the bare tree branches outlined by the soft moonlight. At one point, she consoles Reynald, who is only four. They round a path past the huge pile of leaves and the two older girls roll out, laughing. The children feel completely comfortable and safe with Mlle. They love her very much, even, as Louise says, almost as much as Papa.

Sitting around a bonfire, while an old hermit sings a folk song, roasting apples on a stick, Louise and Reynald think they see a ghost approaching. The figure comes closer and they realize it is their father (Boyer). They rush to him, laughing and giving him hugs. They all get in a buggy for a ride back to their country house, laughing and talking all at once, having had a wonderful day with Mlle. and their papa.

In this and many scenes throughout the movie, the love between the children and Mlle. Henriette is evident. They are easy with one another, and the looks upon their faces show their love for the governess and vice-versa. The children are the primary source of love for Henriette, a single, twenty-five-year-old tutor whose only family is a distant grandfather who has rejected her. Her strength comes from the fact that she knows the children love her, and she them as if they were her own.

Opulence is the key word for *All This and Heaven Too*. This was apparently Jack Warner's real answer to *Gone with the Wind*, a property he let slip through his fingers. No expense was spared on the multitude of sets and costumes. Originally, he planned to turn Rachel Field's novel into a four-star production mimicking Gable, Leigh, de Havilland and Howard. However, this story was a love triangle among Davis, Boyer and Barbara O'Neil (Scarlett's mother in *GWTW*). There was no Ashley Wilkes role.

Originally, Davis objected to O'Neil's casting because she thought her far too beautiful for the duchesse. She needn't have worried because O'Neil played the duchesse as a complete harpie, with little affection for her children. There was no question as to why Boyer's duc avoided her as much as possible.

Throughout the film, Davis is dressed in appropriate nineteenth century costumes, with appropriate hairstyles. The costuming is precise for all the characters, as are the historical settings, providing the appropriate mood for all scenes. Throughout her career, Davis was blessed in being able to wear all sorts of costumes, whether ancient or contemporary, and her hairstyles were also varied and in character.

Director Anatole Litvak helped Davis deliver a touching, sympathetic

Mlle. Henriette (Davis, center) as governess to Louise (Virginia Weidler), Isabelle (June Lockhart), Berthe (Ann Todd), and Reynald (Richard Nichols) in *All This and Heaven Too* (Photofest).

portrayal. Her subtle acting allowed the emotions to come from within and was more powerful because of the restraint. Against this, Barbara O'Neil's outbursts as the duchesse generated even more sympathy for Davis' Henriette.

The children are Praslins, their father a duc and their mother therefore a duchesse. When Mlle. Henriette arrives at the Paris mansion to take up the post of governess, there is turmoil in the household. The parents' relationship is strained. The duchesse, though passionately in love with Theo, is overbearing towards him, possessive and suspicious of his every move. She constantly berates him and neglects her children.

After the new tutor spends time with the family, particularly following a period when Reynald contracts diphtheria, the children come to love their governess. The duc more than admires her ability to teach the children, and display compassion for them as well.

During Reynald's struggle with diphtheria, the doctor and duc keep the duchesse away from Reynald. Essentially it is Mlle. who sees him through the illness when he is near death. With the duc's permission and help, Hen-

13. Not to Be Overlooked

riette opens the windows of the nursery and lifts Reynald over the sill so he can see the spring garden with the almond tree all in bloom. Fresh air and sunshine inspire Reynald to fight through the crisis.

The duchesse writes Henriette a note, thanking her for her devoted care, and gives her a diamond brooch. But when Henriette approaches her to try to develop a closer relationship, she is rebuffed. The duchesse really feels Henriette is undermining her relationship with her husband and children.

The duc has thanked her for bringing peace to their household. The duchesse says she wishes to be first in the mind of her husband and children. Henriette apologizes and says she never intentionally did anything otherwise. She says, "I'll be more careful in the future." The duchesse gets a queer look on her face, almost frightened, and says, "Future?"

The duc and duchesse and their children, without Henriette, go to visit the duchesse's father in Corsica, but the duc soon returns with Louise, who has a toothache. After her dental problem is taken care of, the duc takes Henriette and Louise to the theater to see Rachel in Phedre's play. From their box, opposite the king's box, they have a wonderful view of the play and are well-viewed themselves by the theater crowd. The king bows to the duc's box, drawing even more attention. Subsequently, gossip is printed in a newspaper, questioning the absence of the duchesse and wondering who "Mlle. D." is. During the musical prologue, the duc stares lovingly at Henriette, and she knows it.

When they return home, Henriette plays the harpsichord while the duc and Louise dance in the school room. Henriette thanks him for the play and the evening. They shake hands. He leaves and she snuffs out some candles and puts Louise to bed. Louise expresses her love for Henriette. All the candle snuffing is as if Henriette is suppressing her feelings of love for the duc.

It becomes a silent scene as Henriette roams the outer room extinguishing more candles and lamps. As she reaches the last lamp, she lovingly smells the boutonnière the duc had given to Louise. The look on her face tells all.

Within days, an older servant reads the newspaper to the duchesse, who immediately returns to Paris with her other three children and her father, M. Sebastiani. Henriette is summoned by the father, who shows her the newspaper article.

Henriette remarks, "People who write trash and those who read it."

The duchesse attacks, "...Steal away everything I love. Flaunted your influence over my husband for the king and all of Paris to see."

Henriette defends herself, but M. Sebastiani demands the situation be resolved. Henriette offers to leave, but he rejects that as a solution bound to verify the rumors. Her conduct must be more prudent. Henriette leaves the room and hears the duc acceding to the duchesse's wishes. She goes to her room to pack.

The duc comes to her room and says there are five reasons she mustn't leave, the four children and himself. Henriette replies, "I shouldn't be yielding against my better judgment." Tears are in her eyes.

The duc and duchesse resume a full social calendar, even hosting a ball at their Paris mansion. The three girls watch from a balcony until Henriette finds them and ushers them to bed. After she tucks in the two younger girls, she hears crying coming from Isabelle's room. Davis shows her complete ease with the young actor, June Lockhart, as they discuss her oncoming womanhood, something the abbé has told her will lead to marriage. Isabelle is frightened. Henriette holds her in her arms and lets her know she can be trusted. Isabelle is worried about love and marriage because of her parents' confrontations. Henriette assures her there can be love in marriage, but one must be sure it's right.

The duc comes to Henriette in her chamber, declaring he couldn't stand any more hypocrisy at the ball. He returns to the ball. Then he and the duchesse quarrel in her room.

The duc goes to his own room to discover a new valet, hired by Sebastiani. The duc tells him to get out. A note from the duchesse arrives under the door, which he discards.

Pierre, an old servant, comes to Henriette's room with a gift of a snow globe from the duc. Pierre is impertinent with her. He tells her to "run, run out of this house, for your life." He asks her, "Why do you stand at this window, where you can see the duc's room and the duchesse's room and the unlit passage between? You're caged in the net and you don't even wish to escape."

The next day, the whole family is getting ready to leave for Merlun, the duc's old home area. When the duc goes to see what's holding up the duchesse, he encounters the new valet talking with her. She flies into a rage at the duc. Consequently, Henriette and the children leave for Merlun alone.

After a few days, the duc arrives in Merlun without the duchesse. It is then that he, Henriette and the children have some carefree days together and experience All Hallow's Eve.

Their developing love is expressed when Henriette and the duc stop in a tavern for a brandy. Kneeling to take off her shoes, the duc asks her, "Were you happy as a child?"

"I was always alone as a child ... except for my grandfather." She continues that she will "...never marry. There was some mystery in my birth."

When they return with the children to the Merlun home, the abbé is waiting at the door for the duc. On her way upstairs to the children, who have a gift for her, Henriette runs into the duchesse, who declares Henriette evil and sinful. But she promises to give Henriette a letter of recommendation if she leaves.

13. Not to Be Overlooked

The duc comes to Henriette's room and begs her to stay, asking for her forgiveness.

"We both have known how it had to end," Henriette responds. "You reached out for help, and in my loneliness I reached out to you."

Henriette ends up in a pension, penniless, without the letter of recommendation. The duc and the children visit her infrequently, but he doesn't know about the lack of the letter. Finally, the landlady tells him. He tells Henriette to come to him at two o'clock the next day to get the letter.

When he confronts the duchesse, she appears to read two letters she has written, the first a positive recommendation, the second a vicious attack on Henriette. Then she shows him two blank pieces of paper. She never will write Henriette a recommendation.

The duc becomes enraged and kills her.

Eventually, soldiers come to Henriette's pension and arrest her as an accomplice. The duc is questioned by the House of Lords. He denies his love for Henriette, saying she was in no way involved in the murder.

Henriette is grilled by the jurists, but denies any wrongdoing on the duc's part. A message arrives that the duc has taken poison and is dying. They take Henriette to see him to try to obtain a confession implicating her.

The duc refuses to answer the questions.

When Pierre leans over him, the duc says to tell Henriette, "I love her with every drop of my blood in my soul."

"I think she knows."

"They can never harm her now."

Because of a lack of evidence she is released from prison, but the populace is incensed by her. It's Henry Field (Jeffrey Lynn), a minister from America, who convinces her to go to America to teach in a girls' school in Boston. On the first day, she decides to tell her story to her French class because they, at first, taunt her. Field counsels courage: to teach them patience and tolerance. And so the movie begins.

Litvak directed the two-and-one-half-hour movie with care, care to evoke the proper atmosphere, care with all the actors, care to see that the story was well-told and quite beautifully photographed and care that all the characters were complex and not stereotyped. Even Henriette is not all sweetness and light, but has a purse full of courage (as her landlady says). Davis was in fine hands.

What possessed Davis to make this particular movie? It certainly can easily be discerned that this might have been an Olivia de Havilland vehicle. In the end she signed for perhaps four reasons: 1) she hadn't made a film since she completed *The Private Lives of Elizabeth and Essex* in July 1939; 2) this promised to be the major film of 1940 for Warners, an answer to *Gone with the Wind*; 3) Davis liked the idea of having a major co-star in Charles Boyer; and 4) Davis liked to vary the type of roles she played: queen, socialite, spinster.

Additionally, Davis had just had great success with three costume dramas in a row, and she took pride in her French ancestry.

Jack Warner had spent several weeks ordering/begging her to return from her New England vacation where she had met her second husband-to-be, Arthur Farnsworth. However, she was under suspension. She had needed a substantial break after *Elizabeth* because she had lost a dangerous amount of weight and was on the verge of a nervous breakdown.

All This and Heaven Too wasn't one of Davis' favorite movies, and she was not pleased with Anatole Litvak's style of direction. He planned each scene down to the last detail, which determined the camera position. Unlike William Wyler, who was also meticulous, he did not allow for an actor's interpretation through improvisation, but detailed very movement.

However, his achievement was positive, if not great. He said it was a movie too bogged down in settings and scenery. The positive aspects of the finished production are evident, however, in the extremely well-modulated performances of Boyer and Davis. They respected each other greatly, even though Boyer was apparently going through a personal crisis at the time and wasn't particularly affable or present on the set unless he was required.

Casey Robinson's adaptation of Rachel Field's novel was exceptional. Each and every character was detailed and complex. All the actors had roles which were worth developing. Rachel Field was more than pleased with the final result. In fact, she wrote an unsolicited letter to Jack Warner, thanking him for the care he took in producing it.

Other than Errol Flynn, this was the first time Davis had had a co-star of the magnitude of Boyer, and she appreciated his talent far more than Flynn's.

She had worked with Litvak before, with Flynn as her co-star, on *The Sisters*. So she wasn't unaware of Litvak's style of direction.

Although *All This and Heaven Too* wasn't another *Gone with the Wind*, as Warner had hoped, it was two hours and twenty-three minutes long, allowing for the rich development of the characters, and particularly giving Davis plenty of opportunities to show the full development of Henriette. She was the top female box office draw at the time. The film was nominated for an Academy Award, as was Barbara O'Neil for best supporting actress.

The film appeared at Radio City Music Hall in New York, but because it wasn't in color it never attained the popularity Warner thought it deserved. Also, it didn't have the strong male character personified by Rhett Butler in *GWTW*. This was of much more interest to a female audience.

"Henriette is one of the few impressive tragic figures in modern fiction, and Bette Davis gives her beauty and a plausibility," said *Variety*.[7]

Cast: Henriette Deluzy-Desportes — Bette Davis; Duc de Praslin (Théó) — Charles Boyer; Henry Field — Jeffrey Lynn; Duchesse de Praslin — Barbara O'Neil; Louise — Virginia Weidler; Madame le Maire — Helen Westley; Pasquier — Walter Hampden; Broussais — Henry Daniell; Pierre — Harry Davenport; Charpentier — George Coulouris; Marechal Sebastiani — Montagu Love; Miss Haines — Janet Beecher; Isabelle — June Lockhart; Berthe — Ann Todd; Reynald — Richard Nichols; Abbe Gallard — Fritz Leiber; DeLangle — Ian Keith; Mlle. Maillard — Sibyl Harris; Rebecca Jay — Mary Anderson; Dr. Louis — Edward Fielding; Emily Schuyler — Ann Gillis; Helen Lexington — Peggy Stewart; Gendarme — Victor Kilian; Madame Gauthier — Mrs. Gardner Crane.

Production: Jack L. Warner, Hal Wallis — Producers; Anatole Litvak — Director; David Lewis — Associate Producer; Casey Robinson — Screenwriter; Based on a novel by Rachel Field; Ernest Haller — Cinematographer; Max Steiner — Musical Score; Leo F. Forbstein — Musical Director; Orry-Kelly — Costumes; Carl Jules Weyl — Art Direction; Warren Low — Editor; 1940; Running time — 143 minutes.

Payment on Demand (1951)

Originally titled *The Story of a Divorce*, *Payment on Demand*, filmed in 1949, was Davis' first film after her departure from Warners. She had been apprised of her reputation among Hollywood's population as volatile, temperamental, difficult and unreliable.

It was Howard Hughes' RKO which offered her this production. She was on her best behavior, cooperative and, as always, talented, which shows in her multi-level performance as Joyce Ramsey, a middle-aged woman facing a divorce after twenty years of marriage. Through flashbacks, her young romance with her husband-to-be, David Ramsey (Barry Sullivan), and subsequent initially happy marriage is displayed. Davis' performance was careful, well-modulated and effective.

David divorces Joyce because of her continual social climbing, and because of her seemingly uncaring attitude toward him and his desires. He has taken up with an attractive teacher (Frances Dee).* Joyce is shocked by his action because she believes they have a successful marriage, with two daughters, Martha (Betty Lynn) and Diana (Peggie Castle).

Joyce realizes her drive and ambition are what have alienated David, but because of the adultery she plans to counter-sue unless he agrees to a prop-

---

*Dee played the woman Leslie Howard ends up with in RKO's *1934* Of Human Bondage.

erty settlement and trust funds for their daughters. David tells his lawyer to give her everything she wants.

While waiting for the final decree, Joyce takes a Caribbean cruise and meets Mrs. Hedges (Jane Cowl), a social crony who has been through a middle-aged divorce and now lives on an island, drinking too much and keeping company with much younger men.

On her cruise, Joyce also meets an attractive businessman, Anthony Tunliffe (John Sutton), who is married, with children. She receives a cable from her daughter, Martha, that she intends to marry. Joyce breaks off her relationship with Tunliffe and returns home for the wedding.

At the wedding, she sees David again, who offers to take her home from the reception. At the door of their old house, he asks her if she is willing to give their marriage a second chance. In the original screenplay, she declines emphatically; but months after filming *All About Eve* Howard Hughes called for a rewrite, and the actors had to film the more hopeful ending, much against their wishes. Joyce's reply is that David should think over his request and ask her again later if he still feels the same.

Davis is particularly effective as the young wife who encourages and pushes her husband to succeed in his job. He becomes a successful corporation lawyer and vice-president of a steel company.

As young newlyweds, Joyce and David drop a coin in a wishing well on their honeymoon. Both are glowing with love for each other. A lot was done with lighting, for Davis turned 42 while making this film.

Curtis Bernhardt, who had directed Davis in *A Stolen Life*, helped her give a beautifully restrained performance.

When Joyce goes on her cruise, Davis shows all her concerns and flaws as she sees what has happened to other middle-aged divorcées. With a quiet demeanor, she allows us to see her mind assessing the situation as she views the lonely life of her old friend, Mrs. Hedges.

I first saw this film in February 1951 in Rochester, New York, at what was then called an RKO theater, even though the federal government had caused film companies to divest themselves of their chains of theaters across the country, claiming a monopoly was in existence. Since *Payment on Demand* has yet to be released on videotape or DVD, I've not seen it since. I don't recall it ever being shown on television either, not even on the Turner Classic Movies channel. Recently, some 1930s pre–Code films have been released on DVD and shown on TCM, even some from RKO. So there may be hope that *Payment on Demand* will also one day be available.

At the time of its release, I was a member of the Bette Davis fan club. Members received quarterly publications which provided information from Warners' publicity department. Synopses of her current films were written for the publications. But in this case, the film was released by RKO, and Davis no longer belonged under contract to any one studio. The publicity still of Davis was sent to me as a yearly renewal bonus. The fan club was disbanded after *All About Eve* for the obvious reason that it became a personal expense of Davis' to publish and supply the photos to her fans.

Unfortunately, no real synopsis of *Payment on Demand* was written for the fan publication. There was a magazine at the time called *Screenland* which published screenplays in story form. If it was published in 1951, I never saw it. Therefore, I can only recall from memory my impressions of this film.

Davis as a young Joyce Ramsey in a publicity photograph for *Payment on Demand* (Peter McNally Collection).

Overall, I still admire the film and Davis' performance, but for today's audience it would appear archaic from the standpoint of how divorce is addressed. Today, divorce is not nearly the stigma it was in the 1950s. As the film points out, divorces were not granted overnight, except in places like Reno or Mexico. Even in Nevada, one had to establish residency for a period of six weeks in order to obtain a divorce. New York State, for example, only allowed divorce for the reason of adultery, and even in the 1970s it took two years for a divorce to become final.

The film also depicts Joyce and other divorced women as being unable to carry on a normal, independent life without a husband. Today, society recognizes women in all facets of the workplace and expects them to pursue careers. Not back then. A woman could be a teacher or nurse. But even women teachers had to give up their jobs if they married until after World War II.

So this picture takes on greater significance when viewed from an historical perspective.

Personally, this was a difficult period for Davis because at the time (1949–50) her third marriage to William Grant Sherry was unraveling, and it was not a harmonious time nor an amicable divorce. After she finished *All About Eve*, she received her divorce on July 4, 1950, in Mexico and wed Gary Merrill on July 28, the same day he was granted a divorce from his first wife.

Although Davis received custody of her daughter, she had to pay Sherry some form of alimony to compensate him for the lifestyle he had while married to her. This may sound ludicrous today, but there was some validity to the court's decision. While married to Davis, Sherry, a painter, was prevented from selling his work on the advice of their tax attorney, because if he sold his paintings it would have pushed their joint income into an even higher tax bracket (Davis' annual salary during these last Warners years was over $300,000).

As this movie points out clearly, divorce between two people is not a one-sided issue. If Joyce is willing to forgive David's indiscretion, it will only be because she herself has a clear revelation that her behavior was, in part, the major cause of his adultery. That is not clear at the end of the movie. It is just suggested that David may wish to return to the marriage, not that Joyce has actually changed. Plus, in those long-ago times, adultery was considered unforgivable by most middle-class people in our society.

When filming of *Payment on Demand* (Howard Hughes' choice for a title) was winding down, Davis received the call from Darryl F. Zanuck that changed her life, the offer of *All About Eve*.

At the *Payment on Demand* wrap party the cast and crew gave Davis an ostrich-sized egg on an award pedestal, telling her she had been a "good egg" during production. She had listened to the person at Warners who had warned her about her reputation around Hollywood, and she benefited from his advice.

There was a lasting negative from her reputation at Warners, however. Charles K. Feldman, a producer, came to Davis to ask if she'd be interested in doing the film version of *The Glass Menagerie*. She replied she was too old for Laura. Feldman told her it was the role of Amanda, the mother, that everyone remembers when they see the play. He wanted her for the mother. She agreed that he was right. When Jack Warner got wind of this tentative offer, he absolutely forbade Feldman from allowing Davis on the Warner lot. That's how acrimonious the split had been. It wasn't until 1962 that Warner agreed to publicize and release the Davis/Crawford Seven Arts production of *What Ever Happened to Baby Jane?*

Subsequently, Davis received an offer from David Susskind to play Amanda on TV, but the deal fell through.

"Bette Davis puts forth one of her finest screen efforts," wrote Edwin Shallut in *The Los Angeles Times*. "This is no such flashy performance as she gave in *All About Eve*. It is much finer grained."[8]

Cast: Joyce Ramsey — Bette Davis; David Ramsey — Barry Sullivan; Mrs. Hedges — Jane Cowl; Martha — Betty Lynn; Anthony Tunliffe — John Sutton; Eileen Benson — Frances Dee; Diana — Peggie Castle; Ted Prescott — Otto Kruger; Swanson — Walter Sande; Jim Boland — Richard Anderson; Mrs. Edward Blanton — Natalie Schafer; Mrs. Gates — Katherine Emery; Molly — Lisa Golm.

Production: Jack H. Skirball, Bruce Manning — Producers; Curtis Bernhardt — Director; Leo Tover — Cinematographer; Victor Young — Musical Score; C. Bakaleinikoff — Musical Direction; Edith Head — Miss Davis' costumes; Albert S. D'Agostino and Carroll Clark — Art Direction; Harry Marker — Editor; 1951; Running Time — 91 minutes.

Marked Woman (1937)

Typical in some ways of Warners' ubiquitous crime dramas, *Marked Woman*, written by Robert Rossen, was based on the true-life story of District Attorney Thomas Dewey's assault on "Lucky" Luciano, a crime boss in New York in the 1930s.

Marked Woman was Davis' first film after her abortive departure from Warners to make two pictures in Britain. Sued in British court, Davis lost her case against seven-year contract slavery, and was called a "naughty, overpaid young woman." She lost the battle, but eventually won the war. She was recognized by Warners as their major star. They paid her court expenses and gave her a good script and star treatment.*

Marked Woman is gritty and realistic, and the ending does not have the heroine end up with the D.A. Davis' performance is realistic, knowing and sympathetic, but neither sentimental nor syrupy. "*Marked Woman* gives us Davis as cousin to Blondell and Stanwyck, real Depression grit,"[9] Ethan Morddern remarks in *Movie Star*.

The unique character of *Marked Woman* arises from the solid bonding among the five "hostesses" who work for Johnny Vanning (Eduardo Ciannelli), the crime boss owner of a New York nightclub called Club Intimate, a place for cocktails, dancing, gambling and more. In the first scene, when Vanning takes over the club, he is introduced to the girls who will work for him. He describes his club as a place where out-of-town chumps will come looking for a good time that they can brag about back home. Mary Dwight (Davis) replies, "In other words, a clip joint."

The women room together in a brownstone apartment. They buy their clothes from a salesman who comes to them, also an employee of Vanning's.

---

*Later, Olivia de Havilland challenged the seven-year contract suspension clause and won in U.S. courts.

The gowns are modern 1930s, flashy and pretty — something to attract their clients.

Besides Mary, there is Estelle (Mayo Methot), Emmy Lou (Isabel Jewell), Gabby (Lola Lane), and Florrie (Rosalind Marquis). Their attitude toward their business is that there isn't anywhere else during the Depression they can make the money they're making, which allows them nice clothes. It also enables Mary to finance her younger sister Betty's (Jane Bryan) college education. They live together, trust one another and essentially believe Vanning will protect them from the law. They have no illusions, but Mary tells them she will not be a loser, "Not me, baby, I know all the angles. And I think I'm smart enough to keep one step ahead of them."

Davis had played molls before, tough women, even vicious women, but Mary Dwight is a complex woman, not just a high-priced call girl. She bonds and empathizes with her fellow sex-workers.

Mary is smart. She has a deep love for her sister. She is heartbroken when her sister finds out about her true livelihood, and completely destroyed when her sister is killed. She even shows sympathy for a john who has tried to bounce a check at the nightclub where she works.

D.A. David Graham (Humphrey Bogart) goes to the girls' apartment but is unsuccessful in getting the girls to cooperate in his investigation of Betty's death, even with Mary's pleading. The one eyewitness, Emmy Lou, has been put in hiding by Vanning. Graham threatens them, but it is no use.

Mary shuns the girls and starts to pack to leave when Vanning and his henchman arrive. They've heard of Mary's visit to the D.A. Mary confronts Vanning, asking where Emmy Lou is. He warns her to stay away from Graham. He has his henchman take her to a separate room where she is beaten. Her cheek is cut.

The girls take Mary to the hospital. Graham raids Vanning's club.

Vanning's lawyer warns him that the D.A. is honest and not corruptible. They start to take Emmy Lou elsewhere, but she gets away in the elevator, goes to the basement and is able to escape. She goes to Mary's hospital room, where the other women are with Mary. Mary begs her to help prosecute Vanning. Emmy Lou realizes the future threat to them all and acquiesces to Mary's wishes as do the others. For their own security, they are all placed in jail prior to Vanning's trial.

Vanning's lawyer tells him to plead guilty and throw himself on the mercy of the court, but Vanning refuses. The jury finds Vanning and his henchmen guilty on all four counts. The judge warns Vanning that if any harm comes to the five girls, he will incarcerate him for more than his sentence of 30 to 50 years. Vanning sends word to his killer to lay off.

Left to right, the five "hostesses" in *Marked Woman*: Gabby (Lola Lane), Estelle (Mayo Methot), Mary Dwight (Davis), Emmy Lou (Isabel Jewell), Florrie (Rosalind Marquis) (Photofest).

As they're leaving the courthouse, Graham comes after Mary, asking her where she will go.

"Places. I'll get along ... I always do. We live in different worlds," she tells him. "Goodbye, Graham, I'll be seeing you."

The five women stride off together, arm-in-arm, into the foggy night. Davis shows Mary's different characteristics in some finely delivered acting in significant scenes. Initially she is tough and not intimidated by Vanning when he takes over the Club Intimate. When he makes a remark that Estelle may be too old to continue working for him, Davis moves right in toward him, telling him to give Estelle a chance to prove herself, that it won't cost him anything to do so. Vanning responds favorably to her argument and tries to arrange an intimate meeting with her. However, Mary is too smart to want that connection, and even has the nerve to remind him of what happened to another girl with whom he took up. Vanning is astounded and tells his henchman, "That one is smart."

"Too smart, maybe," the henchman replies.

When Betty, Mary's sister, shows up one morning at the girls' apartment, Davis drops her hardness and expresses her love and happiness at seeing her sister. She carefully reminds her co-workers of their work as "models," and that the reason for the salesman being there is that they're getting ready for a new show. She's protective of Betty, and the other women follow suit.

Mary could be conniving and deceitful, too, when she follows Vanning's orders to dupe the D.A. as to Vanning's involvement in a john's death. Davis acts so sincerely with Bogart that he completely believes her. After crying and behaving in a sympathetic way, she holds a handkerchief up to her mouth. As he turns away, we see a smile on her face. She realizes she has succeeded in her lie.

Later, when the D.A. learns of Betty's death and tells Mary, Davis cries out pitifully. Then when he says he'll help her, she simply cries and places her head on his shoulder and chest. It's all very believable.

Approximately six months before filming *Marked Woman* Davis actually was a marked woman, marked in a lawsuit initiated by her employer, Warner Brothers. She had walked out on her studio and gone to England, via Canada, to do two films abroad, one with Maurice Chavalier. Warners received an injunction against her in the London courts. Subsequently, the judge ruled in Warners' favor. After all, they did have a legal contract with Davis.

All this had been precipitated by Davis' refusal to do a film entitled *God's Country and the Woman*, a lumberjack story. She also had just filmed a loser, *Satan Meets a Lady*. Davis couldn't believe that her Oscar win for 1935's *Dangerous*, and her stellar performance in *Of Human Bondage*, had not led to better scripts, better roles and better directors. She, and even the press, felt she'd never reach her goal of becoming a major actor with the material presently being offered her.

Hence, at age 28, she had the guts to challenge the studio. Her high-powered agent gave Warners a list of ten demands. At first Jack Warner wouldn't even meet with the agent. This was not something new for Warner. He had been confronted earlier by James Cagney with much the same demands. But because he was a man he was treated differently, and differences were resolved with a significant increase in Cagney's salary. He was making thousands of dollars more than Davis.

In the end, of course, Warner did not want to lose a hot property like Davis. So when she returned (as George Arliss, her old mentor, advised her to do), she was finally given the treatment she deserved. Her court costs were paid, she was given better scripts and received star treatment.

Beginning with *Marked Woman*, it all paid off handsomely both for the studio and for Davis. The next three films were A-productions, *Kid Galahad*, *That Certain Woman*, and *It's Love I'm After*, leading to Davis' halcyon years as a star with the release of *Jezebel*. For the next ten years she was the reigning queen at Warner Brothers.

Marked Woman had an excellent script by Robert Rossen (later an excellent director) and Abem Finkel. Warners were still devoted to the gangster film which they had successfully promoted in the early thirties, stories ripped from the headlines, as they say.

Marked Woman used the factual story of New York City District Attorney Thomas E. Dewey, later governor of New York. He, and his office, were largely responsible for the clean-up of criminal gang organization in the city which had been prevalent during prohibition. One of the most notorious criminals was "Lucky" Luciano, upon which the character Vanning is based.

Marked Woman was a first for Humphrey Bogart, because he played the district attorney instead of a crook. Bogart was still a supporting player, featured below the title. It wasn't until 1941 and *The Maltese Falcon* that he became a star. He had actually been in Davis' first film in 1931, *Bad Sister*, which did little for either one of them.

Lloyd Bacon was a contract director who had a long association with crime movies. He knew how to handle action. What was revealing in *Marked Woman* was how well he handled the female actors. More than Vanning, the crime boss, the story really revolves around the hostesses, Davis, Methot, Lane, Jewell and Marquis. Bacon shows their bonding and devotion to one another. Even with their fear of Vanning and what he can do to them, including murder, the women share their feelings, their hopes and their fears.

They disagree with one another and even commit acts which let the others down, but that is done through fear. Given the chance to help the law, they all finally come together to form a solid unit against Vanning. Their solidarity is visibly evident in their words and actions. It is what, in the end, defeats Vanning. He even realizes they can't be intimidated or threatened after he is convicted because the judge will increase his sentence if anything happens to the women.

Davis' role is the catalyst for this unity because it is her younger sister who is killed, but it is that very event which shows the women how vulnerable they are to Vanning's threats.

These complex women realize and accept who they are. There is no happy ending for these women. When Graham questions Mary at the end of the trial about their future, she makes it plain she is not of his class. She joins her "sisters" as they go off into the fog together. It is obvious their lives have been changed forever because they turned state's evidence for the D.A., but they are still who they are. They cannot go out into the daylight of the city and garner legitimate work. Everyone, particularly the underworld, knows who they are. They have no money, no income. What is to become of them is left up to the viewer, but it obviously will be a life of hardship. All they have is each other.

With this film, Davis actually took on a new persona. Compare it with her previous work in films like *Dangerous* and *The Petrified Forest*, two pictures in which she experienced a modicum of success. In *Dangerous*, for which she won her first Oscar, she is an alcoholic, a has-been theater actor. An architect (Franchot Tone) tries to rehabilitate her and sets her on the road to a comeback. Davis' bitchy performance is revelatory of her latent talent, but it is not a mature, modulated performance. It is mostly on a one-note basis — everything played at a highly dramatic, even hysterical level. The script is mundane, the direction worse. It is only the acting between Davis and Tone that is interesting, and even that is not always believable. Davis is still a peroxide blonde with far too many mannerisms.

In *The Petrified Forest* Davis plays an ingénue role as Gaby, an aspiring actor/poet, languishing in her grandfather's desert gas station. It's another of Robert E. Sherwood's polemic plays, distinguished by the Humphrey Bogart reprise of his New York role as Duke Mantee, a gangster on the lam. Here Davis, still a peroxide blonde, has her best scenes with Leslie Howard, her co-star in *Of Human Bondage*. Yet, even in their intimate scenes, Davis is still full of mannerisms, and her voice always seems at one pitch. Her performance is lovely and quiet at times, but it is still waiting for the good scripts and director to come.

Marked Woman gave Davis the concise script she needed and a competent director, along with a well-cast ensemble. She has that "Bette Davis" look, ash-blonde hair, riveting eyes. It is not to say there aren't some lingering mannerisms here, but everything has been modified. One can tell there is a terrifically confident actor here, relishing a well-written role and having a ball acting with her "sisters" and all the other actors, especially Bogart and Jane Bryan, her protégé.

"...Miss Davis has turned in her best performance since... *Of Human Bondage*,"[10] reviewed Frank S. Nugent in *The New York Times*.

"*Marked Woman* gave Davis her first opportunity to use her special alchemy to marry the proletarian, the whore, and the martyr into one person,"[11] observed Bernard F. Dick.

Cast: Mary Dwight — Bette Davis; David Graham — Humphrey Bogart; Johnny Vanning — Eduardo Ciannelli; Betty — Jane Bryan; Gabby — Lola Lane; Emmy Lou — Isabel Jewell; Florrie — Rosalind Marquis; Estelle — Mayo Methot; Charlie Delaney — Ben Welden; Sheldon — Henry O'Neill; Louie — Allen Jenkins; Gordon — John Litel.

Production: Louis Edelman — Producer; Jack L. Warner and Hal B. Wallis — Executive Producers; Lloyd Bacon — Director; Robert Rossen and Abem Finkel — Screenwriters; Seton I. Miller — Additional Dialogue; George Barnes — Cinematographer; Bernhard Kaun and Hein Roemheld — Musical

Score; Leo F. Forbstein — Musical Direction; Harry Warren and Alexis Dubin — Songs; Orry-Kelly — Gowns; Max Parker — Art Director; Jack Killifer — Editor; 1937; Running time — 96 minutes.

Hush ... Hush, Sweet Charlotte (1964)

Hush ... Hush, Sweet Charlotte introduced a hit song by the same title, sung by Al Martino and also recorded by Patti Page. This Gothic melodrama was a cousin to *What Ever Happened to Baby Jane?* but not a sequel, as it was developed from another Henry Farrell story. A much more expensive production, it was to reunite Davis and Crawford. A large photo spread of the co-stars was shot for *Life* magazine in November 1963, but the Kennedy assassination knocked them right off the cover, and the story was never published.

Barely had filming begun in Louisiana when Crawford became "ill" and checked into a hospital. Although she apparently returned, she again was hospitalized, and production shut down until a replacement could be found. Vivien Leigh, among others, turned the role down. Olivia de Havilland, an old compadré of Davis' from their Warners years, returned from Europe to play Charlotte's cousin, Miriam Deering.

Charlotte Hollis (Davis) has written to ask Miriam to come help her fight a state demolition of her home for a highway in Louisiana. Thirty-seven years earlier, Charlotte's married lover, John Mayhew (Bruce Dern), was beheaded, murdered by an unknown assailant. All these years, Charlotte thought, it was her late father (Victor Buono) who had committed the crime. Miriam and Drew Bayliss (Joseph Cotten), a doctor who jilted Miriam after the murder, conspire to drive Charlotte over the edge, to enable Miriam to collect the Hollis fortune. Murder and gore follow.

Surprisingly, when shown, this was the number one movie viewed on TV. Though such popularity stems, perhaps, from the shocks and thrills, *Hush ... Hush, Sweet Charlotte* also offers believable performances from the entire cast. As grotesque as Agnes Moorehead (Charlotte's slovenly housekeeper, Velma Cruther) and Davis look, they perform with total conviction. It is an extremely well-made Gothic thriller, in many respects more complicated than *Baby Jane*.

Davis' performance as Charlotte reveals a complicated woman. The first impression she gives is one of a quiet, lonely woman, living alone in her old family mansion. A group of youngsters approach the house at night, daring, and eventually forcing, one boy to confront Charlotte in her house. They all view her as a crazy old lady who long ago murdered her lover with a cleaver, chopping off his head and hand. Frightened as he is, the boy slowly enters the darkened front door and proceeds to the unlighted library. As he moves around a high wing back chair, he spies a music box. He lifts the lid and a melody begins. The music awakens Charlotte, who's been asleep in the chair. Seeing her frightens the boy, who lunges toward the French doors in order to escape. Charlotte merely looks at him and picks up the music box, uttering her lover's name, "John, John," in a plaintive, sad tone. Outside the house the boys are chanting — a song about Charlotte's long-ago murder of John.

Charlotte awakens in her bed the next morning to the racket of an earthmover machine demolishing a gazebo on her property. Protecting her domain, she rushes to an upstairs balcony with a rifle. She screams at the workmen and tells the foreman to leave. When they continue, Charlotte fires a shot at the machine operator, which hits the rear of the vehicle. She spews a tirade of abuse at the foreman, who tells her he is off to get the sheriff. Velma (Agnes Moorehead), her housekeeper, arrives at the balcony and tries to calm Charlotte.

The foreman discusses the situation with the sheriff (Wesley Addy), who says Charlotte has her moments, but she's not insane. When the sheriff comes to see her, Velma tries to ward him off, but Charlotte appears and recounts how he wouldn't have his job if it weren't for her father's political pull. He takes all her wrath calmly, but forcibly tells her she has ten days to vacate the property.

Davis has shown us a lonely woman, living in the past with her unrequited love for John, but also a woman aware of the political situation which has allowed eminent domain to condemn her property.

When her cousin, Miriam Deering (Olivia de Havilland), arrives to help her, the two reunite in Charlotte's bedroom. Miriam, very sharp looking in her Paris fashion, is a marked contrast to Charlotte's appearance, who's wearing a fuller, not-so-fashionable dress, with her long hair in an unbecoming pony tail of sorts.

Charlotte is thrilled to see Miriam, even though she's a day early. When Miriam moves to start making up Charlotte's bed, Charlotte says, "No, that's Velma's job!" A tiff begins. Finally, Miriam looks over the bed and smiles. Charlotte reciprocates, laughing over the silliness of the issue.

Later that evening, at dinner, they are joined by Drew Bayliss. When Charlotte starts to talk about how Miriam can go to Baton Rouge to fight her eviction, Miriam counters, with Drew's backing, that there isn't anything she can do.

Infuriated, Charlotte asks her why she's here. When Miriam says to help her, Charlotte lets fly her built-up resentment over Miriam and what her father had done for her in years past. She calls Miriam "a vile, silly bitch," as Miriam was responsible for telling Charlotte's father about her and John.

Miriam replies, "How could I know it would end in murder, with John being murdered and butchered?"

Charlotte turns and looks at her father's portrait, saying, "No, you couldn't know that, and that Drew would walk out on you 'cause he couldn't have his fine name linked with ours." Charlotte starts to cry and goes to her room, calling, "John, John."

Angry as she is at Miriam, Charlotte realizes the futility of her situation, but she also reveals she has a tight handle on what happened in the past, and the situation between Drew and Miriam.

Needing someone to trust besides her housekeeper, Charlotte is approached by Mr. Wills, an Englishman and an insurance inspector (Cecil Kellaway) who's in Hollisport to investigate a long-dormant, unclaimed insurance policy involving Jewel Mayhew (Mary Astor), John's wife. He approaches Charlotte as she's placing a bouquet on her father's grave. At first, she starts

Davis and Cecil Kellaway relaxing on the set of *Hush ... Hush, Sweet Charlotte* (Photofest).

to run from him, but his quiet questioning and friendly demeanor calms her down. He tells her she is his favorite mystery. When she asks him if he's ever solved her, he replies she wouldn't be a mystery then, which causes her to laugh.

They go to the veranda for tea, which Velma has provided. Before they've talked much, however, Charlotte sees one of the hired packers holding her music box. She screams at the woman to give it to her. It is her most precious possession.

Davis has again shown Charlotte's rationality in encountering a stranger who is inquisitive but kind, and then how quickly she can turn into a screaming harridan when confronted by a deeply personal threat, the removal of the music box.

Perhaps the most telling scene of this gothic horror is the scene after Charlotte and Miriam have disposed of Drew's supposedly dead body in a swamp. Charlotte is convinced she shot him. Miriam forces her to help dispose of the body. When they return to the house Charlotte is completely distraught. Miriam tells her to go in and go to bed while she puts away the car. Charlotte staggers in and starts to climb the stairs. She breaks down and falls, but remembers Miriam's command to go to bed. She starts crawling up the stairs. The camera moves to show her hand approaching the top step. As her face appears and looks up, she sees a mud-caked man walking toward her, with swamp water dripping from him. Thinking it's Drew, she falls backward, screaming pitiful cries. When she reaches the bottom of the stairs, Miriam is awaiting her. Charlotte's face is full of horror, her mouth agape and eyes crossed and out of focus. Drew and Miriam have succeeded in scaring her into full insanity — or so they believe.

The next night, when they are dressed for dinner and having drinks on the lower veranda, they are unaware that Charlotte has arisen from her bed and is listening to their conversation, their acknowledgement to each other of what they have done to get control of Charlotte's estate. When they embrace, Charlotte has her final revenge by toppling a large stone flower urn from the balcony, which kills them both.

In the final scene, with townspeople gathered around to see Charlotte taken away, Charlotte appears at the front door, serenely dressed in a cape and hat and gloves, carrying her music box. As the door opens and she sees the crowd, she looks at the music box and puts it aside on a table. She is not only leaving the house, she is leaving the past behind her. She is in the present.

When she gets into the back of the car, Mr. Wills hands her a note that Jewel Mayhew had given him to hold until her death. He gives it to Charlotte, telling her she's been waiting for this note for a long time. Charlotte reads it with some surprise, as it reveals that Jewel had killed John, her husband. She turns and waves at Mr. Wills as the car pulls away.

Again working with Robert Aldrich as her director, Davis developed a complex woman, one haunted by her past, her father and her long-lost love. The intrusion of the state, forcing her to leave her life-long home, and the machinations of Drew and Miriam, not only pushes her close to insanity, but enables her to face the truth about her past and the present. Davis plays it very realistically in her reactions to all of the situations. Otherwise, the gothic thrills wouldn't have worked.

One of four films Davis made in 1964, *Hush ... Hush, Sweet Charlotte* underscored her success in *What Ever Happened to Baby Jane?* in 1962. She and Aldrich, the producer-director, reunited for *Charlotte* after their positive experience on the set of *Baby Jane*. During that earlier and quickly produced movie, Aldrich and Davis developed a deep respect for each other.

Charlotte got off to a rocky beginning in Louisiana when co-star, Joan Crawford, caused multiple delays. Finally, the production had to be shut down until replacement Olivia de Havilland accepted the role of Miriam Deering. De Havilland was reluctant to play the role because it was villainous, but she and Aldrich worked out a lighter approach to the character so that the shock of her villainy is that much greater and more treacherous.

Davis had had, over the years, an on-again, off-again friendship with de Havilland. Davis had always made admiring comments about de Havilland and her career. De Havilland probably caused the later rift between them when she appeared at the tribute to Davis in 1977 at the American Film Institute. She was sitting at Davis' table with Robert Wagner and Joe Mankiewicz. When she rose to speak about Davis' career, she said, "...I have been a fan of Bette's since I was a child." Even though only eight years younger than Bette, the implication was that she was far younger. When Davis started making movies in 1931, de Havilland was 15, hardly a child. In fact, de Havilland was 19 in 1935 when Davis (age 27) was making *Dangerous* and de Havilland *A Midsummer Night's Dream*. Davis was not pleased and struck her from a list of speakers for her Lincoln Center honor in 1989.

The two actresses appeared in several Warners films together: *It's Love I'm After*, *The Private Lives of Elizabeth and Essex*, and *In This Our Life*. De Havilland left Warners in 1943 and went on to win Oscars for *To Each His Own* (1946) and *The Heiress* (1949). On *Hush ... Hush, Sweet Charlotte* both actors enjoyed working together, and their performances were exceptionally complementary.

Another co-star, Joseph Cotten, had previously appeared with Davis in 1949's *Beyond the Forest*, and later in the Italian *The Scientific Cardplayer* (1972). In his autobiography, Cotten extolled Davis by saying, "...I defy anyone not to enjoy acting opposite this woman. She is *all* woman." Cotten had a long and important career, making his debut in what is considered by many the best film of all time, *Citizen Kane* (1941), followed by Hitchcock's *Shadow of a Doubt* (1943), *Gaslight* (1944), and Carol Reed's *The Third Man* (1949). He and his wife, Patricia Medina, remained close friends of Davis for years.

A holdover from *Baby Jane* was Victor Buono. In *Charlotte* he played Charlotte's father whom Charlotte believes killed her lover, John Mayhew. Davis loved working with Buono in *Baby Jane* but only had one scene with him here when he confronts, then comforts her in the 1927 portion of the film after she, blood covering the front of her dress, has discovered her dead lover. Buono was a large, imposing figure, making Davis appear even smaller and childlike at her 5' 3" height. His portrait and remembrance haunt Charlotte for the remainder of the gothic thriller, as she continually refers to him as "Daddy."

However, the most intriguing relationship in the film is the one between Davis and Agnes Moorehead. Moorehead received an Academy Award nomination for her supporting role in *Charlotte*. As Velma, she is Charlotte's mainstay. More than her paid housekeeper, Velma tries to protect Charlotte from outsiders and from herself. As a housekeeper, she is certainly lacking in skills. Her idea of cleaning is to slap a dust cloth against a table and call it good. Velma's dress, an off-the-rack housedress with an ill-fitting apron, is unkempt. Her hair is a mess, and her demeanor and walk is slovenly. She is the real threat to any trespasser. She is deeply suspicious of Drew and the newly arrived cousin, Miriam. She openly mocks Miriam's uppity airs.

Velma immediately comes to Charlotte's aid when movers start their destruction of the mansion property. More importantly, she's able to calm Charlotte, even comfort her, when she's delusional, for she can see the cause for Charlotte's distress.

Moorehead and Davis worked well together because they respected each other's talent. Moorehead first came to Hollywood under Orson Welles' aegis when he directed *Citizen Kane*. She played young Kane's mother, who allows him to become a ward to a wealthy man. It's a heartbreaking scene when she has to let go of her son.

The next year Moorehead astounded everyone with her pitiful portrayal of George Amberson Minifer's old maid aunt in *The Magnificent Ambersons*, playing well beyond her age. She later became one of a small group of actors who worked with Charles Laughton studying acting. But she is perhaps most famous for her long-running TV series *Bewitched*.

I first saw Ms. Moorehead, however, along with Charles Laughton, Charles Boyer and Sir Cedric Hardwicke, when they toured the country in George Bernard Shaw's *Don Juan in Hell*, a segment from *Man and Super-*

man. The Drama Quartette, as they were billed, did a "reading" of this work, dressed in evening clothes, with four stools and microphones.

Ms. Moorehead stood out from the males because she was a beautiful woman with flaming red hair, coiffed in a crowning upsweep of hair, and wearing a lovely full evening gown. That was in 1951. They were a phenomenal success across the country in cities, large and small, and on many college campuses.

In 1959, Davis and her then-husband, Gary Merrill, embarked on a similar venture, *The World of Carl Sandburg*, which crisscrossed the country to great ovations and success, particularly in Los Angeles where Davis was once again extolled for her enactment of Sandburg's poetry. By the time the tour had reached New York, however, Merrill had been replaced by Leif Erickson because the Merrills were divorcing. Unfortunately, the chemistry wasn't there between Davis and Erickson. Consequently, the reading was not the success Norman Corwin, the producer, had every right to expect.

It would have been quite something to have seen the theatrical powerhouses Davis and Moorehead together in a worthy movie during their peak years. *Hush ... Hush, Sweet Charlotte* gives us a taste of what could have been.

"Miss Davis ... gives another of her bravura performances [in *Hush ... Hush, Sweet Charlotte*]" concluded Roman Tozzi.[12]

Cast: Charlotte Hollis — Bette Davis: Miriam Deering — Olivia de Havilland; Drew Bayliss — Joseph Cotten; Velma Cruther — Agnes Moorehead; Harry Wills — Cecil Kellaway; Sam Hollis — Victor Buono; Jewel Mayhew — Mary Astor; Sheriff — Wesley Addy; Paul Marchand — William Campbell; John Mayhew — Bruce Dern; Editor — Frank Ferguson; Foreman — George Kennedy; Taxi Driver — Dave Willock.

Production: Robert Aldrich — Producer and Director; Henry Farrell and Lukas Heller — Screenwriters; Based on story by Henry Farrell; Joseph Biroc — Cinematographer; Frank De Vol — Musical Score; Mack David — Lyrics; Al Martino — Title Song; Norma Koch — Costumes; Alex Ruiz — Choreographer; William Glasgow — Art Direction; Michael Luciano — Editor; 1964; Running time — 134 minutes.

Strangers: The Story of a Mother and Daughter (1979)

Playing on Mother's Day, 1979, on CBS, this TV movie, *Strangers: The Story of a Mother and Daughter*, was a triumph for both Davis and her costar, Gena Rowlands.

Winning a Best Leading Actress Emmy for her performance, Davis played a complicated woman, Lucy Mason, a woman at first glad for the return of her daughter, Abigail Mason (Gena Rowlands), after an absence of twenty years. However, Lucy becomes angry when Abigail reveals she has come home because she is about to die from cancer.

In a volatile scene, Abigail is in bed when Lucy attacks her verbally for the nerve she has in expecting Lucy to care for a dying daughter who has neglected her for twenty years. She finds it presumptuous and unforgivable because of the grief she has already suffered during the 20-year absence. She is not about to allow Abigail to get off lightly. Of course, under the circumstances, Abigail cannot reply at all. Lucy has been an independent, self-contained elderly person, taking care of herself without any help from others. She walks to the grocery store and pulls her purchases home in a red wagon; she does her own gardening, working a vegetable patch for her own use. It is only through self-revelation on both their parts that mother and daughter realize even the divisive separation has not loosened their ties of love for one another. Then Lucy is able to see her responsibility and need to care for her dying daughter.

It is interesting that Davis won her Emmy for this particularly modern, gritty role. In it she was able to exhibit her expertness at dealing with up-to-date issues, work in a complementary way with her co-star, Gena Rowlands, and, as always, let herself appear as she thought the character would look. As always, she wanted to be known as an actress, and her talent came through beautifully.

In the Emmy awards arena, she was pitted against an actress she had always admired, Katharine Hepburn. Playing opposite Laurence Olivier, Hepburn was nominated for an old-fashioned romantic tale called *Love Among the Ruins*. Here was Davis challenging herself still, whereas Hepburn was trying to be adorable and playing it safe.

For two years prior to the production of *Strangers*, producers Bob Christiansen and Rick Rosenberg kept pressuring Davis to play the role of Lucy Mason. As changes and modifications were made to the script by Michael De Guzman, Davis became more interested and ultimately accepted. She wished to have either Jane Fonda or Cloris Leachman play her daughter, but when both proved unavailable, she agreed to Gena Rowlands.

A better decision couldn't have been made. Both were excellent actors, and Rowlands had long considered Davis a master thespian. What surprised Rowlands, however, was the fact that Davis was a modern actor, not an old-fashioned one.

Ironically (given the film's subject matter), at the time, both actors were heavy smokers. Reportedly, Davis felt that since it was the daughter who had cancer, it should be the daughter who smokes in the movie. No smoking for Davis!

Davis, in her garden scene, is no glamour queen. This is an elderly woman digging in the dirt, dressed in jeans and wearing a farmer's straw hat. Dirt on her face and gardening gloves on her hands, she is working the earth — growing her food, in her small patch, in order to be self-sustaining, even at her age, an independent soul.

Along comes her long-absent daughter to destroy her orderly existence, her way of living alone. Twenty years of non-communication, twenty years without showing any love. Is it any wonder she's more than skeptical? Yet, underneath she's been living to see her daughter again. She foolishly believes her daughter desires to connect with her mother again after all these years.

Imagine the harrowing discovery when Abigail reveals her encroaching death from cancer. No mother wants to hear that news, least of all an estranged mother who, rightly or wrongly, feels her daughter only wishes to be taken care of in her last days. Much grief and anger must be gotten over before Lucy can feel positively toward Abigail. All the hurt built up over the years has welled up and spilled over. Now she must release the hurt and anger in order to be of use to her dying daughter. The anguish, first displayed in angry tirades, is understandable.

Lucy Mason (Davis), dirty from gardening in *Strangers: The Story of a Mother and Daughter* (Photofest).

All through this mother-daughter love story, Davis shows a full range of emotions through her actions, words and voice. But underlying it all is the determination that she will not let her daughter get away from her again. This is her only chance.

At first, when Davis accosts Rowlands, one is apt to feel pity for Abigail, but in the end one feels pity for Lucy. As the end approaches, they both come to realize that they are lucky to share their lives together, even if it is for only a short while.

Strangers is something of a throwback to *Dark Victory*, where Judith Traherne finally realizes the necessity to face the end of her life with grace, and develops an awareness that she has been useful to her husband. She's had happiness, true happiness, from loving and being a loving person. The circumstances are entirely different in *Strangers*, of course, but the end result is similar. Class does not matter; family and communication do matter.

Strangers came out in 1979, ten years before Davis' own battle with cancer ended. In July 1983, Davis had her mastectomy and suffered a series of strokes. On Mother's Day 1985, less than two years later, Davis' daughter published her memoir about her mother, *My Mother's Keeper*, a book describing the worst attributes of Davis' life. It was relentless in its vicious criticisms of her mother. Davis viewed it as a betrayal. The rift was never healed.

Barbara Sherry Hyman never made an attempt to reconcile with Davis in the four remaining years of her mother's life, a mother who publicly said, "That book was literally as catastrophic to me as the stroke. It was heartbreaking and certainly something that I will never get over. I *worshipped* that girl."

Toward the end of her life Davis was cared for by her personal assistant, Kathryn Sermak, an employee who nursed her throughout her illness to the very end when she died in Paris, France, at the American Hospital. Sermak and Davis' son, Michael W. Merrill, were the only two major recipients of her estate. Merrill had begged his sister not to publish the book, to no avail.

Of Davis' work in *Strangers: The Story of a Mother and Daughter*, critic Gerald Clarke said, "[In] her entire career she has probably never given a better or more poignant performance."[13]

Cast: Lucy Mason — Bette Davis; Abigail Mason — Gena Rowlands; Mr. Meecham — Ford Rainey; Wally Ball — Donald Moffat; Dr. Henry Blodgett — Whit Bissell; Mr. Willis — Royal Dano; Mrs. Brighton — Kate Riehl; Louis Spencer — Krishan Timberlake; Joan Spencer — Renee McDonell; Mildred Sloate — Sally Kemp.

Production: Robert W. Christiansen and Rick Rosenberg — Producers; Milton Katselas — Director; Michael De Guzman — Screenwriter; James Crabe — Photographer; Spencer Deverell — Art Director; Fred Karlin — Music; Millie Moore — Editor; 1979; Running time — 88 minutes.

That Certain Woman (1937)

That Certain Woman was Davis' first film with famous director Edmund Goulding; it helped solidify her star power at Warners. Three films, *Marked Woman*, *That Certain Woman* and *Jezebel*, were the major vehicles, after her return to the studio in 1937, which showcased her ability to play a vast range of women — working class women, prostitutes, mothers or upper middle class and southern aristocracy. "*That Certain Woman* is significant because it reveals Davis' ability to convey strength without becoming overbearing,"[14] commented Bernard F. Dick.

The movie is basically a soap opera, but for its quality performances from Davis, Ian Hunter and Donald Crisp. What makes the film of interest is the iconography of Davis and the total concentration of the director, Edmund L. Goulding, to treat Davis as a glamorous star. Everything is done to make her attractive, from the camera, to lighting, to the costumes. From this and its companion films, it's evident that she was finally on track as Warners' main female star. Even though Henry Fonda receives equal billing in *That Certain Woman*, his role was small, and he was not under contract to Warners. The next time he played opposite Davis was in *Jezebel*, and Davis' name came first and was twice as large as Fonda's in the billing.

Mary Donnell (Davis), a young widow of a gangster, has become the secretary of Lloyd Rogers (Ian Hunter), a married man. She got the job despite the fact that Rogers knew of her past, and over the next few years he has fallen in love with her. However, Mary has become involved with a playboy, Jack Merrick (Fonda), one of Rogers' influential upper class clients. Mary and Jack marry, which infuriates Jack's father (Donald Crisp). When the three meet, the father dismisses her cruelly as unworthy of his son. Jack tries to mollify his father, but does not really stand up for Mary. She is sent away, and the elder Mr. Merrick affects an annulment. Mary refuses to seek out Jack, trusting he will, in time, come to her. Months pass and Mary has a baby, Jack's son. Subsequently she learns Jack has married a childhood sweetheart, Flip (Anita Louise). The newlyweds go to Europe for a honeymoon.

Lloyd Rogers, Mary's boss, comes to love Mary's child and begs her to marry him. He plans to divorce his wife. Before this can occur, however, Lloyd becomes ill. He comes to Mary's apartment, and she tries to get an ambulance to take him home to his wife, but the doctor who arrives says Lloyd is too ill to be moved. His wife (Katherine Alexander) arrives before he dies and is able to hold his hand even though he is crying out for Mary. Unbelievably, the press arrive also and are able to get photographs of Mary and Mrs. Rogers, creating a sensational scandal. Even Mrs. Rogers believes Mary's son may be her husband's offspring. In his will, Rogers leaves Mary and her son extremely well-off.

Meanwhile, on their honeymoon, Jack and Flip have been involved in an auto accident in Europe, which paralyzes Flip. The cause of the accident was Jack's drunken driving. After a few years they return to the U.S. to live.

When Jack learns of Mary's circumstances, he comes to visit her. He sees that her son is his also. He begs her to marry him, even though Flip is his

Jack Merrick (Henry Fonda) pleading with Mary Donnell (Davis) to marry him (Photofest).

responsibility. Mary acquiesces to his wishes. Again, his father interferes and comes to Mary to tell her the family will take his grandson, but Jack will not marry her. Jack arrives in time to tell her he had nothing to do with his father's plan, and he swears he will tell Flip the circumstances and return for Mary and their son.

Flip comes to see Mary later that day and begs Mary to marry Jack because he loves Mary, even though she herself still loves him. Mary can't bring herself to cause such a divorce and tells Jack he must take care of Flip and young Jackie. With her inheritance, Mary goes to live in Europe, away from all her notoriety.

When Flip dies, an emissary from Jack finds Mary and gets Jack on a transatlantic call to speak to Mary, who realizes she still loves him. Thank God for good acting!

In this film Davis transforms her character from a gangster's moll (she married him at thirteen) to a proper, respectable woman. Her language and demeanor, for instance, are strictly working class as she fights off the press in a cemetery where she is putting flowers on her husband's grave. Later, in her role as executive secretary for Rogers, she displays her quick efficiency, her brightness, her resourcefulness, and her ability to meet her boss' demands. She also demonstrates her ladylike behavior in fending off his advances, even though she can tell he really cares for her. She shows genuine surprise and gratefulness when he tells her he hired her in full knowledge of her past, and that she deserved the opportunity.

After her marriage and annulment, Mary throws herself into the care of her growing baby. Mary actually blossoms with love for little Jackie (Dwane Day). When Jack returns to inquire about her after her boss' death, he is ecstatic to have his son and Mary together. As she is dressing little Jackie on the bed, she looks up at Jack with a full, lovely smile, eyes sparkling to see her son and Jack together. Her maternal instincts are beautiful to behold.

Mary's range of emotions gets a complete workout when Flip begs Mary to marry Jack, even though she is crippled and still loves him. Mary, initially ready to fight for Jack, realizes her humanness won't let her behave in such an irresponsible way. From an initial show of anger, her voice and face transform into expressions of sympathy and concern.

In the final scene, Davis is costumed in a long tea gown with a picture hat at a European grand hotel, sitting at a window table for tea. A rubber ball bounces through the open window. She catches it, looks out to see a young boy, smiles and tosses the ball back to him. He expresses his thanks and she smiles at him.

When she turns back to her table, the Merrick emissary, Tilden (Minor Watson), arrives at her table with the news of Flip's death. Mary's face is aglow in close-up as she registers the news. She walks, then runs, losing her hat, then races to answer the transatlantic call. She's in love and at peace with herself.

Mr. Goulding did his job well.

Variety stated, "From start to finish ... she displays screen acting of the highest order."[15]

This movie is a singular example of an insignificant film that is only worth watching because of Davis' performance. Written and directed by Edmund Goulding, it is a reworking of an old Gloria Swanson picture, *The Trespasser*. The soap opera plot is, at times, laughable, but the acting of Davis and company, especially Ian Hunter and Donald Crisp, bring a reality to the situations — just as TV soap operas do.

Many aspects of Davis' performance are worth observing because by this time, 1937, she had really matured as an actor. She had obviously realized her value and worth. Here Warners treated her differently, as a valuable asset, giving her excellent production values and scripts that were tailored to talent. She was no longer expected to play ingénues or participate in really absurd stories. For all the sentimentality of *That Certain Woman*, it was considered an A property, one worthy of a star (as it had been worthy of Gloria Swanson). Goulding was well-regarded as the director of Greta Garbo and many other stars.

Goulding's scriptwriting talent was appreciated by most, and he was known as a top-notch woman's director. Two of Davis' best critical and box office successes, *Dark Victory* and *The Old Maid*, were directed by him. He was slated to direct several other of her films, but was replaced at various times by William Wyler, Irving Rapper and Vincent Sherman. In the case of *The Letter*, Hal B. Wallis and other executives felt he had the wrong slant on the film. It can be conjectured that after *The Great Lie*, Davis, who had input into whom her directors might be, rejected Goulding at times. Goulding's career was sporadic, in all likelihood because he suffered from alcoholism. At one time Davis said, "Mr. Goulding is a genius movie maker, [but] he was also an extraordinarily difficult man.... He did find me difficult...."[16]

In *That Certain Woman*, the focus is definitely on Davis, the star actress, and she delivers. She delivers in several ways. Not only is she presented, photographically, in a beautiful way, but her character is deliberately cast in a sympathetic, positive light throughout the movie.

Whether she is the working class gangster's widow, the working class secretary, the upper middle class divorcée, or the maternal figure, she acquits herself well. There is a point at which she subsumes these characters all into one being. Her character progresses believably throughout her life, changing with her circumstances, adjusting her expectations, and making sacrifices because of her basic desire to be a wife and mother. Davis shows she can play all the stages of this woman's character, and by extension, women of all social classes with all kinds of personalities.

As Mary, her love for Jack trumps all her other feelings. Even when an annulment is brought about by Jack's father, she thinks of Jack first, believing in his underlying worth. When she has her baby, she remains independent, willing to sacrifice rather than force Jack to know the truth.

When her boss, Lloyd Rogers, declares his ongoing love for her and her son, she allows him to persuade her to marry him, necessitating a divorce from his wife. But this is just as much a means of ensuring her son's well-being as her own.

Rogers' subsequent death provides her with an inheritance, but also causes Jack to hear of the news. When he visits Mary, her basic thought is for him to see his son. She even allows him to persuade her to marry him. Again, Mary acquiesces because of her son's welfare. Finally, she reverses her decision, and lets Jack go. Again, Mary's quest for her son's welfare is paramount, as she insists Jack and Flip adopt Jackie. Mary has made the ultimate sacrifice.

Only at the end does she let herself express her undying love for Jack. She has kept that emotion to herself all along, because she put Jack and her son, Jackie, and even Flip ahead of her own wishes and desires.

Today, and even back in 1937, viewers found this utter nonsense. But the point is that, through Davis' skill and conviction, she is completely believable. Her inner emotions flow out through her eyes — her anguish, her resignation, her anger, her overwhelming love for Jackie, and finally her love for Jack and the man he has become.

Goulding encouraged her to play all the facets of Mary. Audiences related to her easily; this kind of role allowed audiences to accept her more dramatic, bitchy roles as well.

After one more comedy, Davis garnered her breakthrough role as a major star in *Jezebel*. *The Marked Woman*, *Kid Galahad*, and *That Certain Woman* were the stepping stones to that mountain peak.

Cast: Mary Donnell — Bette Davis; Jack Merrick — Henry Fonda; Lloyd Rogers — Ian Hunter; Merrick, Sr. — Donald Crisp; Flip Merrick — Anita Louise; Mrs. Rogers — Katherine Alexander; Virgil Whitaker — Hugh O'Connell; Amy — Mary Phillips; Tilden — Minor Watson; Dr. James — Charles Trowbridge; Detective Neely — Sidney Toler; Jackie — Dwane Day.

Production: Hal B. Wallis — Executive Producer; Edmund Goulding — Director; Edmund Goulding — Screenwriter; Ernest Haller — Cinematographer; Max Steiner — Musical Score; Leo F. Forbstein — Musical Director; Max Parker — Art Direction; Orry-Kelly — Gowns; Jack Killifer — Editor; 1937; Running time — 91 minutes.

Mr. Skeffington (1944)

Davis continually referred to *Mr. Skeffington*, even in her autobiography, as *Mrs. Skeffington*. It was "Mr." always and that is the key point of the drama, a romantic look at Fanny's life as a 1900s beauty who ages through the 1930s.

Davis relied on, and gave credit to, technicians — hairdresser, make-up artist and cameraman — for creating the illusion of the beauty she was supposed to be, Fanny Skeffington. They succeed for most of the film. She embodies the differing eras she lives through, the early 1900s, the twenties and thirties. It is after she suffers diphtheria and ages unmercifully that the film falls apart.

Imposing her will on the director, Davis submitted herself to drastic make-up for her aging, and her voice quality, along with far too much grotesque make-up around her eyes and mouth, is not believable. Fanny Skeffington was a totally vain woman who would never have appeared in such horrendous make-up. Even Davis' director, Vincent Sherman, was taken aback when she appeared on the set, but he could not or would not induce her to tone down the garish look.

Jerry Vermilye, in *Bette Davis*, opines, "Her gradual maturation and decline remain a monument ... to the acting art.... She also displays an amazing range, with speech patterns spanning the light frivolity of a young debutante to the low, whiskey-soaked tones of aged dissipation."[17]

Another factor which affected Davis' performance in the movie was the recent mysterious death of her second husband, Arthur Farnsworth. There had even been an inquest. Some biographical information has even implicated Davis in his death. Consequently, she was depressed and nearly impossible to work with on the set, very demanding and temperamental. Toward the end of filming she acknowledged her bitchiness to her director, Vincent Sherman, and then proceeded to have an affair with him.

As a result of this movie, Davis again garnered an Oscar nomination. Regardless of its faults, this is a film to watch to see how Davis could be completely technical and superficial in a performance, when allowed to be, by her so undemanding director.

In *From Reverence to Rape*, Molly Haskell states:

> The super female is a woman who, while exceedingly "feminine" and flirtatious, is too ambitious and intelligent for the docile role society has decreed she play.... She remains within traditional society, but having no worthwhile project for her creative energies, turns them onto the only available material — the people around her — with demonic results.[18]

Chief examples of this "super female" are essayed by Bette Davis in *Of Human Bondage*, *Jezebel*, *The Little Foxes*, *Dark Victory* and *Mr. Skeffington*. Of *Mr. Skeffington*, Edwin Schallert states, "...[Davis] attains as definite a characterization as she has ever proffered."[19]

In 1914, Fanny (Davis) and her brother Trippy Trellis (Richard Waring) are about to grace a dinner party at their Gramercy Park house for all of Fanny's suitors. Three men arrive early in order to see Fanny alone before the dinner. Also arriving is Job Skeffington (Claude Rains), who wishes to speak to Trippy about another matter (Trippy's infractions at Skeffington's stock brokerage firm). Trippy refuses to see him, but Fanny and her cousin, George (Walter Abel), meet with Skeffington in the study prior to dinner. Trippy has embezzled over $20,000 from the firm. Both Fanny and George are shocked, but Fanny believes she has charmed Skeffington when he says he won't see the district attorney immediately.

When Skeffington doesn't send flowers the next day, as Fanny expects, she goes to his Wall Street firm. While there, World War I breaks out and sends the office into a panic.

Soon thereafter, Skeffington commissions a portrait of Fanny. When it is completed, she follows the delivery of the portrait to learn it is Skeffington's. Shortly thereafter, Skeffington and Fanny elope to New Jersey. When they return to the city, Fanny's suitors are there to greet them, still believing themselves protectors of Fanny. Worse, Trippy arrives home drunk and is insulting to Skeffington. When Fanny tries to calm him the next day, Trippy leaves to join the fight against Germany.

Watching a newsreel at home, George and Fanny see that Trippy is part of the Lafayette Escadrille. Fanny faints, but only because she is pregnant.

Then occurs one of Davis' best scenes in the film. Ensconced in bed in the dark, Fanny allows Job to see her, and finally turns on the bedside lamp so he can greet the expectant mother. Job tells her how beautiful she is. Her response is quick as she views herself in a hand mirror: "No, a woman is beautiful if she gets eight hours of sleep a night, visits the beauty parlor every day, and yes, bone structure has a lot to do with it."

All the while she lies languorously in bed, completely made up, in a beautiful negligee, amid exquisite bed linens and pillows. She opens her arms to Job only to allow him to kiss her on the cheek. Before a sedative takes effect, she manages to get Job's promise to let her go to California with cousin George for the birth, so her friends won't see her all swollen.

This is a vain, completely self-centered woman who manages to be fond of her Jewish husband, who has saved her and her brother from financial ruin. Yet, she still maintains her raft of suitors who want to save her from her seemingly selfless husband, Job, who tells George he is a very patient man. Both Job and George serve with the armed service in World War I, but it is Trippy's death that sends Fanny into hysterics. For she only married Job to save Trippy from financial scandal and ruin.

After the war, Fanny takes up with all kinds of new suitors, even a well-known gangster who wants to marry her. He exposes Job's philandering with his secretaries. When Fanny discovers this, she divorces Job and receives a more than generous settlement. Job decides to move to Europe and, at Fanny's suggestion, takes his daughter, young Fanny, with him to be schooled in Switzerland.

During the late '30s, young Fanny (Marjorie Riordan), now a grown woman, comes home because of the encroachment of the Nazis, but Job remains in Berlin.

The elder Fanny is having a romantic relationship with a much younger man, Johnny Mitchell (his actual name). Young Fanny arrives just in time to meet him before her mother and he go for a sail on Long Island Sound. Fanny ends up getting soaked and developing a severe case of diphtheria, from which she almost dies.

When Fanny does recover, it requires weeks of convalescence before she

Jeb Skeffington (Claude Rains) patiently wishing Fanny (Davis), his wife, well after her pregnancy announcement in *Mr. Skeffington* (Photofest).

comes home. The illness has caused her to lose some of her hair, and has aged her well beyond her years. She is devastated and even has hallucinations in which Job appears to her. In the interim, young Fanny and Johnny have decided to wed.

A psychiatrist tells Fanny to accept her age and go back to her husband, who is the only one who still loves her. Determined to prove him wrong, Fanny invites her old beaus and their wives to dinner. Heavily made up, and with her false curls, Fanny is not, all the men realize, the beauty she once was. Even Fanny admits to herself that she saw the disappointed looks upon their faces.

Her cousin, George, comes to her with an earnest request that she visit her former husband, who has escaped from a Nazi concentration camp. She resists his request, thinking only of how she now looks, but George convinces her she has to do it, most especially for herself. He has brought Job to the house.

With much self-doubt, she enters the study and calls out his name. There is complete silence, until finally Job rises from his chair to cross to her. Because he is blind, he falls over a footstool. Fanny rushes to his side, seemingly feeling love and concern for him. She and George help him up, and Fanny tells Manby, her maid (Dorothy Peterson), that Mr. Skeffington has come home. Fanny knows she will always remain beautiful to him.

Never having considered herself, nor been considered, a beauty in the Hollywood sense of the word (à la Garbo or Dietrich), Davis had been able to project a sense of beauty in many of her pictures, particularly from 1937 through 1950. Early on in her career she certainly was attractive in such roles as the southern seductress of *Cabin in the Cotton*, and in *The Petrified Forest*. But it wasn't until *That Certain Woman* that she was actually given a suitable glamorous treatment. She was certainly beautiful in *Jezebel, Juarez, Dark Victory* and *Now, Voyager*.

In *Mr. Skeffington*, Davis had to be a young Gibson girl beauty, and remains attractive through her metamorphosis in the twenties and thirties. Davis achieved this not through physical looks alone, but through her demeanor, voice, and the help of costumer Orry-Kelly and the hair stylist and make-up man. Her director, Vincent Sherman, saw to it that she was presented brilliantly. This makes her devastation when she loses her looks through diphtheria all the more complete.

Fanny assesses herself after her illness with a hand-held mirror. She looks like a little old lady against her pillowed bed — her hair partially gone, eyebrowless, her little mouth and eyes sunken in her head. It mirrors how she looked as a young expectant mother in the 1910s. The contrast is startling. But then, so is the make-up and wig she masks herself with. Everything is too much; it's double the amount of make-up needed, and topped by a wig with far too many curls. Even these cannot hide the deep lines in her face. The physical loveliness is gone, replaced by a grotesque mask.

Davis was never afraid to do whatever was necessary to physically show a character, but it isn't the physicality that personifies her talent in this role.

It is the inner character she allows us to see and hear that matters, and she successfully projects Fanny in all her stages.

In marked contrast are the two bedroom scenes. In the first, she is still a young beauty, assessing her looks via a hand-held mirror now that she is pregnant. She is petulant, yet coquettish, with her husband, knowing he loves her enough to allow her what she wants — a trip to California for confinement and the birth. Her voice practically purrs as she inveigles Job to grant her request, and she looks luscious in the boudoir surroundings.

Years later, in her bed after her bout with diphtheria, no one is at her side. She is alone, viewing the remains of her once beautiful face. Her voice is high-pitched, whiny and tired sounding as she complains to Manby. As much as she is self-deprecating, she is longing for someone, anyone, to find her attractive. Davis' face reflects fear: fear of age, fear of being alone, fear that her self-love will not be enough to live with and for. She is completely frightened to give of herself to anyone. She asks Manby not to leave her. Only her cousin, George, dares to tell her of her need to love and care for someone besides herself.

But this is not a stupid woman — vain, but not heartless. When she sees Job, she sees her role in life is to be a loving caretaker, which she knows will reward her with Job's undying love.

Davis was able to show the complete persona of Fanny, her self-absorption and her denial of reality, yet her ability to fight for change and the protection of her brother; her flirtations with her many suitors, yet her charming rejection of them all. She realizes she has taken Job for granted, yet felt guilty about her non-responsiveness towards him. Finally, she shows a Fanny willing to grow and change as an older, unattractive woman.

Mr. Skeffington was not a picture Davis wanted to make for several reasons. She was 35 at the time and probably did not feel she could impersonate a young beauty. She had no empathy for a character she regarded as useless. She had just been through a disturbing period of her life. Her second husband, Arthur Farnsworth, had died mysteriously on August 25, 1943. Davis made costume tests on March 1, August 19 and then on September 22. Shooting started on October 11. She had basically taken no time off for the grieving process and, in addition, had had to go through a legal inquest as to the nature of Farnsworth's death.

One would hardly expect her mental health to be serene at this point. The picture went way over schedule (59 days), and was completed on February 21, 1944. It had been eight months since she had finished *Old Acquaintance*, an inordinate amount of time for an actor of her stature to be off the screen.

Truth be told, Warners were having a difficult time finding what they considered suitable material for Davis. Hal Wallis, who had provided her with her wonderful movies for years, was gone from Warners, having developed his own production company. The screenplays that came to Warners were less and less suitable for Davis. She made the mistake of turning down *Mildred Pierce* in 1945 in favor of *The Corn Is Green*.

At one point in this slow-moving production, Davis suggested Warner should release her from her newly negotiated contract, which provided her with a top salary and provision for only two pictures a year. It would probably have been profitable for her to obtain a release since she was still box office and young enough to receive some terrific offers from both Broadway and Hollywood (i.e. *A Streetcar Named Desire*).

Mr. Skeffington, however, offered a well-written script by the Epstein brothers. They were also the producers. Both they and Jack Warner became concerned when the production moved so slowly and it was reported that Davis was, in fact, changing their script. In essence, Davis, with director Sherman's consent, was discussing and "directing" not only her scenes but scenes in which she did not appear. It became so troublesome that the Epstein brothers actually left the production.

Davis, as she always did, insisted she only wanted the project to be as perfect as possible. However, some of her artistic choices upset even the director, namely, her use of a high-pitched voice for the younger Fanny, and her grotesque latex rubber mask for the aged Fanny.

When the production was finally completed, Davis attended a screening, and was relieved to find it better than she expected. Warner himself was pleased with the result and its reception. Davis was even nominated for an Oscar.

One can rest assured she delighted in working with Claude Rains, her favorite actor. And during the latter part of the filming, she became less demanding and temperamental because she was having an affair with the director.

At this time also, Davis was spending a great deal of time at the Hollywood Canteen, of which she and John Garfield were the founders. This was a place for U.S. servicemen to meet and mingle with Hollywood stars during World War II.

With *Mr. Skeffington* finished, Davis recalled she developed a certain respect for the kind of woman she played. She received many letters from female fans stating that the woman she depicted realistically represented their experiences regarding what happens to formerly beautiful women when they mature and lose their looks. America has always placed a premium on the beautiful woman, and Hollywood was a major promoter of this trend. Especially in Davis' day, a woman past forty, or one who had physically aged even before forty, virtually lost her career. In everyday life, men divorced older wives to marry younger wives, what we today would call trophy wives. In fact, today it is worse than ever, as our culture worships youth, particularly young women. Even with the advancement of the feminist movement and equality in all aspects for women, the attention to youth and the desire to look youthful via plastic surgery is astonishing.

Davis' career was a remarkable exception to the norm for women, but even she had difficulty finding roles as she got older. When she was seventy, she finally had a face lift because, as she said, she wanted to keep working; it was necessary in order to get jobs. She was a talent who gave some memorable performances when she grew older.

In *Mr. Skeffington* she had to build a performance around a vain, self-centered woman who ultimately can be viewed sympathetically. It was a difficult task. Beautiful women are forgiven much because of their beauty. Davis was able to create that aura, but she had to go beyond this to garner sympathy for the older woman who had fully abandoned motherhood and her husband — not an easy task. Through sheer will she allowed the viewer to experience the torture she felt as she realized how empty her life had become. She was saved from herself only by her final realization that she could and would become a caretaker of her damaged husband, Job.

This was not a very profound lesson for wartime America 1944, but the film still resonated with women, and there was the oblique references to Job's torture in Nazi Germany before he escaped and returned to New York. Basically, he is penniless, and Fanny claims she's no longer well-to-do. So their future is uncertain, at best.

Anthony Lane, in *The New Yorker*, stated, "There is no more sumptuous example of the Warner Brothers melodrama than *Mr. Skeffington*.... Bette Davis as Fanny [is] loud, brittle and precious, like fluorescent Ming porcelain.... Rains vs. Davis: it's a great match of opposition, and the final scene is rightly and movingly, an honorable tie."[20]

Cast: Fanny Trellis Skeffington — Bette Davis; Job Skeffington — Claude Rains; George Trellis — Walter Abel; Dr. Byles — George Coulouris; Trippy Trellis — Richard Waring; Fanny Skeffington — Marjorie Riorden; McMahon — Robert Shayne; Jim Conderley — John Alexander; Edward Morrison — Jerome Cowan; Johnny Mitchell — Johnny Mitchell; Manby — Dorothy Peterson; Chester Forbish — Peter Whitney; Bill Thatcher — Bill Kennedy.

Production: Philip G. and Julius J. Epstein — Producers; Vincent Sherman — Director; Philip G. and Julius J. Epstein — Screenplay; "Elizabeth" — based on her story; Ernest Haller — Cinematographer; Franz Waxman — Musical Score; Leo F. Forbstein — Musical Director; Orry-Kelly — Costumes; Robert Haas — Art director; Ralph Dawson — Editor; 1944; Running time — 145 minutes.

The Sisters (1938)

The Sisters exemplifies Davis' submission to the star system. She received second billing below Warner Brothers' top movie star, Errol Flynn, in this movie, which follows the lives of the three Elliott sisters (Anita Louise, Jane Bryan and Davis). Louise Elliott (Davis), the eldest, elopes with Frank Medlin (Flynn), a San Francisco newspaper reporter. The movie basically revolves around their relationship, but does not neglect the lives of the other two sisters.

Medlin is a temperamental and, at times, irresponsible reporter. He takes his frustrations out on Louise and drinks to excess. Louise becomes pregnant. With the stress and turmoil of her marriage, she suffers a miscarriage. Medlin blames himself for his tortuous behavior with Louise. Medlin approaches his boss for a raise, but becomes verbally abusive when his boss refuses his request. His boss then fires him. Louise insists she will get a job in a department store to help out. Medlin finds this extremely demeaning because he believes it is he who should be the breadwinner. Things get so bad that his newspaper friend, Tim Hazelton (Donald Crisp), tells him that no one will hire him in San Francisco because of his volatile behavior.

Rather than confide in Louise, who would certainly have been willing to move to another town, and who continues to encourage him to write his book, Medlin, having hit bottom, feels he needs his freedom, his freedom for adventure. He leaves a note for Louise and signs on as a deck hand on a ship headed to the Orient.

Louise sees his note and searches the waterfront to try and catch him before his ship sails at midnight. She is thwarted by the law, who picks her up and takes her home to verify the truth of her story. The ship sails at midnight, just shortly before the 1906 earthquake hits San Francisco. Shipmates and the captain have to restrain Medlin from jumping overboard, as he's frantic to get to shore and Louise.

During the two years that pass, Louise becomes an officious executive secretary for the department store owner, William Benson (Ian Hunter). She continues to maintain her belief that Medlin will return to her.

Louise is called home because her youngest sister, Grace's (Jane Bryan), husband is having an affair. Their third sister, Helen (Anita Louise), also arrives to help. Even Louise's boss, Benson, shows up with support because he loves Louise and wants her to marry him. The whole Elliott family goes to a rally/dance for William Howard Taft, the presidential candidate.

Meanwhile, Medlin's old chum, Tim Hazelton, has discovered that Medlin is back in San Francisco looking for Louise. He brings him to the rally and advises Louise to go to the mezzanine to see him. Still in love with

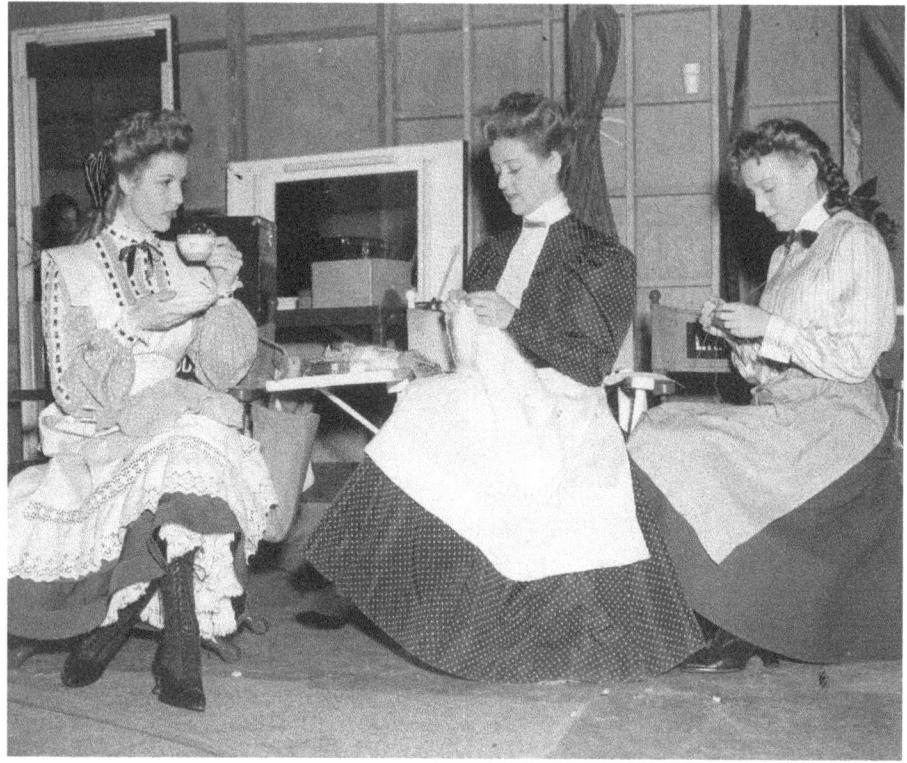

Anita Louise, Davis and Jane Bryan relaxing on the set of *The Sisters* (Photofest).

him, she races up the stairs. He begs her forgiveness, saying that she is the only reason for his whole life. She asks *his* forgiveness for not allowing him to be who he was. They reconcile. Louise goes down to the ballroom to share the news with her sisters. The three of them together, arms locked, smiling, look up to Medlin. They are still the Elliott sisters.

Davis and her two co-stars, the sisters, add believability to this costume drama, as does the historical detail. Davis expresses familial love as well as deep emotion for her wayward husband. She remains resolute and very attractive in love. One reason for the superiority of her performance is Anatole Litvak's masterful direction, a man she respected and with whom she later had an affair.

Davis gives a subtle, quiet performance. There are no histrionics, just a steadfast resolve in her love for her parents (delightfully played by Beulah Bondi and Henry Travers) and for her sisters.

The most touching scene comes when she and Medlin argue over Louise's desire to help by getting a job. Medlin is the upset emotional counterpoint to Davis' quiet certitude. She's determined to be responsible, and resolute in her decision, seeing the need for them to work together equally. She makes her point precisely because she is calm, honest and caring; she is an adult trying to deal with a family issue in a mature, supportive manner.

One also gets to watch Davis do something at which she was an expert. It comes during the scene in which she suffers through the earthquake. Not a word of dialog is spoken. Davis simply reacts to the situation with a determination to survive. In fact, she becomes the comfort and support for an hysterical neighbor, Flora Gibbon (Lee Patrick).

Of her work in *The Sisters*, the *Hollywood Reporter* asserted, "Bette Davis adds still another triumph to her already long list of screen achievements.... Her acting is a joy."[21]

With the triumph of *Jezebel*, Davis honestly expected better scripts to follow. Between the completion of *Jezebel* in January 1938 and the beginning of *The Sisters* in July, Davis turned down what she honestly felt was inferior material. Consequently, she was put on suspension, and drew no salary. *The Sisters* appeared to be better than most scripts she had been offered, even though she was reluctant to accept it. She needed her salary, however, and signed on.

William Dieterle was first assigned to direct, but he balked. Finally, Anatole Litvak was signed. At the time, he was Miriam Hopkins' husband. Hopkins, of course, would become Davis' nemesis in *The Old Maid* and *Old Acquaintance*.

When Errol Flynn was given the part of Medlin, Davis was not pleased, for she didn't have much regard for him as an actor. His signing also caused another problem, one of billing. At the time, he was Warners' biggest star. Flynn was originally to be listed alone above the title which would make for rather odd billing: "Errol Flynn in *The Sisters*." Even with Davis' major success in *Jezebel*, she still didn't have the box office clout of Flynn. A "compromise" was reached and both were listed above the title.

It was Flynn's first straight dramatic role, and he was unsure of his ability to handle it. In fact, repeated takes were often needed when he couldn't remember his lines. As it turned out, however, Davis and Flynn played well together, even if there really was no bond between them.

While their story was the main focus of the movie, the script was full enough to give the audience the value of the other two sisters, Helen and Grace, and their stories (though not in as great detail). As a matter of fact, the central key to this film is the basic study of family and what it means. How the sisters react to each other, and the influence of their parents on each of their lives, is important. They are a close-knit, happy, functioning family. The story gives truth to the notion that happy families are all alike, whereas dysfunctional families are all unique.

In Ned (Henry Travers) and Rose (Beulah Bondi) we have loving, concerned parents. They value each individual daughter and treat each with respect. They give them the freedom to live their lives, even though they certainly have misgivings about their daughters' choices in men.

The daughters make mistakes, but they are grounded women who make their own decisions. When they realize one of the other two may be experiencing marital trouble, they rally together and rely on each other to help solve the personal problems.

Frank and Louise marry after having known each other for only a week when he, as a reporter, is in her hometown to write about the presidential inauguration of Teddy Roosevelt in 1904. With many misgivings, the Elliotts allow Louise to marry. The couple leave Silver Bow, Montana, for San Francisco.

In their big scene with her parents, Davis shows both her sudden overwhelming love for Medlin, and, just as important, her respect and love for her supportive parents. They think she is the most level-headed of their girls. However, it soon becomes evident that Louise and Frank have some problems to work out. Frank is a headstrong young man with a temperament. He's not at all used to being a responsible husband. Louise is a mature young woman, but not really prepared for a marriage where the living is not easy, and where there are financial problems. She also failed to make allowances for Frank's independent nature. He has a lot of maturing to do. Their scenes together are ones of conflict, and both Davis and Flynn express their characters' personalities well. The viewer can easily identify with their emotional and financial struggles.

When Louise takes a job at a department store, Frank feels his inadequacy as a provider more than ever. In his immaturity, plus the social milieu of the times (1904–1910), he cannot respond to Louise as an equal life partner, but feels demeaned by her employment. The fact that she does so well in her job causes him to feel his failure even more sharply when he is fired and unable to gain employment in journalism in the city because of his volatile reputation. His way of solving the problem is to escape, to run off from the too-good Louise and go to sea — a masculine solution, even to the point of abandoning her rather than staying and causing her more trouble and pain.

Surprising to people today is the fact that Louise didn't divorce him and accept the love offered by her department store employer, William Benson (Ian Hunter). Contrary to current myth, people did get divorced in the early twentieth century for reasons of adultery or drunkenness. Divorcées were referred to as "grass widows."

Interestingly, Louise chooses to stay in San Francisco; she does not return to her parents. She is a competent, independent woman. But she does keep in touch with her parents and with her sisters' lives.

When Grace's marriage runs into trouble, Louise and Helen return to Montana to discover Grace's husband is being seduced by a townswoman, whom they "convince" to leave town forever.

Helen has married for wealth, not love, but all does not go smoothly. When her husband dies, an Englishman who's loved her for years comes to marry her. Her sisters and parents are there to support her when she comes home with her tale of love.

Throughout the ten-year period, the bond of the family is shown over and over again to be of the most value to any one person. Even Louise is rewarded for her resolve about Frank. With the help of his old friend, Frank seeks out Louise, realizing her love is the most important part of his life. Just as important, Louise offers her apologies for not recognizing his needs; families must do that to be happy. Respect for each other is non-negotiable.

As Bernard F. Dick expounds in *Dark Victory*:

> *The Sisters* was the bridge between her triumph over an epidemic (*Jezebel*) and her victory over death (*Dark Victory*).... There are two lines in *The Sisters*— both oxymoronic, both spoken by Errol Flynn — that define the Davis woman in terms of a paradox; a hidden harmony, to use the title of Cavaradossi's first aria in *Tosca*, "Recondita armonia." The lines are: "You have a very exciting serenity" and "There is a quiet assurance about you, Louise."[22]

Unwittingly, Flynn summed it all up.

Cast: Frank Medlin — Errol Flynn; Louise Elliott — Bette Davis; Helen Elliott — Anita Louise; William Benson — Ian Hunter; Tim Hazelton — Donald Crisp; Rose Elliott — Beulah Bondi; Grace Elliott — Jane Bryan; Sam Johnson — Alan Hale; Tom Knivel — Dick Foran; Ned Elliott — Henry Travers; Norman French — Patric Knowles.

Production: Hal B. Wallis — Producer; David Lewis — Associate Producer; Anatole Litvak — Director; Milton Krims — Screenwriter; Myron Brinig — Based on his book; Tony Gaudio — Cinematographer; Max Steiner — Musical Score; Leo F. Forbstein — Musical Director; Carl Jules Weyl — Art Director; Orry-Kelly — Costumes; Warren Low — Editor; 1938; Running time — 95 minutes.

The Man Who Came to Dinner (1941)

Davis shows another side of her acting ability in *The Man Who Came to Dinner*, as acknowledged by Charles Affron: "Watching Davis as she subordinates herself to other stars in *The Man Who Came to Dinner*..., we are

Monty Woolley and Davis on the set of *The Man Who Came to Dinner* (Photofest).

attuned to acting as a prodigious feat even when the actress is underplaying with exquisite restraint."[23]

A joyous, raucous comedy (witty, funny, even with some slapstick), the play was a great Broadway hit, one which still gets major revivals. Although Davis' role of Maggie Cutler, Sheridan Whiteside's (Monty Woolley) secretary, is beefed up for the movie, she still plays a secondary character; and she handles the role expertly. She is a part of the ensemble which revolves around Whiteside.

At this time Davis had her pick of roles at Warner Brothers and had just come off a loan-out to Sam Goldwyn for *The Little Foxes*. She went for comedy. In *The Man Who Came to Dinner* Davis received top billing for a minor role. She also had some say on who would play the lead. She wanted John Barrymore, and even secured a test for him. But he was so far gone at this point in his career that he not only couldn't remember lines, he couldn't even use cue cards. Luckily, in the finished film one gets to see Monty Woolley repeat his stage characterization, but he surely knows he wasn't Davis' choice, which is too bad. The reason to watch *The Man Who Came to Dinner* is not only to see Davis do comedy, but to see how a major Broadway hit was successfully transferred to the screen. It still holds up, even though there are specific references to theatrical personages no longer in the public consciousness. The characters are well-written and excellently performed; just seeing Jimmy Durante is enough, let alone the wonderful character actress Mary Wickes (as Whiteside's nurse, Miss Preen) in her first screen role.

Whiteside, an acerbic theater critic and radio personality, based on Alexander Woollcott, a prominent critic of the 1930s and 1940s, is the center of this hilarious comedy, around which everything and everyone revolves. George S. Kaufman and Moss Hart wrote a play which skewers all types of theatrical personalities, as well as satirizing Midwestern American life. The Epstein brothers, Julius and Philip, reworked the play for the screen, doing a masterful job.

Maggie Cutler (Davis) is Sherry Whiteside's major domo. For the most part, she is the one who keeps things on target, and softens his insults against unsophisticated Midwesterners.

Visiting an Ohio town for a speaking engagement at a local woman's club just before Christmas, Sherry slips on the icy steps of his host's house and falls, causing him to be ensconced in the Stanley (Billie Burke and Grant Mitchell) home for recuperation. Of course, Sherry takes over the household, even charming the butler and cook, who find him to be a lovely person. Myriad plot lines emerge concerning the Stanley family and Sherry's famous theatrical friends who visit him. The characters are based on such celebrities of the time as Gertrude Lawrence, Noël Coward, and Harpo Marx.

Maggie falls for a local newspaper reporter/owner, Bert Jefferson (Richard Travis), who has written a superb play. Sherry proceeds to do whatever it takes to break up the relationship because he selfishly does not want to lose his efficient secretary.

Samples of the outrageous comedy include the delivery of four penguins for Sherry—with which the nurse, Miss Preen, has to deal; the arrival of Banjo (Jimmy Durante)—who immediately pursues the nurse; the Christmas Boys' Choir singing for Sherry's live Christmas Eve broadcast from the Stanley home; and the mysterious, elderly sister of Mr. Stanley, who keeps speaking privately to Sherry. She gives him a small, framed portrait of herself as a twenty-year-old. Her image haunts Sherry's memory until he finally realizes she is the axe-murderer of long ago, "Lizzie Borden—who gave her father forty whacks and when she was done, gave her mother forty-one."

Throughout all this, Davis shows she can handle comedy well. She plays in the straight fashion required by the role, essentially only reacting to the other characters' outrageous behavior, and enjoying the humor of fellow actors, especially Reginald Gardiner (Beverly Carlton) as he impersonates a "Lord Bottomly" who is supposedly enamored of Lorraine Sheldon (Ann Sheridan). Davis loved working with Jimmy Durante, a hopeless actor but a very funny person.

Davis is the romantic interest in this movie. She plays it with understated feeling, reacting with humor and love for Bert, and with true hurt and anger toward Sherry when she learns what he has done to try to break up her romance.

Davis' other attempts at comedy were basically thwarted by poor scripts, and heavy-handed direction (i.e. *It's Love I'm After*, *The Bride Came C.O.D.* and *June Bride*). It was only in one of her best pictures, *All About Eve*, that a superior script and a superior director allowed her comedic skills to shine.

William Keighley, the director of *The Man Who Came to Dinner*, kept the mélange of characters constantly on the move, and the interaction was terrific. The film's major weakness, however, is the dated material. Only a theatrical "historian" can appreciate the character references and inside jokes (i.e. Lana Turner's sweater; the significance of all those no-longer-prominent personalities: Coward, Katherine Cornell, Gertrude Lawrence; and "Cream of Mush"). Otherwise, one misses some of the humor.

One of the funniest sequences involves Jimmy Durante, Ann Sheridan and Davis. Lorraine Sheldon (Sheridan), a famous Broadway star, at Sherry's request, has read Bert Jefferson's (Richard Travis) play. Sherry tells her it is a play Katherine Cornell would give her eyeteeth to perform in. Lorraine had Bert read the play to her in her hotel room, and in the process has beguiled him. Maggie sees that she has lost her love because of Sherry's interference. She explains the situation to her friend, Banjo (Durante), a Hollywood comic. Lorraine appears on the scene to see Sherry and thank him for the opportunity. Sherry is in the dining room doing his Christmas Eve radio broadcast. Lorraine is extolling Bert's play to Banjo and Maggie. Being the overly dramatic star she is, she can't resist opening a large Egyptian sarcophagus (which arrived for Sherry as a Christmas gift and now resides in the Stanleys' living room) and standing in it, assuming the pose of an Egyptian queen of long ago. When Banjo sees this he gets the idea to trap her in the sarcophagus and have her shipped to Sherry's place in New York. The fun is in watching Lorraine's hesitation at repeating the pose for Banjo and Maggie. The comic suspense comes from whether or not they'll be able to pull off the prank. On the significant third try, Lorraine succumbs to their flattery and enters the mummy case again. Eyes closed, arms crossed over her chest, she stands in the case. Before she can open her eyes, Banjo has slammed the lid shut and locked it. He and Maggie laugh, and both look like the proverbial cat who swallowed the canary. The audience never fails to laugh.

Perhaps the funniest scene is the last. Upon Sherry's leave-taking of the Stanleys, a call arrives from Eleanor Roosevelt. Sherry turns on the front stoop to re-enter the house and falls again, really breaking his leg. The camera moves to the host, Mr. Stanley. He is banging his head against the fireplace mantle.

Coming off what she considered a more-than-unsettling experience (shooting *The Little Foxes*), Davis was smart to opt for a comedy — and a well-tested one at that. On *The Little Foxes* she had a severe falling out with her favorite director, William Wyler. Back at her home studio Davis pleased Jack Warner with her willingness to take a minor role in *The Man Who Came to Dinner*. He felt she was needed for her star power in order to guarantee the success of this Broadway comedy hit. This practice of putting Hollywood stars in films from New York plays was standard procedure (e.g., from *The Little Foxes* right up to 1962's *My Fair Lady*, in which Warner cast Audrey Hepburn instead of Julie Andrews).

In her long career, Davis played many roles on the screen that other actors had created on Broadway. Nowadays, this practice is moot because there is no longer a studio system, and plays are rarely transferred to the screen. When they are, casting is strictly up to whomever is producing the film. The few musicals transferred because of their fame and success rely on newcomers or offbeat casting. Few serious adult dramas are produced, and they're often original rather than adaptations.

Frankly, I, for one, would like to see what new productions of old classics would look like with modern talent and cinema techniques. It's a shame Meryl Streep has never had the opportunity to remake some of Davis' old treasures. (In the thirties and forties, studios would often remake old pictures. For example, *The Maltese Falcon*, with Humphrey Bogart, was the third filming of the story.) Recently, Nathan Lane acted in a repeat of *The Man Who Came to Dinner*, which was also shown on PBS. What a pleasure!

As a small cog in this large wheel, credit must go to Woolley for a funny, if overacted, performance. Also effective are Ann Sheridan as Lorraine Sheldon, the most actressy actress of all time; Reginald Gardiner as Beverly Carlton, an on-target spoof of Noel Coward; and Jimmy Durante as Banjo, a crazy impersonation of the woman-chasing Harpo Marx.

In addition, there is the teen brother and sister, Richard and June Stanley (Russell Arms and Elisabeth Fraser), whose business Sherry sticks his nose into. Sherry encourages June to elope with her boyfriend, much to the horror of her parents, who are able to get the police to stop them and return June home unscathed. Sherry encourages Richard to follow his desire to be a photographer, to get away and travel all over the world. In other words, Sherry turns everyone's life upside down, skewering the pretentious and helping the downtrodden, all with a major dose of wit and sarcasm.

The Man Who Came to Dinner ranks alongside other great screen comedies like *Bringing up Baby, You Can't Take It with You,* and *Some Like It Hot* for laugh-out-loud performances.

"One palm should be handed Bette Davis ... for playing it so moderately and well," praised Bosley Crowthers in *The New York Times.*[24]

Cast: Maggie Cutler—Bette Davis; Lorraine Sheldon—Ann Sheridan; Sheridan Whiteside—Monty Woolley; Bert Jefferson—Richard Travis; Banjo—Jimmy Durante; Beverly Carlton—Reginald Gardiner; Mrs. Ernest Stanley—Billie Burke; June Stanley—Elisabeth Fraser; Mr. Ernest Stanley—Grant Mitchell; Dr. Bradley—George Barbier; Miss Preen—Mary Wickes; Richard Stanley—Russell Arms; Harriet Stanley—Ruth Vivian; John—Edwin Stanley; Sarah—Betty Roadman; Sandy—Charles Drake; Cosette—Nanette Vallon; Radio Man—John Ridgely.

Production: Hal B. Wallis—Producer; Jerry Wald and Jack Saper—Associate Producers; William Keighley—Director; Julius J. and Philip G. Epstein—Screenwriters; George S. Kaufman and Moss Hart—based on their play; Tony Gaudio—Cinematographer; Frederick Hollander—Musical Score; Leo F. Forbstein—Musical Direction; Orry-Kelly—Gowns; Robert Haas—Art Direction; 1941; Running time—112 minutes.

14

In the Final Analysis

How does one assess an artist, specifically, the actor Bette Davis? As in any art, one must analyze her best performances within her body of work, just as one judges an artist's best paintings or a composer's best symphonies.

In the history of acting, one can only assess theater actors by what was said in recorded observations by their contemporaries. Through articles and books we admire Sir Henry Irving, Ellen Terry, Sarah Bernhardt and Eleonora Duse; and in modern theater, Ethel Barrymore, Katherine Cornell, Lynn Fontanne, Alfred Lunt, Helen Hayes, John Gielgud and Sir Laurence Olivier. These were all basically theater actors — unlike John Barrymore, Greta Garbo, Katharine Hepburn, Lillian Gish, Meryl Streep, James Stewart and Ingrid Bergman, who were film as well as stage actors.

Davis must be judged in terms of her times and her major medium of film. One could discern her style of acting as modern, as initiated by Eleonora Duse rather than Sarah Bernhardt. Duse could be considered the mother of naturalistic acting (exemplified by Stanislavsky), as opposed to declamatory acting (exemplified by Bernhardt). That doesn't mean that Davis and Duse weren't theatrical or larger than life; they were.

An essential point in an analysis of Davis is her full range of performances recorded on film, rather than in the memories of people who saw her on stage. Another ingredient, seen by some as essential, is the roles she essayed. But I disagree. Many great actors do not attempt the Greek tragedies or Shakespeare, or even Ibsen, Williams or Miller, but are known for their superior performances in lesser playwrights' or screenwriters' plays (e.g. Bernhardt and Duse, who both excelled in less than superior works). One must critique their best performances, not their failures or lesser performances. I would stack Davis' top twelve films against any other actor's repertoire of performances.

Davis began her career on stage. After training at the John Murray Anderson School in New York, where she was taught movement and dance by the renowned Martha Graham, Davis honed her theatrical skills with the Blanche Yurka Repertory Company, playing in Ibsen's *The Wild Duck*. She also was hired for Cape Cod summer theater for a few seasons, acting many roles. The Provincetown Players had her perform in *The Earth Between*, and she was seen in two Broadway plays, *Broken Dishes* and *The Solid South*, before going west. Her reviews from critics at the time were generally positive, though at the beginning of her career Brooks Atkinson found her "soft and unassertive."

Davis was trained not only to use her whole body for acting, but, most importantly, her voice. Her diction was always perfect, although as the years went on she acquired some rather odd pronunciations of words. Mostly she spoke "mid–Atlantic."

After working with George Arliss in films, she seemed to acquire a rather declamatory voice in her early pictures. But once she started working with Edmund Goulding and particularly William Wyler, she learned to control her voice so that every word was not played at the same vocal level. Her "voice" fit her roles—English inflection in *The Letter*, southern belle in *Jezebel*, theatrical in *All About Eve*, slatternly in *Baby Jane*, Bostonian in *Now, Voyager*, etc. Her voice became an instrument with many levels, and she used it to expose her character, just as she did with her body.

She developed "star acting," just as Gish and Garbo did. Even though she submerged herself in her character, she also let the star, Bette Davis, show through. She was theatrical, not Actor's Studio. She believed in acting, not to expose her personal inner life, but to expose her character's life. In that process, of course, she exposed herself as well. As has been said many times, she played out the myriad roles she found within herself. She refined her acting for the cinema to enable audiences to see all the colorations of a character, by using her face, her eyes and her voice(s).

Many young New York actors got the call from Hollywood in the 1930s because of the addition of sound, "talking" pictures. Davis joined James Cagney, Humphrey Bogart, Joan Blondell and many other American and English stage-trained actors in films.

Is it fair to judge Davis by her theater work, even if you consider her later stage appearances? Only in one sense. Could she handle the stage's theatrical requirements as they differed from movies? Could she maintain a performance? Could she engage an audience? If you saw her in *The World of Carl Sandburg*, in which she toured for a year before going to NYC, and in Williams' *The Night of the Iguana*, you would have to answer a resounding "yes."

It's worth noting that through the years she was offered numerous stage roles, but studio contracts or personal reasons precluded her acceptance. In 1947 she was offered the role of Blanche in Williams' *A Streetcar Named Desire*, but even if Warners would have allowed it, she was still recovering from the birth of her daughter. In 1957 she was set to do *Look Homeward Angel*, based on Thomas Wolfe's book, but she fell down a flight of stairs and broke her back.

Edward Albee wanted her for *Who's Afraid of Virginia Woolf?* and was later promised by Warners that they'd cast her and James Mason in the movie. His working title for the play was "All About Bette." In 1962 she turned down a road tour of Arthur Laurents' *The Time of the Cuckoo* because Shirley Booth and Katharine Hepburn had already done it. Finally, in 1973, the production of *Miss Moffat* was shut down when she became ill from the previous back injury.

She worked with top directors: Wyler and Mankiewicz and Goulding. Davis was a modern actor working in contemporary movies who was employed during Hollywood's golden age. Three prominent critics, Richard Schickel, David Shipman and David Thomson, have pungent comments about Davis in landmark books they have written about motion pictures.

Schickel, in *Matinee Idylls*, offered the following opinions:

> Over at Warner Brothers, Bette Davis suffered many a sad fate, but there was something feverish, openly neurotic about the way she dealt with circumstances that seemed modern (even when she was in period costume, as she often was) and a lot more entertaining than Garbo's way.
>
> Her fight to assert herself—"I am ambitious to become known as a great actress"...— also forms a significant part of historical record. For in effect it guarantees the truthfulness of her febrile screen presence, reassuring us that it was something more than star acting, a set of mannerisms she could shrug off, like a costume, at the end of a day's work. It is one reason she is a legend...
>
> And everyone was aware that Davis, surely the most logical choice for Scarlett, had been passed over for the role.... On the other hand, *Jezebel* is a much better movie — darker, nuttier, much more tightly wound.

For her conviction, her will, her capacity for self–revelation constantly redeemed improbably tall tales and emotions for believable humanity.[1]

David Shipman, in *The Great Movie Stars*, writes:

> Provided you are taking the retrospective view, that old tag, "The First Lady of the Screen"—after examining all the contenders — belongs decisively and firmly to Bette Davis.
>
> ...[H]er dedication destroyed a lingering belief that stage acting was "superior" to film acting.[2]

David Thomson, author of *The New Biographical Dictionary of Film*, espouses:

Bette Davis trailed the subject of acting across the audience's path with all the preemptive originality of Queen Elizabeth spreading ermine before Raleigh.

Brigid Brophy compared the actress to St. Teresa and remarked at the nature of a great actress's being rooted in an hysterical personality.

Davis was a vulgar, bullying actress who made mannerism a virtue by showing us how it expresses the emanation of the self.

She excelled in the tearjerker *All This and Heaven Too*, and she was at her best in *The Letter* and *The Great Lie* before *The Little Foxes*, which made explicit her command of the emotional woman, thwarted or spurned, who became a malicious tyrant.[3]

In 1977, the American Film Institute chose her as the first woman to receive its Life Achievement Award — a deserved prize.

What is it that enabled Ruth Elizabeth Davis to become the great actress known as Bette Davis? Throughout the analysis of her major oeuvre, one sees various significant factors in her career that allowed Davis to become the icon she is.

Talent alone couldn't guarantee the pinnacle of success Davis achieved, although once her talent was tapped by herself and others, it was the paramount ingredient. Without it, she could never have had the unique ability to essay the number of distinguished roles she was able to delineate. Roles such as Judith Traherne, her favorite, were completely different from the basically unchangeable self-centered character of Regina Giddens. Davis had the talent and intelligence to discern the qualities of both, and through her acting let the audience experience their differences.

That is why one must look at Davis' career in its totality, for only then does one see her talent and her continued growth right up to her last character, Libby in *The Whales of August*, when she and Lillian Gish provide the viewer with an extremely well-wrought look at what it means to be elderly.

Every one of the major characters she played, in her top work, required Davis to not only become that character, which she could do, but also allow the viewers to see Davis and her vulnerability in embodying those people, whether she was Queen Elizabeth I, Margo Channing, Charlotte Vale, Jane Hudson, Leslie Crosbie, Charlotte Lovell, Esther Cimino or Julie Marsden. The variety of characters was remarkable, not just for their outward differences, such as a queen or a New England spinster, a crazed has-been or major Broadway actress, but the variety of inner, complex women she portrayed.

Combining Davis' talent and ability with the terrific ambition she had from the inception of her career let her fight for the career she wanted, the career that allowed her to become a great actress. Without that drive and ambition many talented artists do not realize a major career. That is a major factor in what differentiates an artist from other people. Their art comes first in all cases. Nothing else in life is as satisfying to them as their work. And it definitely takes a toll on their personal lives, just as it did with Davis'. Her personal life, although filled with occasional happiness, led specifically to what she described as the lonely life, the title of her autobiography. She had four failed marriages and numerous affairs, none of which provided lasting happiness. She had three children. Her eldest daughter, whom she adored, wrote a scathing biography of her mother, causing a complete rupture in their relationship. Her second daughter was mentally retarded to the extent that she lives her life in a special home. Her son was the only one who maintained a loving relationship with Davis, and his father, Gary Merrill, though it was a distanced affair, with the two living on opposite coasts. Davis' final close relationship was with her secretary/companion who cared for her after her strokes and while she fought cancer to the end of her life.

Davis admitted having three abortions earlier in her life, two while married to her first husband, in order to not interrupt her budding career, and one later when she was unwed. Davis sacrificed her personal happiness specifically because of her ambitious desire to succeed in her acting career.

Looking at her long career, because it was basically in movies, one can actually see her growth as an actor. First, at Universal and soon thereafter at Warners, she was an ingénue, playing young sweet girls in support of stars like George Arliss. The only time she was allowed to show some overt sex appeal was when she played the southern seductress in *Cabin in the Cotton*, opposite a fading silent star, Richard Barthelmess.

Her well-known breakthrough came when she acted the part of Mildred in *Of Human Bondage*, a Cockney slut. She continually fought with Jack Warner to loan her out to RKO until he finally gave up in frustration, telling her to "go hang yourself." Her talent burst through in this film, shocking audiences and critics alike as to her ability to play such a vile woman.

Subsequently, Warners still did not give her roles she deserved, even though she showed well in *Bordertown* and *The Petrified Forest* in two roles completely different from one another. But aside from these anomalies, Davis was still seen as a supporting actress, not really given lead or star roles. This was most likely because of two major reasons. Even though Warners did prominently feature some females at times in a few pictures, such as Kay Francis and Ruth Chatterton, it was not a studio devoted to making women's pictures. Their claim to success at the time was gangster films with their top stars, James Cagney or Edward G. Robinson. Their musicals were Busby Berkeley spectaculars with the emphasis on his geometric production numbers.

In addition, Davis was not considered a beauty, beauty being defined in her early days as someone like Garbo or Jean Harlow. Davis was given bleached hair, which she kept until 1936 when she reverted to her natural ash blonde hair (which was beautiful but did not photograph as blonde). She had enormous blue eyes and a rather small mouth. It was over time that she exaggerated her mouth line with lipstick to give it a larger look to balance her eyes. Even so, Davis never regarded herself as a beauty and constantly gave credit to hairdressers, make-up artists, lighting and cameramen for the illusion she could give of beauty in many films after her persona was established. What she was interested in was being a great actress, not a movie star beauty.

That said, Davis was beautiful for a period of ten years in pictures, beginning in 1937 when she was, at last, given star treatment. She is absolutely gorgeous in *Jezebel*, and in subsequent films such as *Juarez*, *The Letter*, *The Little Foxes*, *All This and Heaven Too*, and *Now, Voyager*, right up to that significant film made about beauty and what happens to a vain woman who loses her beauty in middle-age, *Mr. Skeffington*.

Davis started to age noticeably in the later forties when she reached 40 herself. Even more careful lighting was needed, but in *All About Eve*, where she has still a certain beauty and certainly a sexual attractiveness, harsh lighting and photography show her years. Such flaws as the heavy bags under her eyes make it very noticeable that she had not aged well.

Today, an actress reaching forty does not face what Davis faced because cosmetic surgery is common and the younger generation apparently leads a more healthy life. Davis was a heavy smoker and drinker, and it took its toll. She never had a face lift until she was 70, far too late to correct skin problems because by then the skin elasticity is gone.

Another issue that Davis faced was the fact that she played characters older than she was, and characters who were not beautiful—characters people tend to remember over the attractive ones.

To say she didn't care how she looked is foolish. She did care. Witness two events which support this. When she came on the set for *Deception*, the technical crew had installed a scrim and a bank of lights. They knew they would need to soften her features. By her own admission she responded by going to her dressing room and crying for more than a few minutes.

The other revealing moment came when she viewed *What Ever Happened to Baby Jane?* for the first time, along with her director Robert Aldrich, at the Cannes Film Festival. Not long into the film, Aldrich heard child-like weeping coming from Davis. When he turned to her, she asked, "Do I really look that ugly?" Even though she had done her own white, pasty make-up and overly made-up eyes and mouth, she was concerned with how she really looked. At fifty-four years old she didn't want to look as old as Baby Jane did.

In her old age, Davis acknowledged that when she met people she could see they were aghast at how she looked, for they had images in their heads of her from *All About Eve* or before.

After her court fight with Warners in 1936, Davis came back to a studio that finally realized her worth. From then on, pictures were developed specifically for her. Her champion in this respect was Hal Wallis, who had become the executive producer for Warner Brothers. She was given literate scripts, the best production values and top directors. All this can easily be seen in *Jezebel*, where no expense was spared to present an opulent southern picture à la *Gone with the Wind* (except for color). The character development is superb, the opening tracking shot of New Orleans is lavish and colorful, the costumes are completely correct for the 1850s, the actors are all perfect for their roles, and the lighting is well thought out. The production starts out brightly lit and increasingly gets darker as the yellow fever takes over. The direction was the best: William Wyler had been borrowed by Hal Wallis from Samuel Goldwyn when Wallis realized intended director Edmund Goulding's concept for the film was not appropriate. No expense was spared on the costumes for this large cast, and the art director bought antiques and furnishings indigenous to New Orleans in the 1850s, as well as having sets made according to factual documents. Three of the opulent sets were the St. Louis bar, the Marsden town house and the country antebellum mansion. The ballroom scene could be photographed completely from all four sides, and the set was large enough to contain the crowd of dancers as well as the orchestra. Obviously, Davis knew she was at the top. She was to become known as the fourth Warner brother!

These were her halcyon years, 1938–48; the pictures and the roles were all A-plus. She was given first rejection on any major film. She basically had director and casting approval, even though it wasn't contractual. She was a superstar and did not really have co-stars of equal wattage. She carried the films, as they were known as Bette Davis films, giving her power as an important creator in all respects.

During this time, she continued to grow and change and was willing to push her limits if she had a strong director who challenged her (e.g., on *The Letter*, *Dark Victory*, *All This and Heaven, Too*, and, notoriously, *The Little Foxes*, when she and Wyler were at loggerheads over the interpretation of Regina).

Significantly, there are critics who say that over this period Davis became rigid in her mannerisms, but I beg to differ. In her performances, Davis has basically dropped those early mannerisms of twisting or tapping fingers. Her physical mannerisms were always consistent with the character. In her vocal manner of definite enunciation a clipped voice sometimes appeared, but she always modified her speech and tonal quality to the role she was playing, i.e., southern, British, New Englandish, and later even a Bronx accent or ordinary American (as in *A Piano for Mrs. Cimino*).

There was a somewhat mannered approach in her later films at Warners when the scripts started to lose quality and the production values were diminished. After 1945, with Hal Wallis no longer there, Warners was having a difficult time finding appropriate material for Davis. *Beyond the Forest, Winter Meeting* and *June Bride* just didn't match previous standards for a Davis movie. Both *Beyond the Forest*, which was one of her worst movies (essentially because of miscasting), and *Winter Meeting* feature some good acting from her, but *June Bride* is really weak and neither witty nor funny, but strained.

After her release from Warners (from a very lucrative contract which had four years to run), Davis made two of her best films, *Payment on Demand* and *All About Eve*, but her career was really a bumpy road thereafter, with some of her best work done on TV. The superstar became a character actress, and the woman's picture went out of fashion. Davis returned to the stage a few times, and basically remained a great actress right up to her death in 1989.

She couldn't have ended with a better vehicle than *The Whales of August*. As sick and physically challenged as she was from the effects of her strokes and her battle with cancer, she remained able to add another lustrous performance to her acting career. The great actress, who so pleadingly begged Jack Warner for help in becoming one, had survived to become an acting legend.

Davis came from a middle-class, divorced family. She had a one-parent relationship and was well-educated at girls' boarding schools, but did not attend college. Most girls in those days did not attend college; plus, it was highly unlikely that Davis' father, a lawyer, would have paid to send her anyway. She went to acting school — John Murray Anderson's in NYC, with her mother's support. Once Davis had attained success and an income, she provided the homes and the income for her mother and her sister. There was no family to go home to in New England, though she remained a Yankee for her entire life, as well as living there for periods of time.

Only one of Davis' top films is a comedy, and that one is the "restoration" comedy *All About Eve*, a satire on the theater scene. In her other movies, comedy occurred as character responses to other characters, or involved select sections laced with humor, such as in *The Private Lives of Elizabeth and Essex* and *The Virgin Queen*, or her over–the–top performance in *What Ever Happened to Baby Jane?* But the few comedies she essayed, like *It's Love I'm After* or *June Bride*, lacked sophisticated comedic writing. Even *The Bride Came COD*, which was a huge hit for her and James Cagney, today seems more hysterical than funny. Only *The Man Who Came to Dinner* had a truly good comedic script. But even here her quiet acting stood amidst a completely overacting cast.

Could Davis have played Rose in *The African Queen*? Because it was a great character, she would have succeeded. Could she have carried off Mrs. Venable in *Suddenly Last Summer*? Easily, and she loved Mankiewicz as a director. Davis reveled in playing all sorts of characters — southern belle, murderers, liars, actresses, historic figures, housewives, working women, old maids, even a Cockney. According to Joe Mankiewicz, "Outside of grand opera, there isn't a thing Bette Davis couldn't do theatrically."

Davis was a master of star acting and always gave of herself to her co-stars and other players, even if she hated them personally (i.e. Miriam Hopkins, who never acted better than in her two pictures with Davis — *The Old Maid* and *Old Acquaintance*). At the prime of Davis' career, Geraldine Fitzgerald extolled her helpfulness in *Dark Victory*, and Mary Astor thanked her publicly when Astor was awarded an Oscar for *The Great Lie*. Vincent Canby, in his review of her last completed film, *The Whales of August*, stated unequivocally that in her performance, Davis gave Lillian Gish something to act with and against, enabling Gish to give a great performance.

In the final analysis one wishes that one of *Davis'* desires would have come true. A great admirer of Katharine Hepburn, she always maintained that she would have liked to have acted in a film with her. Davis admired Hepburn's talent and envied her beauty. Two Yankee women in the same film might have been glorious — or it might have been disastrous. We'll never know.

What we do know is what they showed us separately. Both were powerful movie stars, one continually projecting herself as personality, the other both submerging herself in her role and allowing her emotions to expose the inner personality. The latter, of course, is Davis, the supreme artist of 20th century film.

Davis wanted to be a great actress, not a famous star, and she proved it in the multitude of roles she played in over 100 movies. Even in the worst movies she made she was worth watching. One example is *Beyond the Forest*, the last film she completed under her Warners contract. She admitted she was too old for the part, and didn't believe anyone would believe she wanted to leave Joseph Cotten (she suggested Eugene Pallette); and she fought unceasingly with the great director King Vidor. In one scene as she goes from bar to bar in Chicago, caught in the rainstorm, afraid and alone, not a word is spoken, yet she and Vidor let you inside the desperate woman's heart and soul.

Davis continuously followed her dictum, always giving her best acting in all kinds of movies, with all kinds of scripts, and essaying all kinds of characters. She was always willing to take the risk of hanging herself, the risk of fully exposing her characters and the risk of exposing her inner self.

Davis always acknowledged that her work was the central fact of her life, and that's the way she wanted to be remembered — as a hard worker. As with Duse, that is what she'll be remembered for. The pity is that neither had a happy personal life. They were both larger than life. The young woman who expressed her hope to Jack Warner that she might have a chance to be a great actress was successful, but at a great personal price.

Because of her range, her risk-taking, her accomplishments in her best work, her willingness to stretch her talents, and her viewable results, Davis must be judged the best actress the screen ever produced. Put another way, Davis allowed the medium of the screen to display a rare talent in a career spanning over 50 years and 100 films, one unequaled by any other female actor. She was the female actor of the century in the medium of the century.

In 1987, Carlos Fuentes had this to say:

> [P]robably the best film actress ever ... Bette Davis had the most uncanny way of being in her movies and knowing how to see the camera and be seen by it. No asides, no "Menias" certainly, but certainly the most remarkable way of addressing you and me through the camera, of moving, and looking and feeling in such a way that we have become the camera in response to the actresses' presence.[4]

Afterword

Before the invention of the silver screen, there was really no immortality for actors in theater or whatever medium, for it was all done live — on stage, in a circus, on a street or in an arena. We don't know anyone of that Greek chorus who gave life to the words of Aeschylus, or even any of the original actors for the great Will Shakespeare. We may know the words as the playwright wrote them and some historical notes on the condition of their theaters and how actors performed. It wasn't until the eighteenth century that actors began to be identified and written about by critics and historians.

Actors' performances were all hearsay, one person's opinion of how an actor performed and what kind of theatrical charisma an actor, male or female, possessed. For much of the western world, actors were considered to be from the lowest social level, ranking alongside prostitutes, especially female actors.

In Shakespeare's time women weren't even allowed upon the stage. Right up to the present day there is still a social prejudice against all but the most exalted of artist/actors. There are many of those who have led "storied" lives (e.g., the Ingrid Bergman international scandal when she left her husband for an affair with the Italian director Roberto Rossellini and had a child out of wedlock in 1949).

Social mores may have changed since the 1960s, even in the U.S., but there is still strong disapproval of famous actors who live together and have children out of wedlock, or even those who have acknowledged adulterous affairs. One has only to witness that amid all the hundreds of tributes paid to Katharine Hepburn when she died in 2003 were letters to editors which vilified her as a woman who had a long-time adulterous affair, and questioned the press for its praise of her career and her life.

It wasn't until the invention of the motion picture, and really videotape, that one could look at individual performances of actors to assess not only one performance, but the entire career of an actor. With film, however, there is danger in comparing one actor to another because one is judging players in different roles, and in different genres and from different times. But what one can do that couldn't be done before is assess a single actor's performances over time to see how they hold up, judging them in light of only his or her own career.

Today we admire Chaplin's pantomime almost as much as when he was acclaimed so strongly as the greatest artist in the world. But we also see more clearly the superior artistry of Buster Keaton, his contemporary. We are still enchanted with Lillian Gish's silent film work — her ability to use pantomime, but the characters she essayed seem too Victorian for our taste.

Similarly with Garbo, time has not been kind to this great beauty's talent. Her forte of playing highly-charged, romantic, sexually-destructive creatures has become passé. Her acting seems languorous and rather hard to believe. Her range was terribly limited. But she was a fantastic movie star and the camera loved her (until her later films where she looked aged). One learns from her what star acting was in the '20s and '30s. No one was as "divine" as Garbo.

Just as with Gish, Garbo and Hepburn, one can view in its entirety Davis' film career. She was a star actor. And as one can see over the period of her career, her emphasis was on the acting. She was able to take on a multitude of roles and still be believable today as the modern neurotic woman, the suspicious queen or the total bitch. She excelled in her roles, even when the picture was less than mediocre.

Finally, one must say again that Davis was always willing to take a risk, even though she was terrified of the risk she was taking. As much as she wanted/needed the love an audience gives to a star, she also risked their hatred because she ultimately believed they would love her for the actress she was — one who was able to submerge herself in her character and still have her audience know it was Bette Davis playing the role, a star actor.

Two words apply. *She succeeded.* She was unique; no one was better.

Appendix I

Personal Data

Marriages

Harmon Oscar Nelson, Jr.	8/32–12/38	divorce
Arthur Farnsworth, Jr.	12/40–8/43	death
William Grant Sherry	11/45–7/50	divorce
Gary Merrill	7/50–7/60	divorce

Children

Barbara Davis Sherry	5/46
Margot Mosher Merrill	1/51
Michael Woodman Merrill	2/52

Appendix II

NOMINATIONS AND AWARDS

Oscar Nominations and Winners (*), Picture (**)

1934

Claudette Colbert* (*It Happened One Night***); Grace Moore (*One Night of Love*); Norma Shearer (*The Barretts of Wimpole St.*); (12 movies nominated). Bette Davis, a write-in candidate for *Of Human Bondage*, came in second; she lost to Claudette Colbert for *It Happened One Night*, for which Frank Capra wanted Davis.

1935

Elisabeth Bergner (*Escape Me Never*); Claudette Colbert (*Private Worlds*); Bette Davis* (*Dangerous*); Katharine Hepburn (*Alice Adams*); Miriam Hopkins (*Becky Sharp*); Merle Oberon (*The Dark Angel*); (12 movies nominated); *Mutiny on the Bounty*—Best Picture.

1938

Fay Bainter (*White Banners*); Bette Davis* (*Jezebel*); Wendy Hiller (*Pygmalion*); Norma Shearer (*Marie Antoinette*); Margaret Sullavan (*Three Comrades*); *You Can't Take It with You*—Best Picture; (Ten movies nominated).

1939

Bette Davis (*Dark Victory*); Irene Dunne (*Love Affair*); Greta Garbo (*Ninotchka*); Greer Garson (*Goodbye, Mr. Chips*); Vivien Leigh* (*Gone with the Wind***); (Ten movies nominated).

1940

Bette Davis (*The Letter*); Joan Fontaine (*Rebecca***); Katharine Hepburn (*The Philadelphia Story*); Ginger Rogers* (*Kitty Foyle*); Martha Scott (*Our Town*); (10 movies nominated).

1941

Bette Davis (*The Little Foxes*); Joan Fontaine* (*Suspicion*); Greer Garson (*Blossoms in the Dust*); Olivia de Havilland (*Hold Back the Dawn*); Barbara Stanwyck (*Ball of Fire*); *How Green Was My Valley*— Best Picture.

1942

Bette Davis (*Now, Voyager*); Greer Garson* (*Mrs. Miniver***); Katharine Hepburn (*Woman of the Year*); Rosalind Russell (*My Sister Eileen*); Teresa Wright (*The Pride of the Yankees*).

1944

Ingrid Bergman* (*Gaslight*); Claudette Colbert (*Since You Went Away*); Bette Davis (*Mr. Skeffington*); Greer Garson (*Mrs. Parkington*); Barbara Stanwyck (*Double Indemnity*); *Going My Way*— Best picture.

1950

Anne Baxter (*All About Eve***); Bette Davis (*All About Eve***); Judy Holliday* (*Born Yesterday*); Eleanor Parker (*Caged*); Gloria Swanson (*Sunset Blvd.*). Davis won: NY Film Critics Circle — Best Actress; Cannes Film Festival — Best Actress.

1952

Shirley Booth* (*Come Back, Little Sheba*); Joan Crawford (*Sudden Fear*); Bette Davis (*The Star*); Julie Harris (*The Member of the Wedding*); Susan Hayward (*With a Song in My Heart*); *The Greatest Show on Earth*— Best Picture.

1962

Anne Bancroft* (*The Miracle Worker*); Bette Davis (*What Ever Happened to Baby Jane?*); Katharine Hepburn (*Long Day's Journey into Night*); Geraldine Page (*Sweet Bird of Youth*); Lee Remick (*Days of Wine and Roses*); *Lawrence of Arabia*— Best Picture.

TV Movies

1982

Bette Davis — Best Performance by an Actress for *A Piano for Mrs. Cimino*, International Television Festival — Monte Carlo.

Appendix III
THE "WOMAN'S PICTURE" FACTOR

Melodrama— A drama marked by exaggerated emotions, stereotypical characters and interpersonal conflicts.

Drama— A prose or verse composition, especially one telling a serious story, that is intended for representation by actors impersonating the characters and performing the dialogue and action.

Tragedy—1. A drama or literary work in which the main characters are brought to ruin or suffer extreme sorrow, especially as a consequence of a tragic flaw, a moral weakness, or an inability to cope with unfavorable circumstances. 2. A play, film ... that portrays or depicts calamitous events and has an unhappy ending.

Weepie— A work, especially a film or play, that is excessively sentimental.

Sentimental— Affectedly or extravagantly emotional.

Tear Jerker— Slang, a grossly sentimental story, drama or performance.

The above definitions should help to define the general type of pictures Davis made. In many of the contemporary reviews of her films when they first appeared they were described as "women's pictures," using the term in a derogatory fashion, specifically stating sometimes that they were weepies or tearjerkers.

It must be said, of course, they were women's pictures in the sense that the main characters were women, but the films were not always melodramatic or sentimental. *Medea* is a woman's play; it is a tragedy about a woman.

For example, *Dark Victory*, often referred to in derogatory terms, is actually a tragedy with little if any, excess, of sentimentality. In fact, the heroine, Judith Traherne, never resorts to sentimentality, whereas her secretary/friend expresses deep feelings for Judith's tragedy, acting as a Greek chorus.

What saves some of Davis' films from excessive sentiment is usually the sincerity and realistic way in which she and the other actors perform their believable roles. A perfect example would be *Now, Voyager*, a study of a woman attaining her adulthood and independence. The acting of the entire cast prevents this film from becoming overly sentimental.

Besides, the terms "melodramatic" and "sentimental" can be applied to many other genres of film which are basically "men's pictures" (a term never used in reviewing films), such as crime films, gangster films, westerns, adventure films and comedies or musicals.

This leads to a number of questions regarding Davis' best films:

1. Is *The Letter* merely melodramatic or a great study of a congenital liar?

2. Is *All About Eve* sentimental because Margo and Bill decide to marry, or is it rather a sardonic study of what the aging process does to a woman turning 40 in 1950s New York theatrical society?

3. Is *Dark Victory* merely a weepie or an earnest study of the tragedy of a fatal illness and how the heroine faces certain death?

4. Is *The Little Foxes* a melodrama with excessive sentiment, or is it a serious drama of how greed can infest a family?

5. Is *Now, Voyager* a tearjerker, or is it a careful study of mother/daughter relationships and how a woman becomes an independent adult?

6. Is *What Ever Happened to Baby Jane?* just a horror film, or is Davis able to invest Jane with a character worthy of pity and sorrow?

7. Is *A Piano for Mrs. Cimino* another disease-of-the-week TV movie, or is it a complex study of a woman facing her elderly status as a widow in order to live out her life with dignity?

8. Is *The Old Maid* only a romantic movie about sacrifice, or is it an intelligent characterization of a woman's ability to adjust and live her life to benefit her illegitimate daughter in a rigid 1850s American society?

9. Is *The Virgin Queen* an historic romance, or an historical drama allowing Davis to show the internal conflicts of a queen fulfilling her duty to her country?

10. Is *The Private Lives of Elizabeth and Essex* a romantic view of Queen Elizabeth I and Elizabethan England, or does the drama allow Davis to show an emotionally complex woman as ruler?

11. Is *The Whales of August* a pseudo–Chekhovian comedy, or does it allow Gish's and Davis' talents to delineate two sisters who have treated and been treated by life in very different ways, yet realistically still need each other in their waning years?

12. Is *Jezebel* a melodrama, or does the exquisite characterization of Davis' Julie allow her to reach dramatic heights when she experiences a transformation?

In the end, each viewer will have to decide, no doubt affected by the cultural times in which he or she lives. One can only hope that time and historical perspective will only add to the reality of Davis' true genius.

Appendix IV

MISSED OPPORTUNITIES

- In 1946, producer Irene Selznick offered Davis the role of Blanche in *A Streetcar Named Desire*. John Garfield was later offered the role of Stanley. Davis was 38, but still under contract to Warner Bros., and had to refuse the offer.
- In 1949, producer Charles Feldman approached Davis to consider the role of Amanda in the screen version of *The Glass Menagerie*. At this time Davis and Jack Warner parted company. Warner was so angry with her that he wouldn't even consider allowing her on the lot.
- When *Streetcar* was filmed in 1951, Davis was 43, probably too old to play Blanche, but her sometimes friend, Olivia de Havilland, was offered the role, and turned it down because of her distaste for the character!
- The working title of Edward Albee's masterpiece *Who's Afraid of Virginia Woolf?* was *All About Bette*. She probably could have performed it on stage in 1962, but then lost out to Burton and Taylor in the movie version.
- Ironically, Davis finally essayed a Williams role, Maxine in *The Night of the Iguana*. Apparently, she rejected the Margaret Leighton role in favor of Maxine. At one point during rehearsals/previews, Davis had the director barred from the theater. The play won the NY Drama Critic Circle Award, but Davis left the play in April 1962.
- Davis won the Margo role in *All About Eve* as a replacement for Claudette Colbert, who had injured her back skiing. Initially, Gertrude Lawrence had been considered, but her agent insisted she have a song to sing in the film. Lawrence had played Amanda in the film version of *The Glass Menagerie*.
- Hall Wallis offered Davis the lead in *Come Back, Little Sheba*. She turned it down and regretted her decision.

Appendix V
Film Chronology

A partial chronology of Davis' films. Those in bold are discussed herein.

1931— Arrived in Hollywood
1932— *The Man Who Played God*
　　　Cabin in the Cotton
1933— *20,000 Years in Sing Sing*
1934— ***Of Human Bondage***
1935— ***Bordertown***
　　　Dangerous— first Oscar
1936— *The Petrified Forest*
1937— ***Marked Woman***
　　　Kid Galahad
　　　That Certain Woman
1938— ***Jezebel***— second Oscar
　　　The Sisters
1939— ***Dark Victory***— Oscar nomination
　　　Juarez
　　　The Old Maid
　　　The Private Lives of Elizabeth and Essex
1940— ***All This and Heaven Too***
　　　The Letter— Oscar nomination
1941— *The Great Lie*
　　　The Little Foxes— Oscar nomination
1942— ***The Man Who Came to Dinner***
　　　In This Our Life
　　　Now, Voyager— Oscar nomination

1943 — *Watch on the Rhine*
        Old Acquaintance
1944 — **Mr. Skeffington** — Oscar nomination
1945 — *The Corn Is Green*
1946 — *A Stolen Life*
1948 — *Winter Meeting*
        June Bride
1949 — *Beyond the Forest*
1950 — **All About Eve** — Oscar nomination, NY Film Critics Circle Award
1951 — **Payment on Demand**
1952 — *The Star* — Oscar nomination
1955 — **The Virgin Queen**
1956 — **The Catered Affair**
1961 — *A Pocketful of Miracles*
1962 — **What Ever Happened to Baby Jane?** — Oscar nomination
1964 — *Dead Ringer*
        Where Love Has Gone
        Hush ... Hush, Sweet Charlotte
1965 — *The Nanny*
1978 — *Death on the Nile*
1987 — **The Whales of August**

Television

1972 — *Madame Sin* (Theatrical release in Europe)
1976 — *The Disappearance of Aimee*
1978 — *The Dark Secret of Harvest Home*
1979 — **Strangers: The Story of a Mother and Daughter** — Emmy Award
1980 — *White Mama*
        Skyward
1981 — *Family Reunion*
1982 — **A Piano for Mrs. Cimino** — Monte Carlo Award
        Little Gloria ... Happy at Last — Emmy nomination
1983 — *Right of Way*

Chapter Notes

Preface

1. Whitney Stine, *Mother Goddam* (New York: Hawthorne Books, 1974), p. 3.
2. Ibid., p. 4.

Introduction

1. Bette Davis, *The Lonely Life* (New York: G.P. Putnam's Sons, 1962), p. 69.
2. Gary Carey, with Joseph L. Mankiewicz, *More About All About Eve* (New York: Random House, 1972), p. 87.

Chapter 1

1. Pauline Kael, *5001 Nights at the Movies* (New York: Henry Holt, 1985), p. 419.
2. Stine, *Mother Goddam*, op cit., p. 137.
3. Charles Affron, *Star Acting: Gish, Garbo, Davis* (New York: E.P. Dutton, 1977), p. 8–9.
4. Foster Hirsch, *Acting Hollywood Style* (New York: Harry N. Abrams, 1996), p. 150.
5. Emanuel Levy, *Oscar Fever* (New York: Continuum International Publishing Group, 2001), p. 226.
6. Alexander Walker, *Bette Davis: A Celebration* (New York: Conundrum, 1986), p. 36.

Chapter 2

1. Gary Carey, *More About All About Eve* (New York: Bantam Books, 1974), p. 85.
2. Affron, *Star Acting,* op cit., p. 205.
3. Ibid., p. 295.
4. Hirsch, *Acting Hollywood Style*, op cit., p. 212.
5. Danny Peary, *Cult Movies* (New York: Dell Publishing, 1981), p. 8.
6. Jay Carr, ed., *The A List* (Cambridge, MA: Perseus Books Group, 2002), p. 11–12.
7. Walker, *Bette Davis: A Celebration*, op cit., pp. 115, 117.

Chapter 3

1. Bernard Dick, ed., *Dark Victory* (Madison, WI: University of Wisconsin Press, 1981), p. 18.
2. Ibid., pp. 40, 42.
3. Stine, *Mother Goddam*, op cit., p. 110.
4. Walker, *Bette Davis: A Celebration*, op cit., p. 75.
5. Affron, *Star Acting*, op cit., p. 268.
6. Hirsh, *Acting Hollywood Style*, op cit., p. 25.
7. Gene Ringgold, *The Complete Films of Bette Davis* (New York: Citadel Press, 1990), p. 72.

8. Stine, *Mother Goddam*, op cit., pp. 110–111.
9. John Springer, *They Had Faces Then* (Secaucus, NJ: Citadel Press, 1974), p.81.

Chapter 4

1. Jan Herman, *A Talent for Trouble* (New York: Putnam's, 1996), p. 224.
2. Zoe Caldwell, *I Will Be Cleopatra* (New York: N.W. Norton, 2001), p. 64.
3. Richard Dyer, *Stars* (London: British Film Inst., 1998), pp. 147–50.
4. Hirsh, *Acting Hollywood Style*, op cit., p. 47.
5. Affron, *Star Acting*, op cit., p. 258.
6. Walker, *Bette Davis: A Celebration*, op cit., p. 88.
7. Stine, *Mother Goddam*, op cit., p. 152.
8. Herman, *A Talent for Trouble*, op cit., p. 230.
9. Ringgold, *The Complete Films of Bette Davis*, op cit., p. 112.

Chapter 5

1. Prouty, Olive Higgins (Jeanne Allen, ed.), *Now, Voyager* (Madison: University of Wisconsin Press, 1984), p. 85.
2. Hal Wallis and Charles Higham, *Starmaker* (New York: Macmillan, 1980), p. 105.
3. Hirsch, *Acting Hollywood Style*, op cit., p. 212.
4. Bernard F. Dick, *Hal Wallis* (Lexington, KY: University Press of Kentucky, 2004), pp. 66–7.
5. Affron, *Star Acting*, op cit., pp. 277, 280.
6. Ibid., p. 290.

Chapter 6

1. Charles Higham and Joel Greenberg, *The Celluloid Muse* (Chicago: Henry Regnery, 1971), p. 35.
2. Hirsch, *Acting Hollywood Style*, op cit., p. 133.
3. John Kobal, *People Will Talk* (New York: William Morrow, 1981), p. 274.
4. Higham, *The Celluloid Muse*, op cit., p. 35.
5. Andrew Sarris, *Confessions of a Cultist* (New York: Simon and Schuster, 1970), pp. 81–2.
6. Jeff Simon, *The Buffalo News*, April 25, 2006.

Chapter 7

1. Christopher Nickens, *Bette Davis* (Garden City, NY: Doubleday, 1985), p. 209.
2. Gary Fishgall, *Pieces of Time* (New York: Scribner, 1997), pp. 357–58.
3. Nickens, *Bette Davis*, op cit., p. 209.
4. Ibid., p. 209.

Chapter 8

1. Lawrence J. Quirk, *The Great Romantic Films* (Secaucus, NJ: Citadel Press, 1974), p. 72.
2. Stine, *Mother Goddam*, op cit., p. 119.
3. Quirk, *The Great Romantic Films*, op cit., p. 73.
4. Affron, *Star Acting*, op cit., p. 269.
5. Walker, *Bette Davis*, op cit., p. 81.

Chapter 9

1. Stine, *Mother Goddam*, op cit., p. 119.
2. Alexander Walker, *Stardom* (New York: Stein and Day, 1970), pp. 276–77.
3. David Shipman, *The Great Movie Stars* (New York: Bonanza Books, 1970), p. 150.

Chapter 10

1. Stine, *Mother Goddam*, op cit., p. 57.
2. Ibid., p. 123.
3. Richard Schickel, *The Stars* (New York: Dial Press, 1962), p. 147.
4. Affron, *Star Acting*, op cit., p. 235.
5. Kael, *5001 Nights at the Movies*, op cit., pp. 599–600.
6. Walker, *Bette Davis: A Celebration*, op cit., p. 82.

Chapter 11

1. Gavin Lambert, *Mainly About Lindsay Anderson* (New York: Alfred A. Knopf, 2000), p. 295.
2. Ibid., p. 296.
3. Ringgold, *The Complete Films of Bette Davis*, op cit., p. 209.
4. Hirsh, *Acting Hollywood Style*, op cit., p. 188.
5. Ibid., p. 182.

6. Lambert, *Mainly About Lindsay Anderson*, op cit., pp. 291–2.
7. Walker, *Bette Davis: A Celebration*, op. cit., pp. 132–3.
8. Ringgold, *The Complete Films of Bette Davis*, op cit., p. 209.

Chapter 12

1. *Time* magazine cover caption, March 28, 1938.
2. Affron, *Star Acting*, op. cit., pp. 232–3.
3. Richard Schickel, *Matinee Idylls* (Chicago: Ivan R. Dee, Publisher, 1999), p. 99.
4. Herman, *A Talent for Trouble*, op. cit., p. 177.
5. Molly Haskell, *From Reverence to Rape* (Chicago: University of Chicago Press, 1987), p. 217.
6. Ringgold, *The Complete Films of Bette Davis*, op. cit., p. 86.

The Second Tier

1. Vincent Canby, *The New York Times*, October 5, 1989.
2. Carr, *The A List*, op cit., p. 12.

Chapter 13

1. John Calhaune, *The New York Times*, April 13, 1980.
2. Ringgold, *The Complete Films of Bette Davis*, op. cit., p. 57.
3. Affron, *Star Acting*, op. cit., p. 219.
4. Ringgold, *The Complete Films of Bette Davis*, op. cit., p. 167.
5. Ibid., p. 60.
6. Affron, *Star Acting*, op. cit., p. 231.
7. Ringgold, *The Complete Films of Bette Davis*, op cit., p. 8.
8. Ibid., p. 153.

9. Ethan Mordden, *Movie Star* (New York: St. Martin's Press, 1983), p. 185.
10. Ringgold, *The Complete Films of Bette Davis*, op cit., p. 76.
11. Dick, *Dark Victory*, op cit., p. 20.
12. Ringgold, *The Complete Films of Bette Davis*, op cit., p. 76.
13. Gerald Clarke, *Time* magazine, April 14, 1980.
14. Dick, *Dark Victory*, op cit., p. 20.
15. Ringgold, *The Complete Films of Bette Davis*, op cit., p. 81.
16. Judith Crist, *Take 22* (New York: Viking Penguin), 1984, p. 40.
17. Jerry Vermilye, *Bette Davis* (New York: Pyramid Publications, 1973), p. 92.
18. Molly Haskell, *From Reverence to Rape* (Chicago: University of Chicago Press, 1987), p. 214.
19. Ringgold, *The Complete Films of Bette Davis*, op cit., p. 128.
20. Anthony Lane, *The New Yorker*, January 8, 2007.
21. Ringgold, *The Complete Films of Bette Davis*, op cit., p. 89.
22. Dick, *Dark Victory*, op cit., p. 22–3.
23. Affron, *Star Acting*, op. cit., p. 294.
24. Ringgold, *The Complete Films of Bette Davis*, op cit., p. 114.

Chapter 14

1. Schickel, *Matinee Idylls*, op cit., pp. 43, 95, 98, 99, 100.
2. David Shipman, *The Great Movie Stars*, Vol. I (Boston: Little, Brown, 1995), p. 150.
3. David Thomson, *The New Biographical Dictionary of Film* (New York: Alfred A. Knopf, 2002), p. 208–9.
4. Carlos Fuentes, *The New York Times*, March 14, 1978.

Bibliography

Affron, Charles. *Star Acting: Gish, Garbo, Davis*. New York: E.P. Dutton, 1977.
Allen, Jeanne, ed. *Now, Voyager*. Madison: University of Wisconsin Press, 1984.
Barris, Alex. *Hollywood's Other Women*. New York: A.S. Barnes, 1975.
Basinger, Jeanine. *American Cinema*. New York: Rizzoli International Publications, 1994.
Caldwell, Zoe. *I Will Be Cleopatra*. New York: W.W. Norton, 2001.
Carey, Gary. *More About All About Eve*. New York: Bantam Books, 1974.
Carr, Jay, ed. *The A List*. Cambridge, MA: Perseus Books Group, 2002.
Carr, Larry. *More Fabulous Faces*. New York: Doubleday, 1979.
Carter, Graydon, and David Friend. *Vanity Fair's Hollywood*. New York: Penguin/Putnam, 2000.
Davis, Bette. *The Lonely Life*. New York: G.P. Putnam's Sons, 1962.
_____. *This 'n That*. New York: G.P. Putnam's Sons, 1987.
Davis, Daphne. *Stars!* New York: Stewart, Tabori and Chang, 1983.
Dick, Bernard F., ed. *Dark Victory*. Madison: University of Wisconsin Press, 1981.
_____. *Hal Wallis*. Lexington: University Press of Kentucky, 2004.
Dyer, Richard. *Stars*. London: British Film Institute, 1998.
Ebert, Roger. *The Great Movies*. New York: Broadway Books, 2002.
Fishgall, Gary. *Pieces of Time*. New York: Scribner, 1997.
Haskell, Molly. *From Reverence to Rape*. Chicago: University of Chicago Press, 1987.
Herman, Jan. *A Talent for Trouble*. New York: G.P. Putnam's Sons, 1996.
Higham, Charles. *Bette*. New York: Macmillan, 1981.
_____ and Joel Greenberg. *The Celluloid Muse*. Chicago: Henry Regnery, 1971.
Hirsch, Foster. *Acting Hollywood Style*. New York: Harry N. Abrams, 1996.
Hurrell, George. *Hurrell's Hollywood*. New York: St. Martin's Press, 1992.
Kobal, John. *Hollywood Color Portraits*. New York: William Morrow, 1981.
Krenz, Carol. *100 Years of Hollywood*. New York: Friedman/Fairfax Publishers, 2000.
Lambert, Gavin. *Mainly About Lindsay Anderson*. New York: Alfred A. Knopf, 2000.
Lawton, Richard, and Hugo Lecky. *Grand Illusions*. New York: McGraw-Hill, 1973.

Levy, Emanuel. *Oscar Fever*. New York: Continuum International Publishing Group, 2001.
Mankiewicz, Joseph L. *All About Eve*. New York: Random House, 1951.
McDowall, Roddy. *Double Exposure, Take Two*. New York: William Morrow, 1989.
Nickens, Christopher. *Bette Davis*. Garden City, NY: Doubleday, 1985.
Peary, Danny. *Cult Movies*. New York: Dell Publishing, 1981.
Quirk, Lawrence J. *The Great Romantic Films*. Secaucus, NJ: Citadel Press, 1974.
Ringgold, Gene. *The Complete Films of Bette Davis*. New York: First Carol Publishing Group, 1990.
Robinson, Jeffrey. *Bette Davis*. New York: Proteus Publishing, 1982.
Sarris, Andrew. *Confessions of a Cultist*. New York: Simon and Schuster, 1970.
Scherman, David E., ed. *Life Goes to the Movies*. New York: Time, 1975.
Schickel, Richard. *Matinee Idylls*. Chicago: Ivan R. Dee, Publisher, 1999.
_____. *The Stars*. New York: Dial Press, 1962.
Shipman, David. *Cinema*. New York: St. Martin's Press, 1993.
_____. *The Great Movie Stars*. New York: Crown Publishers, 1970.
Simon, Jeff. *The Buffalo News*, April 25, 2006.
Springer, John. *They Had Faces Then: Hollywood in the Thirties, the Legendary Ladies*. Secaucus, NJ: Citadel Press, 1974.
Stine, Whitney. *Mother Goddam*. New York: Hawthorne Books, 1974.
Thomson, David. *Hollywood: A Celebration!* New York: D.K. Publishing, 2001.
_____. *The Whole Equation*. New York: Alfred A. Knopf, 2005.
Trent, Paul. *The Image Makers*. New York: Harmony Books, Crown Publishers, 1982.
Vermilye, Jerry. *Bette Davis*. New York: Pyramid Publications, 1973.
Walker, Alexander. *Bette Davis: A Celebration*. Boston: Little, Brown, 1986.
_____. *Bette Davis Legends*. London: Conundrum, 1986.
_____. *Stardom*. New York: Stein and Day, 1970.
Wallis, Hal, and Charles Higham. *Starmaker*. New York: Macmillan, 1980.
Whitman, Walt. *Leaves of Grass*. New York: Penguin Books USA, 1986.

Index

Abel, Walter 204
Acting Hollywood Style 17, 31, 45, 57, 68, 80
Actor's Equity 36
Actor's Studio 222
Addy, Wesley 190
Adler, Jay 162, 165
Aeschylus 231
The African Queen 228
Aherne, Brian 171
Akins, Zoe 102, 109, 111
Albee, Edward 223
Aldrich, Robert 78, 83, 85, 87, 193, 226
Alexander, Katherine 199
Alice Adams 160
Allred, Julie 79
American Film Institute 28, 224
Anderson, Lindsay 131, 137
Anderson, Maxwell 123
Arliss, George 186, 222, 225
Arsenic and Old Lace 49
Astor, Mary 191
Atkinson, Brooks 222

Bacon, Lloyd 187
Bad Sister 187
Bainter, Fay 141, 144, 145, 146
Bancroft, Anne 85
Bankhead, Tallulah 28, 39, 52, 54, 57, 62, 140
Barrat, Robert 167
Barrymore, Ethel 221
Barrymore, John 217, 221
Barthelmess, Richard 225

Barton, Anne 79
Bates, Barbara 26
Baxter, Anne 22, 29, 33
Becky Sharp 109
Bergman, Ingrid 221, 231
Bergner, Elisabeth 28
Bernhardt, Sarah 153, 221
Bernhart, Curtis 180
Berry, David 137
The Best Years of Our Lives 28
Bewitched 194
Beyond the Forest 26, 100, 193, 228, 229
Blanche Yurka Repertory Company 222
Block, Bertram 39
Blondell, Joan 109, 183, 222
Bogart, Humphrey 43, 184, 186, 187, 188, 219, 222
Bondi, Beulah 212, 214
Booth, Shirley 223
Borgnine, Ernest 162, 164
Born Yesterday 33
Boyer, Charles 172, 173, 174, 178, 194
Brando, Marlon 115
Brecht, Bertolt 89
Brent, George 40, 45, 46, 47, 48, 102, 111, 141, 142
Brent, Romney 116
Brewer, George Emerson, Jr. 39
The Bride Came COD 228
Broken Dishes 222
Brooks, Richard 162, 165, 166
Brown, Harry 121

249

Bryan, Jane 106, 111, 184, 188, 211, 212
Bunny O'Hare 100, 165
Buono, Victor 82, 189, 194
Burke, Billie 217
Burnett, Marlene 104, 112
Burton, Richard 121
Cabin in the Cotton 146, 160, 225
Cagney, James 28, 186, 222, 225, 228
Camden, Joan 163, 165
Cannes 33, 87, 226
Capra, Frank 49, 158
Carey, Harry, Jr. 132, 135
Carlson, Richard 58
Castle, Peggie 179
Catherine d'Medici 116
Chaney, Lon 87, 88
Chaplin, Charles 232
Chase, Ilka 64
Chatterton, Ruth 47, 109, 225
Chayefsky, Paddy 161, 162
Chekhov, Anton 97
Chevalier, Maurice 186
Christiansen, Bob 196
Ciannelli, Eduardo 183
Citizen Kane 28, 194
Colbert, Claudette 27, 158
Collinge, Patricia 52
Collins, Joan 116, 119, 120
Come Back, Little Sheba 32
Cooper, Gary 52
Cooper, Gladys 17, 64, 69, 71, 72, 73, 74, 75, 76
The Corn Is Green 97, 136, 209
Cornell, Katherine 17, 19, 221
Corwin, Norman 195
Cotten, Joseph 189, 193, 194, 229
Cowan, Jerome 104
Coward, Noël 217, 220
Cowl, Jane 180
Crawford, Joan 78, 80, 81, 85, 87, 88, 89, 189, 193
Crews, Laura Hope 111
Crisp, Donald 103, 125, 199, 201, 211
Cromwell, John 154, 160
Cromwell, Richard 141
Cukor, George 109, 160
Curtiz, Michael 124, 146

Day, Dwayne 201
Deception 225
Dee, Frances 157, 179
De Guzman, Michael 196
De Havilland, Olivia 89, 122, 124, 128, 173, 177, 189, 190, 193
Denny, Reginald 157
Dern, Bruce 189
Design for Living 109
Dewey, Thomas E. 183, 187
Dietrich, Marlene 19, 27

Dingle, Charles 51
Don Juan in Hell 194
Douglas, Robert 116
Duke, Patty 89
Dunne, Irene 64, 146
Durante, Jimmy 217, 220
Duryea, Dan 52
Duse, Eleonora 33, 153, 221

Eagles, Jeanne 17
The Earth Between 222
Emmy 196
Epstein, Julius J. 209, 217
Epstein, Philip G. 209, 217
Erickson, Leif 195

Fabray, Nanette 124
Farmer, Frances 19
Farnsworth, Arthur, Jr. 48, 64, 178, 204, 208
Farrell, Henry 85, 189
Fashions of 1934 160
Faulkner, William 109
Feldman, Charles 85, 182
Ferdinand 4
Field, Rachel 172, 173, 178
Finkel, Abem 187
Fitzgerald, Barry 162, 164, 165
Fitzgerald, Geraldine 39, 40, 49
Flynn, Errol 122, 123, 125, 126, 144, 178, 211, 213, 215
Fonda, Henry 109, 140, 147, 199, 200
Fontanne, Lynn 124, 221
Ford, Harrison 3
Ford, John 28
Francis, Kay 225
Frankenstein 4
From Here to Eternity 159
Fuller, Penny 92, 96

Gable, Clark 144, 173
Garbo, Greta 45, 159, 202, 220, 222, 225, 232
Gardiner, Reginald 220
Gardner, Ava 85
Garfield, John 109
Garson, Greer 19
Gaslight 194
Gaudio, Tony 15
Gielgud, John 221
Gillespie, Gino 79
The Girl from Tenth Avenue 165
Gish, Lillian 132, 133, 134, 137, 138, 221, 222, 223, 229, 232
The Glass Menagerie 85
Godfrey, Arthur 132
God's Country and the Woman 186
Goldwyn, Samuel 18, 51, 56, 217, 227
Gone with the Wind 34, 45, 49, 124, 144, 173, 177, 178, 227
The Good Earth 170

Gordon, Gavin 168
Goulding, Edmund 38, 39, 45, 46, 47, 49, 102, 103, 109, 110, 111, 136, 146, 199, 201, 202, 203, 222, 223, 227
Graham, Martha 67, 222
Grand Hotel 46
Granville, Bonita 65
Grayson, Jesse 55
The Great Lie 26, 45, 48, 202, 229
Guest, Christopher 93, 95, 96

Hale, Alan 125, 135
Haller, Ernest 49
Hampton, Walter 34
Hardwicke, Sir Cedric 194
Harlow, Jean 225
Hart, Moss 217
Harvard 61, 72
The Hasty Heart 121
Hayes, Helen 221
Hearn, George 92
The Heiress 193
Heller, Lucas 85
Hellman, Lillian 51, 52, 56
Henreid, Paul 63
Hepburn, Audrey 219
Hepburn, Katharine 19, 89, 144, 160, 196, 229, 231
Hicks, Russell 52
Hitchcock, Alfred 84
Holliday, Judy 33
Hollywood 15, 24, 26, 28, 30, 39, 47, 85
Hollywood Canteen 209
Holm, Celeste 23, 27, 29, 33, 25
Hopkins, Miriam 102, 103, 108, 109, 110, 111, 140, 213
Hopper, DeWolf 105
Housewife 171
Howard, Leslie 109, 154, 155, 158, 173, 188
Hughes, Howard 18, 46, 180, 182
Hull, Josephine 89
Hunter, Ian 199, 201, 211, 214
Hurrell, George 47, 49
Huston, John 142
Hyman, Barbara Sherry 198

Ibsen, Henrick 221, 222
If 131
In This Our Life 48
Indiana Jones 3
International Television Festival Award 91
Irish Republican Army (IRA) 45
Irving, Sir Henry 221
It's Love I'm After 186, 193, 228

Jarvis, Graham 92
Jewell, Isobel 184, 185, 187
John Murray Anderson School 67, 222, 228
Juarez 102, 171

Juarez, Benito 170
June Bride 228

Kabuki Theater 87
Kaufman, George 217
Kaye, Sammy 36
Kazan, Elia 23
Keaton, Buster 232
Keighley, William 102
Kellaway, Cecil 191
Kenin, Alexa 92, 96
Kennedy, John F. 189
Kennedy, Madge 162
Kid Galahad 202
Kidman, Nicole 7
Koch, Howard 5
Koch, Norma 88
Koster, Henry 118

Ladd, Margaret 131
Laguna Beach 62
Lane, Lola 184, 185, 187
Lane, Nathan 219
Laughton, Charles 129, 135, 194
Laurents, Arthur 223
Lawrence, Gertrude 27, 217
Leigh, Vivien 19, 45, 49, 124, 173, 189
Leighton, Margaret 88
Lester, Bruce 10, 18
A Letter to Three Wives 33
Levy, Emmanuel 17
Life 189
Lindsay, Margaret 140, 168
Little Women 160
Litvak, Anatole 18, 178, 213
Lockhart, June 172, 173, 174
Loder, John 68
Loew's 112
Loftus, Cecilia 103
Look 89
Look Homeward, Angel 32, 223
Lord, Mindret 117, 121
Lord, Robert 18
Louise, Anita 199, 211, 212
Love Among the Ruins 196
Luciano, "Lucky" 183, 187
Lundigan, William 106
Lunt, Alfred 124, 221
Lynn, Betty 179
Lynn, Jeffrey 177

The Magnificent Ambersons 194
The Maltese Falcon 187
Man and Superman 194
The Man Who Played God 160
Mankiewicz, Joseph L. 4, 22, 26, 27, 28, 30, 34, 36, 122, 138, 193, 223, 228
Marlowe, Hugh 24, 29, 31
Marquis, Rosalind 184, 185, 187
Marriott, John 54

Marshall, Herbert 10, 17, 18, 19, 51, 56, 114, 119
Martino, Al 189
Marty 162, 165
Marx, Harpo 217
Mason, James 121, 223
Maugham, W. Somerset 15, 154
Mayo, Archie 167
McDaniel, Hattie 49
Merrill, Barbara 79, 85
Merrill, Gary 5, 23, 27, 28, 29, 34, 120, 195, 225
Merrill, Margot 121
Merrill, Michael W. 28, 32, 198
Methot, Mayo 184, 185, 187
MGM 144, 162, 165
A Midsummer Night's Dream 22, 193
Mildred Pierce 209
Miller, Arthur 221
The Miracle Worker 85, 89
Miss Moffat 32, 136, 223
Mitchell, Grant 217
Monroe, Marilyn 24, 27
The Moon and Sixpence 159
Moore, Grace 158
Moorehead, Agnes 189, 190, 194
Morning Glory 160
Mother Courage 89
Muni, Paul 87, 102, 167, 170, 171
My Fair Lady 219
My Mother's Keeper 198

Nelson, Harmon O. 39, 46 161
New England 61, 62, 67
New Hampshire 48, 62
New York Drama Critic's Circle 5, 85
New York Film Critic's Circle 33, 45, 124
Newell, David 10
Nichols, Richard 172, 173, 174
The Night of the Hunter 135
The Night of the Iguana 5, 85, 88, 89, 136, 222
Norman, Maidie 83
Nye, Carrie 17

Oberon, Merle 19
O'Herlihy, Dan 117
Old Acquaintance 208, 213, 229
Olivier, Laurence 123, 196, 221
O'Neil, Barbara 172, 173, 178
O'Neil, Patrick 88
Orr, Mary 28
Orry-Kelly 49, 124, 207
Oscar 49, 78, 85, 89, 162, 165, 186, 188, 204, 209

Page, Patti 189
The Painted Veil 159
Pallette, Eugene 167, 229
Paramount Pictures 19, 109

Pasteur, Louis 170
Patrick, Lee 213
Perkins, Anthony 84
Peterson, Dorothy 40, 207
The Petrified Forest 188, 225
Picasso, Pablo 1
Players Club 22
A Pocketful of Miracles 85
Polito, Sol 72
Price, Vincent 125, 135
Prince Valiant 119, 132
Production Code 159
Prouty, Olive Higgens 64
Psycho 81, 84

Quartet 159
Queen Elizabeth I 114, 117

Radio City Music Hall 154, 178
Rains, Claude 64, 65, 66, 67, 72, 204, 206, 209
Rapper, Irving 64, 202
Ratoff, Gregory 24, 31
Reagan, Ronald 43, 45
Reid, Carl Benton 51, 60
Remick, Lee 17
Reynolds, Debbie 162, 163, 164, 166
Right of Way 100
Riordan, Marjorie 205
Ritter, Thelma 24, 30, 33, 162, 164
RKO 51, 158, 160, 179, 180, 225
The Robe 119, 121
Robinson, Casey 38, 46, 49, 178
Robinson, Edward G. 109, 225
Roebling, Paul 96
Rogers, Ginger 64
Rogers, Roy 4
Roosevelt, Eleanor 132, 219
Rossellini, Roberto 231
Rossen, Robert 183, 187
Rowlands, Gena 195, 196, 197

Sadie McKee 75
San Francisco 27
Sanctuary 109
Sanders, George 22, 29, 33
Satan Meets a Lady 186
Schaefer, George 91, 100
Schultz, Leroy 92
The Scientific Cardplayer 193
Screenland 181
Selznick, David O. 144
Selznick, Irene 85
Selznick, Myron 144
Sergeant York 52, 62
Sermak, Kathryn 137, 198
Shadow of a Doubt 194
Shakespeare, William 97, 221, 231
Shaw, George Bernard 194
Shearer, Norma 64, 158

Shepherd, Sam 97
Sheridan, Ann 219
Sherman, Vincent 202, 203, 204, 207, 209
Sherry, Barbara Davis (B.D.) 27
Sherry, William Grant 27, 182
Shipman, David 223
Siddons, Sarah 22, 26, 34
Simon, Robert 162
Singin' in the Rain 3
Sir Walter Raleigh 121
Smith, Pete 4
Snow White and the Seven Dwarfs 4
Solid South 222
Sondergaard, Gale 14, 18
Sothern, Ann 135
Stage Fright 121
Stanislavsky 48, 221
Stanwyck, Barbara 19, 109
The Star 32, 121, 165
Star Wars 3
Steenburgen, Mary 131
Steiner, Max 20, 45, 49
Stephenson, Henry 125
Stephenson, James 17, 103
Sterling, Tisha 132
Stevens, George 160
Stewart, James 89, 100, 221
Stickney, Dorothy 165
A Stolen Life 180
Stork Club 25
Storm Center 5, 97
The Story of Temple Drake 109
Streep, Meryl 17, 219, 221
A Streetcar Named Desire 85, 209, 223
Stricklyn, Ray 164, 165
Stroheim, Erich 61
Suddenly Last Summer 229
Sullivan, Barry 179
Sunset Blvd. 23, 33, 84
Suskind, David 182
Sutton, John 180
Swanson, Gloria 23, 33, 201, 202

Tallichet, Margaret 146
Taylor, Rod 162
Taylor, Elizabeth 121
Terry, Ellen 221
The Third Man 194
Thomson, David 223
Three on a Match 165
The Time of the Cuckoo 223
To Each His Own 193
Todd, Ann 172, 173, 174
Todd, Richard 114, 117, 119
Toland, Gregg 18, 59, 87
Tone, Franchot 188
Tracy, Spencer 45
Travers, Henry 40, 212, 214
Travis, Richard 217, 220

Trio 159
Truman, Harry S 132
Turner Classic Movies 180
20th Century–Fox 33, 120
20,000 Years in Sing-Sing 160, 165
Two's Company 100, 165

Universal 225

Vallee, Rudy 87
Vidal, Gore 162
Vidor, King 229

Wagner, Robert 193
Wallis, Hal 18, 19, 39, 46, 64, 68, 110, 147, 170 209, 227, 228
Walters, Barbara 34
Waring, Richard 204
Warner, Jack L. 38, 39, 45, 110, 122, 129, 144, 154, 173, 178, 182, 186, 209, 219
Warner Brothers 19, 26, 27, 28, 45, 47, 85, 97, 114, 121, 122, 123, 144, 158, 160, 161, 167, 179, 182, 183, 186, 187, 189, 208, 217, 225, 227, 228, 229
Watch on the Rhine 26
Watson, Minor 201
Wayne, John 28
Wedding Breakfast 162
Weidler, Virginia 172, 173, 174
Welles, Orson 28, 194
Westmore, Perc 52, 87
Wharton, Edith 108, 109, 111
Who's Afraid of Virginia Woolf? 121, 223
Wickes, Mary 69, 217
The Wild Duck 222
Wilder, Billy 23
Williams, Tennessee 5, 85, 88, 97, 221
Willock, Dare 79
Wilson, Janis 68
Winter Meeting 26, 228
Winters, Shelley 89
The Wizard of Oz 39
Wolfe, Thomas 223
Wolfington, Peg 28
Wong, Anna May 18
Woollcott, Alexander 217
Woolley, Monty 216, 217, 219
The World of Carl Sandburg 136, 195, 222
Wright, Teresa 52, 60
Wyler, William 15, 16, 17, 18, 19, 20, 28, 46, 51, 52, 56, 58, 87, 140, 142, 145, 146, 147, 148, 178, 202, 219, 222, 223, 227
Wynn, Keenan 93, 95, 96

Young, Victor Sen 11

Zanuck, Darryl 27, 120, 122, 182

www.ingramcontent.com/pod-product-compliance
Ingram Content Group UK Ltd.
Pitfield, Milton Keynes, MK11 3LW, UK
UKHW041935140426
5217IPUK00014B/495